The Davidson Family
of Rural Hill, North Carolina

The Davidson Family of Rural Hill, North Carolina

Three Generations on a Piedmont Plantation

JIM WILLIAMS *and* ANN WILLIAMS

McFarland & Company, Inc., Publishers
Jefferson, North Carolina

LIBRARY OF CONGRESS CATALOGUING-IN-PUBLICATION DATA

Names: Williams, Jim, 1939– author. | Williams, Ann, 1940– author.
Title: The Davidson family of Rural Hill, North Carolina : three generations on a Piedmont plantation / Jim Williams and Ann Williams.
Description: Jefferson, North Carolina : McFarland & Company, Inc., Publishers, 2020 | Includes bibliographical references and index.
Identifiers: LCCN 2019058870 | ISBN 9781476680484 (paperback) ∞ ISBN 9781476638522 (ebook)
Subjects: LCSH: Davidson family. | Davidson, John, 1735–1832. | Plantation owners—North Carolina—Mecklenburg County—History. | Plantations—North Carolina—Mecklenburg County—History. | Rural Hill (N.C.)—History.
Classification: LCC F262.M4 W54 2020 | DDC 929.20973—dc23
LC record available at https://lccn.loc.gov/2019058870

    ISBN (print) 978-1-4766-8048-4
    ISBN (ebook) 978-1-4766-3852-2

BRITISH LIBRARY CATALOGUING DATA ARE AVAILABLE

© 2020 Jim Williams and Ann Williams. All rights reserved

No part of this book may be reproduced or transmitted in any form or by any means, electronic or mechanical, including photocopying or recording, or by any information storage and retrieval system, without permission in writing from the publisher.

Front cover: inset portrait of Robert (Robin) Davidson (image from the private collection of Dr. Douglas Marion); the ruins of Rural Hill, 1890 (photograph in the collection of the authors, a gift from the May Davidson Estate)

Printed in the United States of America

McFarland & Company, Inc., Publishers
  Box 611, Jefferson, North Carolina 28640
    www.mcfarlandpub.com

IN MEMORIAM

Brevard Davidson, 1808–1896
E. L. Baxter Davidson, 1858–1944
Chalmers Gaston Davidson, 1907–1994

Gatherers and Guardians of History

Acknowledgments

THIS BOOK ORIGINATED as a research project under a grant from the Arts and Science Council of Charlotte, North Carolina. It was distributed in 2012 as a monograph to be used by historians, researchers, family members and the staff at Historic Rural Hill. Today Rural Hill is a 265 acre Mecklenburg County Park in the northwest part of the county lying along a horseshoe bend in the Catawba River. It is a portion of the large plantation farmed by six generations of the Davidson family. The last three siblings of the sixth generation—none of them married and with no heirs— sold the property to the County in 1990. They had great respect for their heritage and correctly envisioned that the park would be interpreted as an historic farm and would be of interest to a modern urban population.

We wish to thank the Arts and Science Council for funding the original research and Ed McLean, then director of Rural Hill, for obtaining that grant. Jeff Fissel and Zac Vinson of Rural Hill opened their files to get us started. Robin Brabham, professor emeritus of Atkins Library, University of North Carolina at Charlotte, built the Special Collections and University Archives, which include the Davidson Family Papers. These original records made this work possible. We are truly grateful for his work and for that of his staff. Mary Boyer has tirelessly researched Mecklenburg history for decades and generously opened her files to us, providing much essential information. Jane Johnson, director emeritus of the Robinson-Spangler Carolina Room of the Charlotte Public Library, and her staff gave an extra measure of effort in providing us with facts gleaned from newspapers and other contemporaneous sources.

The works of the late Dr. Chalmers Gaston Davidson, professor of history at Davidson College, have contributed greatly to this history of

Rural Hill. Dr. Davidson was descended from the Rural Hill Davidsons and wrote several histories of the area and biographies of some of his ancestors. Most were written from the 1940s to the 1970s; some were published, others exist only in manuscript form. Dr. Davidson was an author, history professor, director of the Davidson College Library and, in retirement, college archivist. His research is well documented, but many resources are available today that were not readily accessible when he did his work. Dr. Davidson died in 1994 and is buried in the Rural Hill Burying Ground. Consult Appendix B for more details about Davidson College.

An extensive and thoroughly researched genealogy of the Davidson family has been compiled by Dr. Douglas Marion of Chester, South Carolina. Dr. Marion, also a Davidson descendant, has spent many years on this project and regularly corrects and updates his records as new information becomes available.

John Blythe, historian, genealogist and Davidson descendant, helped fill in many details. His knowledge about north Mecklenburg County is legion.

Finally, we wish to thank the members of the Charlotte History Roundtable and the staffs at regional historic sites who have provided the questions, answers, and general encouragement that kept us going on this project.

Table of Contents

Acknowledgments	vii
Preface	1
Introduction	5
1. Isabella Ramsay Davidson Hendry, Mother of Major John Davidson	9
2. Samuel and Mary Wilson, Parents of Violet Wilson Davidson	14
3. The First Generation at Rural Hill: Major John and Violet Davidson	23
4. The Davidson Children and Rural Hill	37
5. Holly Bend: Robin and Peggy Davidson	50
6. Robin and Peggy: Family, Wills and Estates	66
7. The Second Generation at Rural Hill: Jacky and Sallie Davidson	88
8. The Third Generation at Rural Hill: Brevard and Mary Davidson	99
9. Brevard and Mary: Mills, Wills and Children	119
10. Scientific Farming at Rural Hill	130
11. Rural Hill: The Last Three Generations	147

APPENDICES:

A. Davidson Family Genealogy	153
B. Davidson College	156
C. Hopewell Presbyterian Church	158
D. The Lunacy of the Rev. Alexander Caldwell	159
E. The Story of Plum, Enslaved Man, Freedman, Property Owner	161
F. A Marriage Deed of Trust	162
G. Naming Conventions and Other John Davidsons	165
H. Brevard's Slave Inventories	168
I. Road and River Work	174
J. Iron Making in North Carolina	175
K. The Value of Money	179
L. A Confusion of Counties	183
M. Land Acquisition by Grants and Deeds	185
N. Major John's Earliest Land Transactions	193
O. Land Acquisition by Robert Davidson	203
P. Courts and Legal Structure	205
Q. The Court House Law of 1774	210
Notes	213
Bibliography	223
Index	231

Preface

JOHN DAVIDSON CAME to the North Carolina backcountry about 1751 as a teenager with his sister and widowed mother. Here he worked and prospered, married well and built a large plantation he called Rural Hill. This is the story of the early settlers of this area, how they established themselves in a wilderness and how John Davidson's sons and grandsons built on that foundation. The story covers the period from 1750 to 1860 and includes not only detailed information about who the Davidsons were and how the families developed, but also about how they made their livings, built their fortunes and raised their families. For further details see Appendix A. Davidson Family Genealogy.

The Davidsons of Rural Hill were among the earliest settlers in this area. They were active in the American Revolution, developed the iron industry in the area and were early practitioners of scientific farming.

This work originated as a research project under a grant from the Arts and Science Council of Charlotte, North Carolina, at the request of Historic Rural Hill. It originally was issued by the authors in 2012 as a monograph to be used by historians, researchers, Davidson descendants and the staff at Historic Rural Hill. This book is an expansion and extension of that 2012 work.

This investigation began with the early histories, dating to 1846, discussed in the bibliography. Although these are interesting stories, they were only a starting point. Genealogical abstracts by Herman Ferguson and Brent Holcomb added to that base as a launching point into the original records. Fortunately the early grants, deeds and wills for this area are extant. The Mecklenburg County Court records are also available, although those for the first 25 years, prior to 1774, are missing. One of the things that made this book possible was the fact that the family papers, which date from the beginning, are in Special Collections at the University of North Carolina at Charlotte, UNC Chapel Hill, and Davidson College.

These family papers, including letters, contracts, receipts and journals, added greatly to this research, which was extended by investigations of ancillary topics such as the little-known shad fisheries on the Catawba, the development of iron manufacturing in Lincoln County, scientific farming, and the extensive slave records kept by Brevard Davidson. A number of these topics are documented in separate appendices.

The earliest settlers in this area were Palatine Germans, but the Scots-Irish who came shortly after soon dominated government and society in Mecklenburg and surrounding counties. Major John Davidson was fairly typical of these Scots-Irish and an outstanding example of the hardworking Carolina backcountry settlers. In general, early settlers like the Davidsons, arrived in extended family groups with little more than basic farming tools, a modest amount of money to purchase the very cheap royal land grants, and the determination to make their way on their own terms and to be free and independent of overbearing authority. During the Colonial Period in North Carolina, up to 1776, unoccupied land could be granted by the Royal Governor, in the name of the King. These early settlers were loyal British citizens who purchased and improved their land and gladly paid the quit rent and other taxes required of every citizen. They formed their own county justice of the peace courts and sent representatives to the Colonial Assembly when it was called into session. For a complete discussion of land acquisition see Appendix M. Land Acquisition by Grants and Deeds.

This is the story of the main line of the Davidson family that lived at Rural Hill and of several of their branches, illustrating how their lands and fortunes were developed and distributed and how these fiercely independent people built a lasting legacy in the Carolina backcountry.

The spelling in the quotes from Brevard's journals has been retained. He wrote for his own edification in making himself a better farmer. He never intended for the journals to be read or studied by others. As long as he could read and understand what he wrote, spelling was unimportant.

In the language of the 19th century prior to the Civil War, the most prevalent term for those of African descent was "Negro." Most were enslaved; those who were not were referred to as free blacks or free people of color. The word "slave" occurred in legal documents but rarely in letters, journals or other personal records. The next most common terms of the period were "servants' and "hands." These could be simply job descriptions—hands worked in the field, servants worked in the house. They were also used as euphemisms as the words "slave" and "Negro" were beginning to acquire baggage. Prime examples refer to black church members as "servants in the congregation" or the "servants' quarter" in graveyards. "Our family" and "our black family" are also seen. The word "African" often meant people born in Africa but not their descendants. They were noteworthy for preserving African culture and folklore. The word "black" was also used, and it seems to be a purely descriptive term that never has borne baggage from the earliest days to the present. The terms "African American," "the enslaved," or "enslaved people" are modern terms.

Slavery was a cruel and despicable institution. By the mid–19th century it had been abolished in much of Europe, and sentiment toward abolition was growing in America. This movement was hindered by the extremely prosperous cotton economy. America became the world's leading producer of cotton by 1830, and by 1860 it represented 60 percent of all American exports and two-thirds of the world's cotton supply. This benefited the North as well as the South, which is why many Northern states had a "not in my backyard" attitude toward the institution. From the earliest days of European settlement in America, slavery had been universally experienced and generally tolerated, another hindrance to ending the system. Gradually the abolition movement gathered steam and the Civil War ensued.

This didn't mean that people in the North thought blacks were equal to whites. Northerners generally objected to the concept of people owning other people, but many Americans, in the North and in the South, believed that black people were simple, childlike, and needed a great deal of care and supervision. This misperception was challenged during the 1860s when educated, highly literate black citizens became influential.

In the Carolina Piedmont the vast majority of people were Presbyterians, and their ministers preached against harsh punishment of Negroes or using the women sexually. This doesn't mean that those things didn't happen. It might have prevented people from writing about whippings or rapes in letters or private papers. Presbyterians were also encouraged to teach their young servants to read from the Bible or the catechism in spite of the 1831 law prohibiting the teaching of reading. When religion was involved, the law was openly ignored. As the conflict between North and South intensified, North Carolina passed nearly draconian laws to maintain slave labor. Other than by a will, it was nearly impossible to emancipate a slave. The owner had to guarantee that the newly freed person would leave the state, assure that he would be accepted by the state to which he moved to, and post a large bond —usually $1,000—in case these promises were broken. Many planters were beginning to realize that it might be easier to pay a labor force than to provide food, clothing and shelter for a large number of people, but doing so would probably cut into their profits.

The cruelty of slavery cannot be debated, but remember that those captured in Africa were victims and were not responsible for their victimization. It was their white purchasers who bear the guilt and shame for the peculiar institution. In spite of their captivity, black Americans contributed much to our nation.

Introduction

IN 1823 MAJOR JOHN DAVIDSON, at the age of 87, wrote his will, distributed his property and retired to a life of ease. Violet, his wife of 57 years, had died four years before. Six of his ten children were still living, and most of his 65 grandchildren were well established. Having started in life with nothing but his skill as a blacksmith, he looked back on his accomplishments with great satisfaction. As a pioneer in this new country, he had accumulated a great deal of land, proudly served in its revolution and in its government, and started and succeeded in two major industrial ventures. This is his story.

The plantation John Davidson called Rural Hill lies in the northwest corner of Mecklenburg County in the North Carolina backcountry. At one time it consisted of nearly 2,000 acres (over three square miles) in the great bend of the Catawba River.

John Davidson was born in 1735 in Lancaster County, Pennsylvania. His father, Robert, had come over from Scotland or Ireland, married Isabella Ramsay and fathered two children before dying at an early age. His untimely death left his widow and two small children to live with relatives. As John grew toward manhood he learned the blacksmith's trade to help support his widowed mother and orphaned sister. Note: Children whose father had died were legally referred to as orphans, whether their mother was living or not. Mothers reared babies until young childhood, when they were generally put out to an apprenticeship or placed with other relatives to be raised and taught the skills of a farmer or housewife.

In about 1750 the extended Ramsay and Davidson families, along with many others in that part of Pennsylvania, moved to the Carolina backcountry, which had just been opened to settlement. Land had become expensive in Pennsylvania and their future lay in this more southerly place. Shortly after arriving in the backcountry, Isabella met and married a prominent local widower with small children and, for the first time in many years, was able to set up housekeeping in her own home. John continued his blacksmith business and saved his money towards setting up on his own.

In the spring of 1759, when John Davidson was 23, he bought land on Coddle Creek just east of the present-day city of Davidson and began farming. Two years later he and Violet Wilson were married and soon two daughters were born. In 1765 the little family moved to land on McDowell Creek, just east of the Catawba River. There John built Rural Retreat, a rude log cabin, to house his family. Over the years, as eight more children joined the family, he added on to that cabin until it had eight rooms. Then, finally, in 1788 he built the magnificent manor house they called Rural Hill. These two buildings were home to the Davidson clan for the next four generations.

John bought the land on McDowell Creek from his father-in-law Samuel Wilson for 45 pounds. This was a fair price but no bargain. These Scots-Irish settlers prospered by being shrewd businessmen as well as skillful farmers and craftsmen. One year after John and Violet moved to McDowell Creek, they sold the land on Coddle Creek at a nice profit.

During the American Revolution John served as a major in the militia and after that was customarily called Major John. This title will be used here in order to avoid confusion with his many descendants also named John Davidson and with other John Davidsons who lived in the area at the time. Major John's son and namesake will be referred to as Jacky, as he was usually called.

In 1795 Major John made a gift of a portion of his land to his oldest son, Robert, called Robin. This was the only time John gave away any land until he distributed his estate near the end of his life. In about 1800 Robin built a magnificent house, now called Holly Bend, where he and his wife, Margaret Osborne, who went by Peggy, lived the rest of their lives. That house still stands in the Cowan's Ford Nature Preserve about a half-mile from the ruins of Rural Hill. They had no children but served as benefactors to many of their nieces and nephews.

Also in 1800 Major John's second son, Jacky, married Sarah Brevard. They settled in the old home place, Rural Retreat, where all of their ten children were born. In 1823 Major John, now widowed, went to live with his daughter and son-in-law, Betsy and William Lee Davidson, Jr.; Jacky and his family moved into Rural Hill.

Jacky's son Adam Brevard Davidson, called Brevard, married Mary Laura Springs in 1836. They moved into Rural Hill with his parents and began their family of sixteen children. A year later Jacky and Sarah moved back to Rural Retreat, where they lived out the rest of their lives.

Rural Hill burned in 1886, although portions of the foundation and some porch columns remain, and Rural Retreat burned in 1898. The ruins of Rural Hill, some of the outbuildings and a substantial portion of the land form the historic site today. An old log kitchen building, much modified and expanded over the years, stands near the Rural Hill ruins. This is where the last Davidsons who lived at Rural Hill resided until they sold the remaining property to Mecklenburg County in 1992. Those members of the family left no heirs and lie buried at the Rural Hill Burying Ground. However, Major John's many children, grandchildren, and subsequent generations left thousands, perhaps tens of thousands, of descendants.

In addition to the Rural Hill ruins there are a number of small original outbuildings on the site plus an 1890 schoolhouse and the 1900 Bethesda School, where black children were taught. A large reproduction barn now stands on the original barn site and a log cabin has been built to give an idea of what Rural Retreat may have originally looked like.

Through a bequest from May Davidson, of the last generation to live at Rural Hill, the Scottish Heritage Center was built and is used for weddings and other celebrations.

The Rural Hill Burying Ground, on Neck Road across from the Rural Hill ruins, is owned and maintained by the Davidson Family Trust. In it are buried Major John and Violet, many of their children and grandchildren, and descendants of later generations. The last Davidsons to live at Rural Hill now lie in this beautiful burying ground.

Chapter 1

Isabella Ramsay Davidson Hendry, Mother of Major John Davidson

LITTLE IS KNOWN FOR CERTAIN about the parents of John Davidson. Almost all that has been previously published has come from family stories and early histories rather than from documented evidence. The following is based on the best information available today and is followed by a discussion of the evidence that supports this narrative.

Among the few hard facts are these: Major John was born, by his own account, in 1735 in Chestnut Level, Lancaster County, Pennsylvania. His sister, Mary, was born several years later. Their parents were Robert Davidson and Isabella Ramsay Davidson. Robert Davidson died a few years after Mary was born.[1]

Given the marriage customs of the time, Isabella was probably about 20 when her first child was born, meaning she herself had been born about 1715. This birth date tallies well with later events. When her husband, Robert, died, Isabella Ramsay Davidson was left a young widow with two small children. It was customary at the time for a widow with small children to be taken in by her relatives until she remarried.

There were other Ramsays and Davidsons in the Chestnut Level area, and Robert Davidson was probably related in some way to the brothers John and George Davidson. After her husband's death, Isabella might have looked to the Ramsays for support, but with a son named John Davidson she was probably taken in by the Davidsons.

About 1750 a number of extended families from the Chestnut Level and nearby Thyatira Church areas of Lancaster County moved to North Carolina. These included many members of the Davidson, Ramsay, and

Brevard families. They settled between the Catawba and Yadkin rivers in Anson County.

The brothers John and George Davidson settled in that part of Anson County that would become Rowan County the next year. John spent a few years there and then relocated 80 miles to the west. Despite building a fort for protection from the Indians, he and his wife died at the hands of the Cherokee during the Revolution. The location of that fort is marked today by the town of Old Fort, located on Interstate 40 between Morganton and Asheville.

George Davidson stayed on Davidson Creek near present-day Davidson College and the town of Davidson. Isabella and her children, John and Mary, probably lived with them as there is no record that she purchased any land or had any other dealings with local or state courts.

When these Davidsons moved to North Carolina, young John was about 16. He had been trained as a blacksmith and, while he had not yet reached his majority (age 21) and could not enter into contracts, he was able to set up a business and practice his trade. Some of his income may have gone to help support his mother and sister, but he apparently saved most of it to buy land and set up on his own.

About ten miles from the Davidsons lived the Hendry family. Henry Hendry, with his wife and one or more small children, had arrived in the area about the same time that the Davidsons did. They had settled in Anson County on Coddle Creek in what is today northwestern Cabarrus County. Sometime between 1750 and 1765 Hendry's wife died, and sometime after that the widower Hendry married the widow Davidson. The evidence of this is a property deed of the time recording that Henry Hendry; his wife, Isabella; and John Davidson sold a piece of land in 1765.

Considering their ages at the time, the marriage of Henry and Isabella was probably closer to 1750 than to 1765. Isabella was at least 35 when she arrived in North Carolina, and Hendry was probably about the same age. Living just ten miles apart, they certainly knew each other. In those days making a living and raising children were two full-time jobs, and widows and widowers with young children often remarried as soon as possible. Henry and Isabella were well matched for each other; Henry was becoming established and Isabella was capable of raising Henry's children. Also, Isabella's remarriage would relieve her brother-in-law George Davidson of the burden of caring for the family. In the sparsely settled Carolina backcountry of that time there were few other choices.[2]

Hendry had settled in Anson County in 1751 with a land grant of 300 acres. He served as clerk of the Anson County Court in 1754 and perhaps other years. From that year until April 1756 he was the registrar of deeds for Anson County. These offices were unsalaried but he received fees for performing various official duties.

Anson County at the time consisted of all the land west of the Yadkin and Pee Dee rivers between Virginia and South Carolina. It extended west to "the Great South Sea," or the Pacific Ocean. In a census taken in 1754, Anson County had 810 families.[3]

Court was held for one week every three months in Anson Court House on the Pee Dee River near the South Carolina boundary, about 60 miles from where Hendry lived. As county clerk and/or registrar of deeds, Hendry attended these court sessions, traveling two or three days each way on horseback.

When court was not in session he kept the books at home, where he copied records and performed services for people who brought him deeds and contracts to be registered. In those early days when Anson County was rapidly being settled, serving as county clerk or registrar of deeds brought in a sizable income to supplement his farm crops, and Hendry probably accumulated the beginnings of a family fortune.[4]

In 1759, when John Davidson was 23 years old, he bought a 300-acre parcel of land on Coddle Creek. This land had originally been granted to Henry Hendry and had been auctioned off to settle a lawsuit. Another party to the suit was Samuel Wilson, John's future father-in-law. John paid £50 for the land, and the deed was witnessed by Henry Hendry.

John Davidson and Violet Wilson were married on 2 June 1761, when she was 18 and he was 25, and they set up housekeeping on Coddle Creek. Their first child, Rebecca, was born nine and a half months later, on 20 March 1762. For the next 25 years Violet had a child about every two and a half years until her 10th child, Benjamin Wilson, was born 20 May 1787, when she was 44 years old.

In January 1765 John bought 250 acres of land on McDowell Creek from his father-in-law, Samuel Wilson, for £45. This was the land that would be the basis for Rural Hill Plantation. John, Violet, and their two daughters moved onto this land and lived in the log cabin that came to be known as Rural Retreat. A year later they sold the land on Coddle Creek for a very tidy profit.

Not much more is known of Henry and Isabella Hendry. It is said that when Hendry died (date unknown), Isabella moved in with Major John or with his sister Mary, and her husband, James Price, and lived with them for the rest of her life. No wills for Henry or Isabella Hendry have been found. Henry Hendry appeared often in court records from 1751 until 1772.

His sudden disappearance from these records could well signal his death at about that time, at the age of perhaps 65 years. There is no record of Hendry's service during the Revolution.

The evidence that Henry Hendry had been married before and was left a widower with several small children is circumstantial but convincing. Hendry first appeared in Anson County records in 1751. Nineteen years later a Mecklenburg deed of June 1770 records that "Henry Hendry, Jr." bought land on the Catawba, in the Hopewell area. It was witnessed by "Henry Hendry, Sr."[5] Since the son had to be 21 years of age to buy and sell property, Junior had been born before 1749. Henry Hendry, Sr., must have been married and had one or more children before his wife died. It is not known who Hendry's first wife was, where they lived, or when she died.

Eight years after the last court appearance of Henry Hendry, the name "Henry Henry" begins to appear. He served as a juror, patroller, road hand, road overseer and river overseer. This is probably the Henry Hendry Jr. mentioned in the 1770 deed. The variation in spelling of the last name was not unusual. County clerks kept the records and spelled names as they heard them. This spelling change is very sharp as "Hendry" never appears after 1772 and "Henry" never appears before 1780.[6]

The story of how Major John Davidson's mother got to Mecklenburg has come down in the family and was written in various versions in the early histories. However, none of those stories matches the facts as revealed in court records of the time. Among the major sources for this era are J. B. Alexander, Chalmers Davidson, and Charles Sommerville. A passage from Davidson will serve to represent the others.

> The widow Isabella Davidson is thought to have settled near the present town of Salisbury in Rowan County rather than in the Center Church vicinity. There was an attraction near Salisbury in the person of a teacher by the name of Henry Henry or Hendry. Hendry is credited with a Princeton education by local historians but there is no record of his matriculation at that University.... John and Mary Davidson are said to have been educated by Mr. Hendry. Sometime about this period he married their mother.[7]

The problem with this story is that Henry Hendry is present in the Anson and Mecklenburg County records as owning land on Coddle Creek, but he is completely absent from the Rowan County and Salisbury records. Also, school teaching at that time was generally a temporary occupation for young men just starting out in life or for Presbyterian ministers who established academies. Hendry owned and farmed 600 acres, had one or more small children and served in responsible positions in Anson County government. He was no schoolteacher.

Other histories have different accounts, all equally wrong. One such has Robert and Isabella migrating to Pennsylvania in 1715 as a married couple. This would mean that she had been married for 22 years and was 37 years old when her first child was born and 54 when they moved to North Carolina. Another has Isabella settling in Salisbury in 1740, long before that region was settled.[8]

Many of the stories say that Samuel Wilson gave the land where Rural Hill is located to John and Violet Davidson as a wedding present. It is clear from the court records that John bought his first farm two years before he married Violet and bought the Rural Hill land from his father-in-law three years after they were married. This is described in detail in "Major John's Earliest Land Transactions" in Appendix N.

CHAPTER 2

Samuel and Mary Wilson, Parents of Violet Wilson Davidson

ACCORDING TO SEVERAL EARLY HISTORIES, Samuel Wilson came from England, Ireland or Pennsylvania, and came to Mecklenburg via Charleston, South Carolina, or down the Wagon Road from Pennsylvania.[1] It is said that he was related to the famous English portrait painter Benjamin Wilson and to the likewise famous English general Sir Robert Thomas Wilson. There is also an account that Sir Robert Wilson, or a relative of his, visited the Wilson family "in after years." No documentary evidence has been found confirming any of these stories.[2]

Although it is not known what country Samuel Wilson originally came from, there is some evidence that he may have moved to North Carolina from Lunenburg County, Virginia. In any event he was one of the earliest settlers in the part of Anson County that later became Mecklenburg County. In 1749, the first year that land was granted in the area, he applied for and received a large number of land grants. In 1751 he executed one of these grants for 600 acres in Anson County. This is the land on McDowell Creek where he and his wife, Mary Winslow, their five children and other members of their extended family settled and where he spent the rest of his life. Their oldest child was Violet, nine years old at the time, who would later marry John Davidson.[3]

In North Carolina Mary bore one more child before dying in 1758, leaving Samuel a widower with six children under the age of 16. He remarried soon thereafter, to Sarah Howard, and they had one child named Margaret. Sarah died in early 1765.

Samuel Wilson's third wife was Margaret Jack, a daughter of the Char-

2. Samuel and Mary Wilson, Parents of Violet Wilson Davidson   15

lotte tavern owner Patrick Jack. Her brother was Captain James Jack, who in June 1775 carried the Mecklenburg Declaration of Independence to Philadelphia. The date of this marriage is generally given as 1765, indicating that Sarah must have died early in the year, and Samuel remarried soon thereafter. Samuel was 54, Margaret was 19. When Samuel died in 1778, Margaret was 32 and apparently never remarried. She is buried near Samuel in Baker's Graveyard; the grave is marked "Margaret Wilson."

The early histories differ from one another in the names and numbers of the Wilson children. The best sources are the contemporaneous ones: Wilson's will, written near the end of his life, four tombstones in Baker's Graveyard, and county records of wills, deeds and court minutes.[4]

The names and birthdates of the children of Mary Winslow Wilson were probably Violet, 1742; Benjamin, 1744; Mary, called Maria, 1746; David, 1748; Samuel, 1750; and John, 1752.

When Mary died in 1758, Samuel married Sarah Howard. Early histories and family stories give her maiden name as Howard but do not list her given name. J. B. Alexander gives her last name as Potts. These early sources say she died soon after delivering her only child, a daughter named Margaret. However, a deed from Samuel dated 16 January 1765 says that "Samuel Wilson & wf Sarah" sold the land. From this we know not only the given name of Samuel's second wife but that she lived until at least January 1765.

After Sarah Howard died, Samuel soon married Margaret Jack. His will of 1778 leaves bequests to the four children of this union, Sarah, Charity, Lillie and Robert, plus a bequest to "the infant which my beloved wife, Margaret Wilson is now pregnant with." Both Hunter and Sommerville name this child as William or William Jack. When John Wilson died in 1795, his will mentioned William as his half-brother. William Jack Wilson appears in a guardianship document in Samuel Wilson's estate papers. Margaret's children were all under the age of ten when their father died.[5]

Left a widow at the age of 32, Margaret inherited enough real estate and personal property to raise her young children without the necessity of marrying again. In March 1779 she purchased a fill-in grant for all of the vacant land between her land and that of Garret Wilson, Ezekiel Wallace and Alexander Campbell. In August of the same year she bought two lots in Charlotte for £100. running along Church Street from Trade to Fourth Street. They were next to the two lots owned by her father, Patrick Jack, where Jack's Tavern is said to have stood. Margaret sold her lots in 1801.

Samuel Wilson was not a signer of the Mecklenburg Declaration of

Independence and was age 64 in 1775 when the Revolution began. He died in 1778 and so had no part in the war. There is no record of his having served in the militia at any time.

During this period there were a number of men named Samuel Wilson in Onslow, Anson and Rowan counties. Sometimes it can be difficult to determine whether the public record is referring to our Samuel Wilson or someone else. As mentioned previously, our Samuel Wilson had a son named Samuel Wilson. References to Samuel Wilson, Sr., and Samuel Wilson, Jr., probably refer to those two.[6]

In 1751 Samuel Wilson, at the age of 38, was granted 600 acres in Anson County on McDowell Creek. Over the years recorded deeds show that he bought an additional 1,425 acres, making a total of 2,025 acres. He sold 1,717 acres prior to his death in 1778. This land went to his three sons for token sums, to a widow for a token amount, and to his son-in-law John Davidson at a good price. This left a plot of 308 acres on which he continued to live and which he disposed of in his will.

Hunter recounts an interesting anecdote connected to Samuel Wilson's family and the American Revolution that occurred after his death.[7]

> After General Davidson was killed at Cowan's Ford, on the morning of the 1st of February, 1781, Major David Wilson, and Richard Barry, Esq, both of whom participated in the skirmish at that place, secured the body of their beloved commander, and carried it to the residence of Samuel Wilson, Sr., to receive the usual preparatory attentions for burial. Mrs. Davidson, who resided about ten miles distant, in the vicinity of Center Church was immediately sent for; she came as hastily as possible in the afternoon, under the charge of George Templeton one of her neighbors, and received, on that solemn occasion, the heart-felt condolence and sympathy of numerous sorrowing friends and relatives. In consequence of this necessary delay, those true patriots and friends of the deceased (Wilson and Barry) moved with the body late in the evening of the same day, and committed it to the silent tomb, *by torchlight*, in Hopewell graveyard.

Samuel Wilson had died in 1778, and in 1781 his widow, Margaret Jack Wilson, was living at the home place with her minor children. The family story is that General William Lee Davidson was found naked, stripped by British soldiers, and was dressed by Mrs. Wilson in clothing that belonged to her brother, Captain James Jack.

The term "naked" in the 18th century could mean, as we think of it today, completely stripped of all items of clothing. However, "naked" was also used to refer to someone who was without a coat or without a coat and waistcoat. In any event, clothing supplied by Mrs. Wilson to cover the general most probably had belonged to her recently departed husband rather than belonging to her brother, James Jack. The captain was very much alive at that time and probably needed all of the clothing he owned. Their father, Patrick Jack, had owned a tavern in Charlotte. It is said that the tavern burned in the fall of 1780 during the British occupation.

Samuel Wilson's last will and testament is recorded in Mecklenburg County Wills, and his estate papers are at the state Office of Archives and History in Raleigh. Images of these papers are available on microfilm at the Charlotte Library and at FamilySearch.org. The 49 estate papers document the inventory and auction of personal effects, guardianship of the minor children and the settlement of the estate.[8]

Wilson's will is dated 9 March 1778 and says he was "sick and in a low state of health, but of sound mind and memory." He died four days later and his will was entered into court during the next session, on 15 April 1778. The will appointed his son-in-law John Davidson and his two sons, Benjamin and Samuel, as his executors. Those men relinquished their rights, and the court issued letters of administration to Colonel Ezekiel Polk and Captain James Jack. Polk was the husband of Samuel's daughter Mary, and Jack was the brother of his widow, Margaret. The administrators posted bonds of £10,000 each, indicating an expected value of the estate of £5,000. This was a very large amount of money at the time, but it was in North Carolina currency, which probably had begun to depreciate by early 1778.

In his will Samuel Wilson left bequests to his wife, twelve children and two grandsons. The money bequests totaled £1,330.

His bequest to his wife, Margaret, consisted of £385 plus a feather bed, the house and kitchen furniture, a saddle, the Eagle mare and the enslaved man named Peter. Margaret was to occupy the mansion house and garden and have whatever else she needed to raise the minor children.

By the laws of North Carolina at that time, when a man died intestate (without a will of any kind) his widow was entitled to "the widow's third." This was a life interest in one-third of his real estate. She also received one year's provisions for her and her children. Under this law the widow and each of the children inherited equal shares of the personal property while the children divided the remaining real estate equally.[9]

Most recorded wills were similar in this regard, making provision for the widow during her lifetime. If the will did not give the widow her third, she could go to court to claim it. Most wills conveyed this real estate to her during her lifetime or until she remarried. By law, when a woman married, all real and personal property she owned immediately became the sole property of her husband, no matter how she had acquired it. The provision "until she remarries" kept a man's property from falling into the hands of his widow's second husband, which would have effectively disinherited his own children.

Margaret did not receive a bequest of real estate in her husband's will but did receive the right to occupy the manor house and garden. The home place ("the plantation on which I now live") was divided between two of his sons, John, age 20, and Robert, age four, so Margaret continued to live in the manor house with her minor children. The "kitchen garden was probably several acres on which she raised everything they ate except for corn, wheat and other grains and animals for meat and milk."

Token bequests of 20 shillings (£1) went to five of the six children of Samuel's first wife, Mary. They were the three sons, who had purchased land from their father for token amounts, and the two daughters, who had already married and had received a dowry of some sort.[10]

John, the sixth child of Mary, was born in 1757 and was still a minor at his father's death. He received a large inheritance, including "a negro man named Plumb," several horses, half of "the plantation on which I now live," and half of a 600-acre survey in Burke County.

Margaret, the daughter of Samuel Wilson's second wife, Sarah, was 17 and unmarried. She was to receive a horse and four cows, some household furniture and the sum of £20. Presumably the daughter Margaret was to live with the widow Margaret on the home place until the daughter married.

The remaining children were the minor sons and daughters of Samuel Wilson's third wife, the widow Margaret Jack Wilson.

Robert Wilson, age four, received half of the home place and half of the 600 acres in Burke County, plus £20.

Sarah, Lillie and Charity each received £200.

Finally, "the infant which my beloved wife, Margaret Wilson is now pregnant with," received £200. When this child was born, he was named William Jack Wilson.

There were also bequests of £50 each to two grandsons, Samuel C. Polk, son of Mary and Ezekiel Polk, and a Samuel Wilson who does not appear elsewhere and may have died young.

The remaining personal property was to be sold and divided between the seven minor children. The final settlement of the estate amounted to £3,144.

These amounts were very large but, as noted, they were in North Carolina currency, which had probably begun to depreciate by that time. Throughout the Revolutionary War the currencies of the states and of the

2. Samuel and Mary Wilson, Parents of Violet Wilson Davidson

United States were paper money with no backing in gold or silver specie. The value of these currencies declined steadily until by the end of the war they were "not worth a Continental." The actual value of these amounts, in gold or silver at any particular time is impossible to determine.

In the October 1778 court session the two executors were appointed as guardians for the minor beneficiaries. At that time the term "guardian" did not mean what it does today. When a minor inherited a bequest, from their deceased father the court appointed a guardian, not for the minor person but for their assets In almost all cases the child did not live with the guardian. In many cases the court authorized a guardian to make payments from the child's assets to support the child, who was being raised by the widow or another relative.

Guardians were generally bonded in an amount equal to twice that of the expected inheritance. When the youngest child reached his or her majority, the court terminated the guardianships and paid out the inheritances to all of the children. If a guardian was not performing his duties properly, the court could relieve him of that duty and appoint another guardian.

If a deceased father did not have sufficient assets to leave bequests to his minor children, those older than seven years of age were often put out to an apprenticeship to learn a trade or skill. Frequently these apprenticeships were to learn "the art and mystery of housewifery" or of a spinster or a farmer.

One of the guardians of the Wilson children was James Jack. The story of Captain Jack, the Paul Revere of the South, is well known in Charlotte and in North Carolina. He rode as an express rider to carry the Mecklenburg Declaration of Independence of 20 May and the Mecklenburg Resolves of 31 May 1775 from Charlotte to Philadelphia to lay them before the Second Continental Congress. It is said that this intrepid lad was a well-known and well-liked tavern keeper who risked his life to carry a treasonous document through enemy territory. The story is widely known, and his life and accomplishments are celebrated each May 20. His fame is immortalized in a larger-than-life bronze statue on the Charlotte Trail of History showing him on horseback.[11]

However, a close examination of the wills, deeds and county court minutes of Mecklenburg and surrounding counties, and of Georgia, reveals much more.

First of all, it should be noted that he was an express rider who was frequently hired for tasks like this. He was hired for the express purpose of carrying something, usually a letter or other piece of paper, from one point to another. The word "express" does not imply any sort of unusual speed. Since at that time there was no organized postal service, express riders were necessary to carry papers throughout the colonies. After Boston was occupied by the British Army in 1768, Committees of Correspondence were organized in all of the colonies and they communicated with each other by means of express riders.

These express riders were in no particular danger, other than the usual ones of accidents or bandits. The idea of interrupting the correspondence of these committees never occurred to the colonial authorities and would have been completely impractical.

Until recently, nearly everything known about James Jack and his family came from the historian C. L. Hunter, who wrote an account of the Jack family in *Sketches of Western North Carolina* in 1877, a hundred years after the fact. He tells that the Jack family came from Pennsylvania, lived in Rowan County for a few years, moved to Mecklenburg County and finally to Georgia at the end of the Revolutionary War. Hunter includes extensive genealogy of the Jack family but little detail of their life in Mecklenburg, except that James ran a tavern, was captain of the town militia company, carried the Declaration to Philadelphia and served in the militia during the Revolution.

The only account from James's own hand is what he wrote in 1819, then living in Georgia, regarding his connection with the Mecklenburg Declaration of Independence. That account was included in the history of the Declaration written and published by the State of North Carolina in 1831.[12]

Rowan and Mecklenburg county records reveal additional information about the Jack family in North Carolina from 1763 to 1783. The whole family—the father, Patrick; his wife, Lillis, and their three sons and five daughters—migrated from Pennsylvania to North Carolina in late 1763. Patrick bought land in Rowan County, where the family lived and worked until they moved to Mecklenburg. Despite the fact that six of his eight children were over 21 when the family moved to Rowan, no land records have been found for any of them in that county, and they probably lived there with their parents.

Seven years later the family members moved to Mecklenburg County one by one. The two younger sons bought land and farmed, while Patrick and his eldest son, James, lived in Charlotte and kept a tavern. James speculated in Charlotte town lots, perhaps making a good deal of money, and also participated extensively in the county court and in local politics. He served as town commissioner, militia captain, tax assessor, and overseer of the poor. It also appears that James served in the militia in some of the Revolutionary War activity in the area.

When the will of Samuel Wilson was submitted for probate at the April 1778 session of the Mecklenburg County Court, letters of administration were issued to Colonel Ezekiel Polk and Captain James Jack.

When the estate was settled six months later, the surplus was over £3,000 in cash. By the terms of the will the minor children received individual monetary bequests, and any additional funds were to be divided among those seven children. These funds were to be held and kept secure by the court-appointed guardians until the children reached their majority. This was a great deal of money at the time, and it seemed that the minor children's education and future prospects were assured.

However, court records reveal that four years later, in late 1782, Captain James Jack left the state and moved to Georgia without accounting for the inheritance of his nieces and nephews. The court proceedings state, "James Jack hath removed himself out of this State so that the ordinary process of Law Cannot be Served upon him." A Georgia deed six months later places him in that state, and other records show that his wife and children, as well as his two brothers, John and Samuel and his sister Jean Jack Barnett and her husband William Barnet, had gone with him.

James Jack's performance as guardian of his nieces and nephews had been guaranteed by two friends in the amount of £6,500, and they were left holding the bag. Since James Jack had left the state, they were liable for the children's inheritance. The court issued orders for the sheriff to search for any assets Jack had in North Carolina, but all that could be found were six city lots that were virtually worthless.

After Jack had left the state, Samuel Wilson, Jr., the half-brother of the Wilson children, was appointed their guardian. In July 1783 James Jack returned briefly to Mecklenburg. He bought and quickly sold a prime town lot, clearing a £300 profit. Jack paid Samuel Wilson Jr. £315 toward settling the estate and quickly returned to Georgia.

In the following years there were lawsuits in Mecklenburg and in Wilkes County, Georgia, related to monies owed by James Jack. First Samuel Wilson, Jr., and then Margaret Jack Wilson served as guardian of the children. They each succeeded in collecting a good deal of property and money from James Jack in the Georgia courts.

Captain James Jack and his extended family never returned to North Carolina and had no further connection to Mecklenburg County, except once, in 1819, when a delegation went to Georgia and recorded his account of his famous ride with the Mecklenburg Declaration of Independence.

Samuel Wilson's will included a bequest to his son John. John died 17 years later, and his will gave Plum his freedom and both land and personal property. John's half-brother William contested the will. A jury found the will to be valid, and the court officially manumitted Plum. For a full description of this interesting and illuminating story, see "The Story of Plum, Enslaved Man, Freedman, Property Owner" in Appendix E.

As mentioned earlier, a family story holds that Samuel Wilson was related to the famous English portrait painter Benjamin Wilson and his son, the likewise famous British general Sir Robert Thomas Wilson, and that the general or a relative of his visited Mecklenburg "in after years." No documentary evidence has been found confirming these stories, and it seems clear that neither of these famous Wilsons ever visited North America. However, there is an account regarding a famous North Carolina spa that may explain at least part of this story.

In the first half of the 19th century, a spa called Catawba Springs on the South Fork of the Catawba River was famous and patronized by well-to-do individuals and families from South Carolina and Alabama as well as many from the surrounding area. Several of the guest books from 1838 to 1854 are in the Davidson College Library Archives.

In addition to many famous names, these books list some names which are perhaps too famous. It seems that students from Davidson College occasionally stayed at Catawba Springs on their way to or from the college. Each guest signed in with his name and address. Several of those showing the address of Davidson College, founded in 1837, seem suspect, such as General William Lee Davidson (who died in 1781), General William Henry Harrison of Tippecanoe fame (who became U.S. president in 1841), and so on.

One that is clearly suspect is from 1847. It is "Major General Thomas A. Wilson, Esquire, of Davidson College." At that time there was a student at Davidson named Thomas A. Wilson, and it might have been he who signed in as a famous person and was the source of the family story that the Wilsons were related to the famous British Wilsons.[13]

Chapter 3

The First Generation at Rural Hill: Major John and Violet Davidson

JOHN DAVIDSON ARRIVED in the Carolina backcountry with his widowed mother and younger sister around 1750. Over the next 82 years he would make his mark on history and leave a legacy in north Mecklenburg County that would endure for ages.

He had been apprenticed as a blacksmith, and he was able to practice his trade and help support his family, although at the age of fifteen he was well short of his majority and could not enter into contracts. His sister, Mary, was a few years younger and perhaps helped out in some way as well.

They came from Lancaster County, Pennsylvania, along with other families from that area and settled with the George Davidson family in Anson County (later Rowan County, today Iredell County). They were on Davidsons Creek near the Catawba River and the present-day town of Davidson, North Carolina. John's deceased father, Robert, is thought to have been either a brother or a cousin of the brothers George and John Davidson. George was the father of General William Lee Davidson, who died at Cowan's Ford at the head of his troops opposing the British Army as it crossed the Catawba River into Mecklenburg County in 1781. Other families that came from the area around Chestnut Level and Thyatira Church in central Lancaster County included the Ramsays and Brevards.

After young John Davidson reached his majority and accumulated sufficient funds from his blacksmithing business, he began to acquire land and establish himself as a farmer and planter. This was at first on Coddle Creek, then on McDowell Creek at the Catawba River. Eventually his land holdings exceeded 1,000 acres. He married Violet Wilson, who lived nearby, and they raised a family of ten children, all of whom lived to maturity and many of whom rose in prominence and prosperity. John, along with two of his sons-in-law, pioneered the manufacturing of iron across the river in Lincoln County. He was an early adopter of cotton cultivation, which, if it did not make his fortune, did ensure its continuation.

Once he was established, John took part in public life, serving two terms in the Colonial Assembly and was one of the men who met at the courthouse in Charlotte on 19 May 1775 and adopted the famous Mecklenburg Declaration of Independence. During the Revolution he served as a major in the Mecklenburg Militia on campaigns against the Cherokee in the Carolinas and in opposing the invasion of North Carolina by the British Army under Major General Charles, Lord Cornwallis in 1780 and 1781.

Davidson continued as an active farmer until 1823, when, at the age of 87, having been widowed for five years, he "broke up house keeping," distributed most of his property to his children and retired to a life of ease. He spent the rest of his life living with his daughter Elizabeth and her husband, William Lee Davidson, Jr., at their plantation, Beaver Dam, near present-day Davidson College. Major John Davidson died at the age of 96 in 1832.

As related in Chapter 1, when John; his mother, Isabella; and sister, Mary, first came to Carolina and stayed with George Davidson, they lived 10 or 12 miles from another new settler named Henry Hendry. He had arrived in the area with his wife and small children about the same time that the Davidsons did and settled on Coddle Creek in what is today northwestern Cabarrus County. Hendry's wife died shortly after they arrived in the area and soon the widow Davidson and the widower Hendry were married.

In 1759, when John was 23 years old and had been in Carolina for nine years, he bought his first piece of land. This was on Coddle Creek, near his mother and stepfather. He farmed that land for two and a half years before marrying Violet Wilson, whose family lived nearby.

A deed in the county records shows the details of this first land purchase, 300 acres on Coddle Creek for which he paid £50. The land had been originally granted to Henry Hendry and later was auctioned off to settle a lawsuit. A counterparty to that suit was Samuel Wilson, John's future father-in-law, and the deed was witnessed by Henry Hendry. Three years later John bought an additional 19 acres in the same area.

The early histories tell the story that John's father-in-law, Samuel Wil-

3. The First Generation at Rural Hill: Major John and Violet Davidson

son, gave them a piece of land neighboring his on McDowell Creek as a wedding gift in 1761 and that this was where John and Violet first settled and built Rural Retreat. However, the county records of the time tell a different tale. They show that John and Violet lived on Coddle Creek for three and a half years after they were married and that two of their 10 children were born there. Then, in 1765, John bought 250 acres of land on McDowell Creek from his father-in-law for £45, where he built a modest cabin later called Rural Retreat and moved his family. A year later they sold the land on Coddle Creek for a tidy profit.

In their long life together John and Violet had ten children. The eldest, Rebecca, was born in 1762 and married Captain Alexander Brevard of Iredell County in 1784. Eight or ten years later Rebecca and Alexander moved to Lincoln County, where he went into the iron-making business with his father-in-law and brother-in-law.

John and Violet's next child, Isabella, was born in September 1764 and married General Joseph Graham of Mecklenburg County in 1787. They also moved to Lincoln County, where he became a partner in the iron-making business. For the lives and children of these couples, see the discussion of the iron-making business in the next chapter and in "Iron Making in North Carolina" in Appendix J.

Mary, called Polly, was born in December 1776 and married Dr. William Maclean in 1792. Maclean, born in 1757, attended Queens College and served in the Mecklenburg Militia at the beginning of the Revolution. From 1779 to the end of the war he was a surgeon's mate (an officer and physician) in the Fifth Regiment, North Carolina Continental Line. After the war he trained as a doctor in Philadelphia and became a member of the American Medical Society.

He was active in politics in Lincoln County, as a justice of the peace and militia officer. He served in the assembly and the state senate and in both Constitutional Ratification Conventions. William and Mary were married at Rural Hill in 1792 and lived at Willow Plain in Lincoln (now Gaston) County, where they raised ten children.

Robert, called Robin, was born in April 1769 and married Margaret Osborne, called Peggy, in 1801. They made their home on land, just to the west of Rural Hill, given to Robin by his father. There Robin built a magnificent house for his new bride that still stands and is known today as Holly Bend. Robin and Peggy had no children, and the legend is that Peggy had no toes. They took in and/or educated numerous nieces and nephews and left many of them handsome inheritances. Robin was a very successful farmer and planter, among the richest men in the county when he died.

Peggy outlived him by 11 years, dying during the Civil War. For details of their lives see chapters 5 and 6.

Violet was born in August 1771 and married William Bain Alexander in 1791. He was a justice of the peace and appointed registrar of deeds in 1792, replacing his father, John McKnitt Alexander, who had resigned the post. Violet and William had 14 children.

Sarah was born in June 1774 and married the Reverend Alexander Caldwell in 1794. He had become the pastor of Rocky River Presbyterian Church just one year before they married. Three years after this marriage the Reverend Caldwell was removed from the pastorate because he had become mentally deranged. The next year, in October 1798, a jury of the Mecklenburg County Court found him to be in "a State of Lunacy as not to be able to take care of his own property, and further that he has lost property for the want of that capacity." The jurors, one of whom was Major John, recommended that Alexander's brother, the Reverend Samuel C. Caldwell, be appointed as his guardian to take charge of his property.[1]

There were three children from this union; the youngest was born after his father was declared to be a lunatic. Martha "Patsy" Caldwell, their first child, was born in July 1795 and David Alexander Caldwell in January 1799. Between these two was John Hancock Caldwell. His birth date is not known, and given names weren't included in the census until 1850, but the evidence of the census of 1800 indicates that he must have been born between Patsy and David in order to have been younger than 10 years old in 1800 . He was probably born in 1797.

After the court declared in 1798 that Alexander was a lunatic, evidence from the 1800 U.S. Census shows that Sarah and her three children had moved to Rural Hill. Either her husband was not capable of taking care of them and providing for them or perhaps he was violent or abusive to her or to the children.

The censuses of 1800 through 1820 indicate that Sarah continued to live at Rural Hill. The family tradition is that Sarah lived there the rest of her life, but she is not listed there in the 1830 census and was probably living with one of her adult children by that time.

Margaret Davidson was born to Violet and John in February 1777. On 10 December 1813, at the advanced age of 36, she married Major James Harris, a wealthy and prominent citizen of Cabarrus County. By that time all of her sisters had married, and her father gave her a sizable dowry, making it possible for her to continue to live the life to which she had become accustomed. This gift consisted of seven slaves plus cash, bonds, notes, cattle, horses and furniture; the total value was $1,250.

3. The First Generation at Rural Hill: Major John and Violet Davidson 27

According to the laws of the time, anything a wife brought into a marriage, or acquired thereafter, immediately became the sole property of her husband, to do with as he wished. Before the wedding Major John executed legal and binding agreements with the prospective bridegroom and others in order to safeguard her property. These documents ensured that Margaret retained full title to the property given to her by her father and that she was able to dispose of it as she wished on the event of her death. The marriage was said to have been held on 10 December but these agreements are dated 14 and 15 December and refer to "the Marriage intended to be had & Solemnized." This may indicate that the wedding was actually held sometime after 15 December.

On 14 December Major John executed a deed of trust by which he sold, for the nominal sum of ten shillings, seven named slaves and their children, to his son-in-law William Bain Alexander and his son Robert Davidson as trustees for Margaret. In doing so Major John said:

> For & in consideration of the natural love & affection which the said John Davidson hath for his daughter Margaret Davidson, for the purpose of making a Suitable provision for her on her Marriage intended to be had & Solemnized with Major James Harris of the County of Cabarrus, and for the purpose of securing to her the absolute right of disposing of the property hereafter mentioned ... that the said Margaret Davidson, for & during the joint lives of her self and James Harris her intended husband shall receive and have all the benefit & advantage which may arise from the use, hire or labor of the said Slaves and their future increase.

Finally, the agreement specifies that if James Harris were to predecease Margaret, William and Robert were to deliver the slaves to her to have and hold. If Margaret were to die before James, he was to receive one-third of the slaves and the other two-thirds would go to her brothers and sisters. If Margaret died, "leaving issue of her body" (that is, leaving children), the slaves were to be divided among her children.

In a separate document dated the next day James Harris bound himself to the same two men in the amount of $2,500. The condition of this bond was that, since James Harris had received a considerable personal estate valued at $1,250 in cash, bonds and notes plus cattle, horses and furniture in consequence of his marriage, that he was to allow Margaret, his intended wife, to enjoy the use of that property during their joint lives and permit his wife to enjoy a personal estate valued at $1,250. The document also stipulated that James Harris was to leave this property to Margaret in his will and give such property to beneficiaries of her will and similar property to the children of their marriage. And he was to abide by the obligations of the preceding deed of trust.

In this marriage James and Margaret had one daughter, whom they named Violet after her grandmother.[2]

Violet and John's son John was born in November 1779 and married Sarah Brevard in 1800. Known as Jacky, he lived and farmed with his parents until his father retired from farming. Jacky and his wife spent most of their lives at Rural Retreat (see Chapter 7). Their son Adam Brevard Davidson later inherited Rural Hill (see Chapters 8 and 9).

Elizabeth, called Betsy, was born in September 1782 and married William Lee Davidson, Jr., in 1805. William Lee Davidson was the youngest child of General William Lee Davidson, who had died at the head of his troops in the Battle of Cowan's Ford in 1781. Son William Lee was born after his father's death. Betsy and William Lee, Jr., had no children.

During the latter part of Major John's life, William Lee was his trusted adviser and the executor of his will. After Major John broke up housekeeping at Rural Hill, he moved in with Betsy and William Lee and lived there the rest of his life.

Benjamin Wilson Davidson, called Wilson, was born to John and Violet on 20 May 1787 and married Elizabeth Latta in 1818. Benjamin and Elizabeth lived at Oak Lawn Plantation on land he bought from his father, and he served as a justice of the peace. Wilson died in 1829, leaving six sons under the age of 11. Six years later his widow married Major Rufus Reid of Mount Mourne near Centre Church in Iredell County.

Oak Lawn is located off McCoy Road in northern Mecklenburg County. It has been preserved and restored, is privately owned and is designated a Mecklenburg County Historic Landmark.

Because Wilson was born on May 20, there is a family tradition that as a boy he was called Independence Ben. However, the historian Chalmers Davidson, in his typescript biography of Benjamin Wilson Davidson, states that local people did not take much note of this historic date until 1819, when Wilson was 32 years old. Therefore the historian doubts that the name Independence Ben was used to refer to the boy in childhood.[3]

There is also some doubt as to whether he was called Ben at all. In 1828 his sister-in-law Nancy Latta married Rufus Reid. Benjamin Wilson's niece Mary Graham Morrison wrote to her brother: "Nancy Latta is married to Rufus Reid. All the friends are pleased, but Uncle Willson. He went and heard the ceremony and left the house." "Uncle Willson" is believed to be Benjamin Wilson Davidson, so it is quite possible that he was called by his middle name. The use of middle names was common during this time, when many extended family members shared the same names.[4]

In 1772 John Davidson was elected as one of two Mecklenburg County representatives to the lower house of the North Carolina Colonial Assembly and took his position in January 1773. Martin Phifer of Rocky River was the other representative from Mecklenburg. During this session Phifer introduced a bill "praying a Law may pass for establishing a public Seminary of Learning in the Western part of this Province." This was just after the king had disallowed the bill authorizing Queens College in Charlotte. This new bill did not pass.

In the same session Davidson introduced a bill that "a Law may pass for establishing a court house in the Town of Charlotte in Mecklenburg County and other purposes." This bill was passed by the assembly and sent to the Upper House of the North Carolina General Assembly but was not passed into law.

Since these bills did not pass and become law, we have only the title of the bills and do not know what was in them. For more on courts and legal structure, see Appendix P.

Throughout the session of the assembly John Davidson is mentioned in the minutes many times as carrying bills and other messages between the assembly and the council. This was a task of some honor and speaks to his place in colonial society. Assembly members received no pay for attending the sessions but did receive expenses. John Davidson received an expense payment of £23.11.3 for this session.[5]

In December 1773 John Davidson was again elected to the assembly. This time the other member was Thomas Polk. On 21 December Polk presented a bill "for establishing a court house in the Town of Charlotte in Mecklenburg County and for Regulating the said Town." This may have been the same bill that Davidson proposed in the previous session. This time the bill was passed and sent to the council, which approved it and sent it to the governor. He in turn gave his approval, and it became one of the laws of 1774.[6]

This is an interesting omnibus law that tells us something about life in the village of Charlotte just prior to the Revolution. For the complete text of this law, see "The Court House Law of 1774" in Appendix Q.

The title says that the purpose of the law is to establish a courthouse in Charlotte, but there already was one. The law was actually to ensure that the courthouse would stay in Charlotte.

One of the laws passed in 1768 had formed Tryon County from the western part of Mecklenburg. The dividing line was the Catawba River, so the Mecklenburg County courthouse was then near the western edge of the county. This first law stated, "The Court House of the said County of Mecklenburg already built is not central" and provided that after seven years the courthouse could be sold and a new one built in the center of the county. The second law, passed six years later, said that the courthouse should stay in Charlotte, for moving it "would be inconvenient to many of the Inhabitants of the said County and discourage the Trade and Commerce of the said Town."[7] Appendix L elaborates on the complexities that prompted and resulted from the creation of new counties.

Probably the leading men had come to realize that the area along the Catawba River and around Charlotte represented most of the wealth and political power in the county. Moving the courthouse would involve taxing the county population to buy the land and finance the new courthouse. They could try to sell the old courthouse, but it is hard to see that anyone would pay very much for a single-room building on 10-foot brick pillars with no fireplace and located in the middle of the intersection of Trade and Tryon streets. It would have to be moved somewhere else. Therefore they decided to keep the courthouse in Charlotte.

Mecklenburg County at that time included an area that would later be split off as Cabarrus and Union counties. If the county had built a new courthouse as allowed in the law of 1768 "at any other Place in the said County more central," that new courthouse might have been built in what is today Union County.

There were a number of other provisions in that law "for regulating the said Town." One section provided for the prohibition of actions that disturbed the peace, including horse racing, firing guns (except to kill pigs and cattle for butchering), and "playing at long bullets."[8]

The law of 1768 establishing the town of Charlotte required every lot owner to build a house of minimum specified dimensions within three years of buying the lot. This provision seems to have been honored more in the breach than in the execution. A provision in the 1774 law eliminated that requirement except for lots fronting on Trade or Tryon streets.

The streets must have been in pretty bad shape, for this law also required that every taxable person (white men 21 and older) in the village be required to put in six days of labor on the streets each year.

Some of the original town trustees had died or moved away, so four more trustees were appointed. Finally, all fines arising from this act, for engaging in a public nuisance or for refusing to work on the city streets, would be applied to repairing those streets.

On 21 December 1773 John Davidson (spelled Davison in the minutes of the assembly) presented "a Bill for altering the dividing line between the Counties of Rowan, Mecklenburg and Tryon."[9]

Josiah Martin, Royal Governor of North Carolina prorogued the assembly on 21 December to reconvene the following March. He did not dismiss the assembly but rather told its members to go home and come back later to finish the session. He apparently thought they had not accomplished what he wanted, so he told them to think things over and come back to pass the laws he had requested.

John Davidson did not return for the remainder of that session, but his bill had already passed and was approved by Governor Martin and issued in the laws of 1774. It provided for the building of a courthouse in Tryon County and established the Catawba River as the boundary between Mecklenburg and Tryon counties. This line had been specified when Tryon County was established, but there had been some disputes about the line that were resolved by this law.[10]

John Davidson served as a major in the Mecklenburg Militia in 1775 and 1776. On 9 September 1775 he was appointed second major of the Mecklenburg Militia under Colonel Thomas Polk and on 22 April 1776 was appointed first major in the Mecklenburg Militia under Colonel Adam Alexander.[11]

In 1832 Samuel Wilson, Jr., age 82, filed an application for a federal pension for his Revolutionary War service. He stated that he had served for six months in the militia against the Cherokee as a captain under Colonel Alexander, Colonel Phifer, and Major John Davidson.[12]

In the late fall of 1775 Major John served in the Snow Campaign under Colonel Thomas Polk against the Scovilite loyalists in western South Carolina. In 1776 he served in Rutherford's campaign against the Cherokee.[13] Griffith Rutherford entered the war in 1775 as a colonel in the North Carolina militia following his appointment to the Rowan County Committee of Safety. Throughout that year, his regiment helped to disarm and disperse Loyalist groups in the South Carolina back country, most notably during the Snow Campaign in Ninety Six, South Carolina. In 1776 he raised an army of 2,400 men to campaign against local Cherokee Indians, who had been attacking colonists on the western frontier since their alliance with the British.

Minutes for sessions of the Mecklenburg County Court, from its founding in 1763 to July 1774, have not been found, so we have no information about John Davidson's public service in the county up to that date. The family tradition is that he served as a justice of the peace for Mecklenburg County, a lifetime appointment on good behavior. The justices of the county presided over the court sessions, which were held for one week every three months. The justices also adjudicated minor matters on their own, generally from their homes.

When the assembly met in 1776 and passed laws establishing the government as a state rather than as a British colony, the members issued a list of justices of the peace for the various counties. John Davidson of Mecklenburg was one of those so appointed. However, the county records do not mention him as ever having being sworn in or as serving as a justice. If he had been a serving justice, his name should have always appeared with the honorific "Esquire" or "Esq." and it does not. He also should have appeared in the county court records at least at the annual meeting where all of the JPs voted to appoint people to such offices as sheriff, clerk and registrar of deeds and to decide which of them would preside over the quarterly court sessions. He does not appear in those records. There were a number of other men at that time who were similarly appointed but did not serve.[14]

Family tradition also has it that Major John served on the Mecklenburg County Committee of Safety in the years before the Revolution. That committee is mentioned in the minutes of the Provincial Congress of North Carolina on 31 August 1775, regarding the purchase of gunpowder, but the minutes of that organization have not been found and it is not known who served on the committee.[15]

On the subject of the Mecklenburg Declaration of Independence, we are on much firmer ground. In a sworn affidavit published in *The NC Pamphlet* of 1831, Major John testified that he was a delegate to the convention that adopted the declaration. This is confirmed by the statement of James Jack in that same publication.

The most recent and complete description of this important event is in Scott Syfert's 2014 book, *The First American Declaration of Independence?* An earlier book, V. V. McNitt's *Chain of Error*, provides a rigorous analysis of the various wordings of that document. McNitt's book was first published in 1960 and reprinted by the Mecklenburg Historical Association in 1996.[16]

In the earliest extant Mecklenburg County court records, beginning in July 1774, the name John Davidson appears from time to time, as do the names of most leading citizens. However, at that time there was a prominent merchant in Charlotte named John Davidson, and others of the same name in the county, so in many cases it is not possible to tell which John Davidson the court entries refer to.

A man named John Davidson often served on juries in both the Court of Common Pleas and Quarter Sessions in Charlotte and the District Court, held in Salisbury. He declined to serve as executor of the will of Andrew Bowman in 1775 but did serve as executor of the will of Margaret Bowman

3. *The First Generation at Rural Hill: Major John and Violet Davidson* 33

in 1777. He also was the executor of the will of Henry Walls in 1777 and of Samuel Cowen in 1789. And he served in other public capacities such as a tax assessor and as a juror to value and apportion property and to resolve real estate disputes. Some or all of these entries may have referred to Major John or to the Charlotte merchant or to someone else.[17]

In 1778 Major John's father-in-law Samuel Wilson died. The will listed "John Davison" as one of the executors, but he declined to serve and the will was administered by Colonel Ezekiel Polk and Captain James Jack. In 1782 Major John Davidson was elected as one of the overseers of the poor.[18]

In 1793 Major John and 23 of his neighbors issued a public notice that was registered in the county deed book, saying in part, "We do forbid & prohibit all persons whatsoever to drive deer or hunt deer with dogs on any of our lands." Other names on this notice include James, William B., and J. McKnitt Alexander and James Knox. Copies were posted at Crocket's Mill, Allison's Mill and John McKnitt Alexander's gate.[19]

Nine years later Major John and 68 of his neighbors issued a legal notice and registered it in the deed book: "Every person without exception is hereby prohibited from hunting in any manner or way for game on the lands of the Subscribers without a written permit from the owner under the penalties inflicted by Law." These notices were posted at Major Davidson's Mill, Robeson's Mill and Wm. Price's Blacksmith Shop.[20]

In 1795 John Davidson served as an executor of the will of John Wilson, who lived in the Hopewell community. This was almost certainly Major John. The will was challenged in court by other family members regarding the manumission of the Negro named Plum.[21]

John and Violet Davidsons lived most of the rest of their lives on their 250-acre tract on McDowell Creek. In addition to this home place he acquired a great deal of land in a number of locations over his lifetime. For some of this land there are good records, but there were a number of John Davidsons in the area so there are questions about exactly who owned some of this land.

It was required that all land grants be registered at the colony or state level. It was usual and customary for the purchaser to prove all grants in the county court and to register them in the county deed books. This protected the buyer by providing a local public record of the grant. However, a fee to the county registrar of deeds was involved, and this registration was sometimes not done. The grant had been registered in the colonial or state land patent books, so the grantee may have felt no need to pay a fee to also register them in the county books.

Likewise, all deeds were to have been proved in the county court and registered in the county deed books. However, there was no legal requirement to do this and no penalty for not doing so, and a registration fee was involved. The buyer of the land had the deed that had been signed by the seller and may have felt he had no need to pay another fee. It appears that most property acquired by inheritance was not registered.

In some cases the only evidence of the ownership of a piece of land is in a chain of title in a later deed. Sometimes deeds were registered many years after the sale. When there was likely to be a question of ownership, the owner brought the old deeds into court and had them registered.

Thus it is that there are difficulties in determining exactly how much land Major John bought and sold and how much his heirs received. Even wills are of little help since bequests were often in the form of "the Johnson Place" and very often "the place whereon I now live" with no further indication of location or amount of land.

Many grants and deeds refer to the property as being on a particular creek or river. Unless the metes and bounds specifically state that the land was on the bank of a creek or crossed it, this phrase means only that the land lay "on the waters of said creek" and is located somewhere in the watershed of that creek, which can be a very large area.

A further complication is that land could be abandoned when a man moved away, in which case it would escheat to the state. Also, land could be seized by the sheriff for delinquent taxes. In these cases, when the land was sold by the state's agent or at a sheriff's sale, a new dead was issued. It showed the name of the seller as the University of North Carolina or the name of the local sheriff, and the chain of title was broken.

As we have described, John Davidson's first land acquisitions were on the banks of Coddle Creek, a tributary of Rocky River in the Yadkin River watershed. He bought 300 acres in that area in 1759 and 240 more in 1762 after he and Violet were married. In 1765, one month after he had moved to McDowell Creek, he and his mother and father-in-law sold 180 acres on Coddle Creek. On the same day Major John sold a 19-acre tract and nine months later an additional 228 acres, all in the same area. Finally, four years later he bought a royal land grant for 104 acres in that area. No other records of his purchases or sales in this area have been found, leaving 217 acres unaccounted for.[22]

Major John's land acquisitions in the McDowell Creek watershed began in 1765 with the purchase of 250 acres from his father-in-law. This was the land where he built Rural Retreat and Rural Hill and where he and Violet are buried. Starting in 1770, and over the next 30 years, he bought seven tracts of land totaling 970 additional acres in that same area. Three of these were fill-in grants claiming vacant land between his property and that of his neighbors. These grants were at a very cheap price and totaled 435 acres, nearly half of the land that he purchased. For the land he bought by deed, he paid about £100 per 100 acres. The land grants were purchased for one and a half pounds per hundred acres.

The only land that he disposed of during this time was the 430 acres he gave to his son Robin. Counting his original plantation plus the land he acquired, less that which he gave away, by 1804 Major John Davidson owned a total of 790 acres, or about 1.25 square miles.

During that same period a John Davidson bought two parcels on the west side of the Catawba River totaling 240 acres. He may have farmed or held this land for speculation, and no record has been found of the disposition of this land. It is also possible that this was a different John Davidson.

Between 1778 and 1787 a John Davidson purchased 12 grants for himself and six in partnership with others in Burke County totaling 3,429 acres. Although this might have been Major John Davidson, it was more likely one of the Lincoln or Iredell County John Davidsons. At that time Burke County consisted of all the land west of the Catawba River, north of Lincoln County and south of Wilkes County.

Starting in 1791 Major John, along with his two sons-in-law, Joseph Graham and Alexander Brevard, and his friend Peter Forney formed partnerships to go into the iron-making business in Lincoln County, across the river from Rural Hill. Over the next thirteen years the various partnerships acquired a total of 7,852 acres and ran a very successful iron-making business. In 1804, after 13 years in the iron business, Major John sold all of his interests in this property and other iron-making assets to his sons-in-law for $12,200, a large fortune at the time.

In 1793 Major John Davidson bought two lots in the town of Lincolnton. There is no indication that he built on those lots and no record that he sold them. He may have bought them on speculation and, when Lincolnton did not develop as he had hoped, let them be taken by the sheriff for taxes.

In 1795 Major John bought a tract of 31 acres from his son Robin for a token sum and on the same day gave to Robin "for love and affection" 430 acres in three tracts. The 31-acre tract was part of a land grant that Robin had received just six months before. This was a fill-in grant for all of the vacant land between his father's property, that of Francis Bailey, and the Catawba River. The three tracts he received from his father included the land where Holly Bend stands today. This is the only land Major John gave away until he dissolved his estate near the end of his life.

Finally, in 1819 Major John made provisions for the future of his two younger sons with a complicated sale and land swap. In one deed he sold 425 acres to his third son, Benjamin Wilson Davidson, known as Wilson. In another deed Wilson sold 300 acres to his brother Jacky.

Twenty years earlier, in 1800, when Benjamin Wilson Davidson was 13, he had inherited land from his uncle Benjamin Wilson. Uncle Benjamin had no children and left all his land to his two nephews named Benjamin Wilson and Benjamin Wilson Davidson. That will does not identify the land except to say that it was "the part of my plantation west of the spring branch adj Allison Knox and the wagon road." The part east of that line went to Benjamin Wilson Davidson.

By 1819 Wilson Davidson was 31 and recently married. In one of the two deeds mentioned above, Wilson paid $1,000 to his father, Major John, for the title to the land inherited from his uncle plus the additional 425 acres on Torrence Creek. It is probable that Major John had been farming this land as his son's guardian, and had not formally transferred it to Wilson ten years before when he reached his maturity. Or it could be that Wilson had been farming this land ever since he was old enough to work in the fields. When he married, he needed to take formal possession of his inherited land.

In the second deed on the same day, Wilson sold a tract of 300 acres located between Beatties Ford Road and McDowell Creek to his brother Jacky for $100. This appears to be the inheritance Wilson had received from his uncle.

In these transactions Major John made legal provisions for his two youngest boys to own substantial amounts of land. Jacky owned land connected to Rural Hill, and Wilson owned a larger piece of land a little farther off. This is the land where the historic house Oak Lawn stands today, a listed Historic Property in private hands.[23]

Chapter 4

The Davidson Children and Rural Hill

REBECCA, THE ELDEST CHILD of John and Violet, was born in 1762 and married Captain Alexander Brevard of Rowan County in 1784. They moved to Lincoln County in the last decade of the 18th century; there he went into the iron-making business with his father-in-law and brother-in-law.[1]

During the American Revolution Captain Brevard had a distinguished military career. He served in the militia in the Snow Camp Campaign, then as an ensign under Colonel Thomas Polk in the Fourth Regiment of the North Carolina Continental Line. He was promoted to lieutenant and was in the battles of Brandywine and Germantown.

After spending the winter at Valley Forge, he returned home an invalid. Recovering his health, he continued to serve as a captain in the militia. When the theater of war shifted to the south, he rejoined the Continental Line as a first lieutenant and served as quartermaster under General Horatio Gates. When the American Southern Army was destroyed at the Battle of Camden, Brevard managed to save a large amount of military supplies and was later promoted to captain. Near the end of the war he commanded a company at the last major battle of the Revolution in the Carolinas, at Eutaw Springs, South Carolina, just 20 days before the British surrender at Yorktown, Virginia.[2]

Captain Brevard resigned his commission in 1783 and returned to Rowan County. There he purchased land near his family, married Rebecca and took up housekeeping. In 1791 he partnered with his brother-in-law Joseph Graham and his father-in-law Major John to enter the iron-making business. Vesuvius Furnace and Mt. Tirzah Forge produced large quantities of pig iron and cast iron goods, making individual fortunes. In 1804 Major John sold his interest in the business to his sons-in-law. Later Joseph Graham sold out to Brevard, who continued the business with his sons through several generations until after the Civil War.[3]

Alexander and Rebecca Brevard were the parents of eight children. The interesting stories of three of their sons were recorded in a journal kept by Keziah Brevard, the wife of one of them, from July 1860 through April 1861.[4]

Their son Joseph was born in 1801, and married Keziah Goodwyn Hopkins of South Carolina in 1827. They settled in Lincoln County, where he served in the assembly for one term. Then their marriage quickly fell apart as Joseph began drinking heavily. Keziah left him and fled to her father's home, Oldfield Plantation, near Columbia, South Carolina. Joseph followed her and stayed with her family while trying unsuccessfully to convince her to come home. He was admitted to the South Carolina lunatic asylum in 1835, diagnosed with monomania—he was obsessed by jealousy and the idea that Keziah had a paramour. He was released two months later not much improved, and Keziah's father and brother were appointed his legal guardians.

His derangement continued and his health declined as he came to believe that people were trying to poison him. He died at Oldfield in 1842 after another brief stay in the lunatic asylum. Joseph and Keziah had no children.

Alexander and Rebecca Brevard's son Theodore, born in 1804, graduated from South Carolina College and began practicing law in Columbia. He married Caroline Hopkins in 1826, one year before his brother Joseph married her sister Keziah. In their short marriage they had two sons, both of whom died young. Caroline died soon after the birth of her second son in 1828. Three years later Theodore married again, this time to Caroline Mays of Edgefield, South Carolina. In 1833 they moved to Alabama, and then to Florida, where he served as state comptroller from 1855 to 1860. Brevard County, Florida, established in 1855, is named in Theodore's honor. Cape Canaveral and the town of Melbourne are located in Brevard County.

Alexander and Rebecca Brevard's son Franklin was born in 1788. He married Margaret "Peggy" Conner in 1820.[5] During their brief marriage they had four children, three of whom died in infancy or early childhood. After seven years of marriage Peggy was left a widow with one child, just two months before her brother-in-law Joseph married Keziah Hopkins. These two sisters-in-law, one widowed and the other with an insane husband, became great friends. Their exchange of letters is detailed in Keziah's diary.

A woman named Juliana Conner of Charleston, who kept a diary as a bride in 1827, wrote of visiting her new husband's family in Mecklenburg as well as several Alexanders and Brevards in Lincoln County, and Robin and Peggy Davidson at Holly Bend. Her husband's name was Henry Conner.[6]

John and Violet's second child, Isabella, was born in September 1764. When she was 23, she married Joseph Graham of Mecklenburg County in 1787 and moved to Lincoln County seven or eight years later. Her husband was born in 1759, raised in Mecklenburg County and was educated at Queens College. He witnessed the reading of the Mecklenburg Declaration of Independence on 20 May 1775.

Beginning in 1781, at the age of 18, Graham served in the militia, taking part in 15 engagements and rising in rank from private to major. Perhaps the high point of his service was in commanding the militia at the Battle of Charlotte. This was a rearguard action opposing the occupation of Charlotte by the British Army under General Cornwallis on 26 September 1780. As the much outnumbered American forces retreated, there were a number of skirmishes. In one of these Graham received three gunshot wounds and six saber cuts and was left on the field for dead. He recovered and continued to serve his country to the end of the war.

After the war he continued his public service as Mecklenburg County sheriff from 1783 to 1791 and as delegate to both of the conventions called to ratify the U.S. Constitution. In later years he was a state senator, on the founding board of the University of North Carolina, and served as a general in both the War of 1812 and the Creek Indian War of 1813–14.

After 1820 he wrote his reminiscences of the Revolution. These were published in 1904 by his grandson. They provide the only existing eyewitness accounts of many of the seminal events of that era, including the public reading of the Mecklenburg Declaration of Independence.[7]

Notable among the eleven children of Isabella and Joseph was Mary, who married Dr. Robert Hall Morrison, who became a renowned Presbyterian minister and the founder and first president of Davidson College. Among Mary's daughters were Anna Morrison, who married the Confederate general Stonewall Jackson, and Isabella Morrison, who married the Confederate general Daniel Harvey Hill.

Another notable child of Joseph and Isabella Graham was William Alexander Graham, who served as governor of North Carolina from 1845 to 1849 and as a U.S. senator and secretary of the navy.

In 1788 the North Carolina General Assembly passed a law designed to encourage the manufacturing of iron. Patents (conveyances of public land) would be issued for up to 3,000 acres of land, free of charge, and free of taxes for ten years, if the land was not fit for cultivation and the grantee produced two and a half tons of iron within three years. Iron manufacturing had been going on in North Carolina since before the Revolution and in Lincoln County since at least 1784. One of the early iron makers was Major John's friend Peter Forney.[8]

Seeing this opportunity, Major John formed a partnership with two sons-in-law, Joseph Graham and Alexander Brevard, to engage in the ironmaking business. Along with Peter Forney they sought a grant of 3,000 acres in 1791. The next year, without Forney, the three of them entered for another grant of 2,640 acres. Both grants were issued in 1795, although the partners had begun to develop the ironworks before that time.

The partners continued to purchase land grants and land from others through the years as the iron business prospered, finally amassing 7,852 acres (over twelve square miles). Then, in 1804, as he neared his 70th year, Major John sold all of his interests in this property and in other iron-making assets to his sons-in-law for $12,200, a large fortune at the time.

A ridge of good quality iron ore, called the Big Ore Bank, runs northeast to southwest through Lincoln County. This deposit supported a thriving iron-making industry from 1780 to 1880. Reminders of that industry survive today in place names in the area such Vesuvius Furnace Road, Brevard Place Road, Ironton Township, Ore Bank Branch (creek) and the town of Iron Station.

North Carolina colonial records indicate that iron making was an active industry in various parts of North Carolina well before the Revolution. Recognizing that iron goods such as cannons, cannon balls and wagon parts were vital to the war effort and could no longer be obtained from England, the assembly passed a number of laws to encourage domestic production. Bonuses were awarded to the iron makers, and their workers were exempt from being drafted into the militia. When General Cornwallis came into the area in 1780, he made a special point of destroying William Hill's Iron Works, located on Allison Creek in South Carolina near the North Carolina border. This was the earliest recorded ironworks in the area, established about 1776.[9]

There had always been a great demand for iron goods of all types in the American colonies, and backcountry Carolina was no exception. The traditional source of supply had been England but that supply began to end with the various nonimportation agreements made in response to the Stamp Act of 1765.

Even when iron ware was available, the expense of transporting these heavy goods by wagon from the nearest head of navigation was excessive. After the war the iron-making business continued and increased. The earliest recorded iron-making activity in Lincoln County was in June 1784 when John Sloan contracted with William Hill of South Carolina to build an ironworks.[10]

When Davidson and his sons-in-law joined with Peter Forney to develop an iron-making business, they were forming a partnership with one of the most experienced iron makers in the backcountry. Of French Huguenot extraction, the Forney family had been early settlers to the west of the Catawba. They had fought on the American side during the Revolution, including at the Battle of Cowan's Ford, where they served with Major John under General William Lee Davidson.[11]

Starting as early as 1784, Peter Forney and others began buying land and land grants on their own and in various partnerships and going into the ironworks business. There were a number of other iron makers in Lincoln and surrounding counties during this time, and many of these furnaces and forges survived and prospered throughout the antebellum period.[12]

When Major John and his partners sought land in 1791 and 1792, it took them nearly four years to complete the grant process. The Lincoln County Court was ordered to appoint a jury of twelve men to examine the proposed area, agree that it was "not fit for cultivation" and report to the court. It was not until after they sought the second grant that this jury was appointed. In addition to determining that none of the land was fit for cultivation, the jurors were to lay out and mark a road "from the Dutch Meetinghouse past the forge now abuilding by Brevard, Davidson & Co."

The county surveyor was then ordered to lay out the land and file the plat with the secretary of state, who then issued the grant. On 16 January 1795 the first grant was issued. The second one was issued nearly a year later in December 1795. The tasks of cutting trees and making charcoal; digging ore and limestone; and building the furnace were well under way by the time the grant was formally issued.

When a blast furnace was built, a forge often was built nearby. A blast furnace burns charcoal mixed with iron ore and limestone. A continuous blast of air into this mixture makes the charcoal burn hot enough to melt and extract molten iron. This iron is cast into goods such as pots and pans, firedogs and backs, various wagon parts and "pigs" of cast iron. These pigs were reheated at a separate location called a forge and beaten to improve purity and to form wrought iron goods. Pig iron could be converted to steel by repeated heating and beating.

From 1795 to 1798 Major John and his two sons-in-law bought additional land in various plots to reach a final total of 7,852 acres. Major John's share of these purchases amounted to an investment of $2,585. During these years the three of them built the Vesuvius blast furnace and the Mount Tirza Forge. They produced and processed the raw materials of charcoal, iron ore and limestone and made and sold a great deal of iron and steel goods. When Major John sold his interest in the partnership to his two sons-in-law in October 1804, the sale included not only all the land but also the furnace and forge, raw materials, finished goods, buildings and enslaved people.[13]

An ironworks required a great deal of land for quarrying the iron ore and limestone, and much more was required for raising the trees which were cut and made into charcoal to run the blast furnace. A typical blast furnace in this area produced about 340 tons of iron in the five-month winter production season. This required 170,000 bushels of charcoal, which consumed the trees on 120 acres of woodland. New trees were planted as the old ones were cut, but it took 25 years for those trees to grow big enough to be used for making charcoal. It took about 3,000 acres of woodland to sustain a continuing iron-making operation.[14]

In 1801 Alexander Brevard and Joseph Graham established a private family cemetery north of Leeper's Creek, midway between their homes. They called it Machpelah in honor of the Cave of the Machpelah in Hebron, the burial ground of Abraham, Isaac and Jacob. The Brevard-Graham cemetery is located near the present-day town of Iron Station, beside the road from Beatties Ford to Lincolnton that later became the Plank Road. Today this cemetery is still in use; Graham, Brevard and the Rev. Robert Hall Morrison lie buried there with many of their prominent descendants.

In 1848 Machpelah Church was build on the site, using a bequest from Alexander Brevard, deceased. The Reverend Morrison was the founding pastor, and services were held there through the Civil War.[15]

In 1765, when Major John bought the land on McDowell Creek and moved his family there, he selected a likely spot and built a two-room log cabin. This became known as Rural Retreat where the rest of their children were born. The family lived there for 23 years, until the construction of Rural Hill in 1788. In 1800 John and Violet's son Jacky married Sarah Brevard and set up housekeeping at Rural Retreat, where all their children were born. Over the years first John and then Jacky added on to Rural Retreat until in the end it had a total of eight rooms. This house burned in 1898, and those who remembered it described it as having one-and-a-half stories, covered inside and out with wide boards.[16]

Such simple cabins were the usual residences of the early settlers as building them required few tools—just a felling axe and a broad axe—and very few nails. In *Albion's Seed. Four British Folkways in America*, David Hackett Fischer describes the cabins and methods of construction used in the southern backcountry by Scots-Irish settlers. It is likely that this is the kind of cabin that housed the Davidson family in those early days.

In this construction the first building was a simple "single-pen" one-room log cabin measuring roughly 16 by 22 feet. The logs were notched at the corners in half-dovetail joints that grew stronger as the building settled. The structure was supported by a large stone at each corner. Doors were cut in the front and rear walls, there was a fireplace at one end and perhaps a window or two. As the family grew, the owner kept adding on to the original cabin.

Adding an identical cabin to one end sharing a common wall, with a second fireplace at the far end, made it a "double-pen" cabin. Removing the roof and raising the structure made a low-ceilinged second floor for children's bedrooms. Finally, a second identical four-room cabin was built behind the first one, again sharing a common wall. Thus the original single-room cabin became an eight-room family home.

The construction was all of hewn logs, usually oak, which was readily available, with a puncheon floor, half-dovetailed corners and a cypress shake roof. The log walls were daubed or chinked with clay, mud and straw in a futile attempt to keep the winter winds out. As the chinking dried out and the logs shrunk in the dry winter air, the chinking soon fell out. As soon as nails became available and a sawmill opened in the neighborhood, the owner covered the outside with lap siding and the inside with vertical planks.[17]

By 1788 the country had recovered from the ravages of the Revolutionary War and Major John had prospered mightily. All of his 10 children had been born and it was time—and he had the resources—to build a fine new manor house for his family. It was a timber-framed brick house made from trees cut on his land and bricks made from local clay and sand.

Because of the time it takes to cut and season timber, make bricks and order nails, doors and windows, and other accouterments from far away, it generally took two or three years to construct such a house. He designed the manor house, which became known as Rural Hill, in the

Georgian or Federal style and built it on a rise a few hundred yards south of Rural Retreat and a half-mile from the Catawba River. It consisted of two stories with a full basement and a high attic, making four floors in all. With a hipped roof and four brick chimneys, two on each end, it was an imposing edifice.

In *Major John Davidson of "Rural Hill"* Chalmers Davidson gives a description of the house, based on family letters and other sources. The floor plan of the homestead in the days before the Civil War was as follows:

> The basement contained the dining room on the east (entire length), a hall, and a kitchen, a pantry and a store-room on the west. The last was the only room in the house without a fireplace.
> The first floor was divided by a central hall about ten feet wide. To the west was the great parlor with a smaller room at the north which was separated by a folding partition. When the partition was folded to the walls the west side of the first floor was thrown into one large apartment. To the east of the central hall were two bed chambers. The second floor was divided by a similar hall with two bed rooms on either side. The rooms to the west of the upstairs hall could be thrown together by raising a hanging partition to the ceiling. Ceilings on both main floors were about ten feet high. The garret was one great room with windows only in the gable ends.[18]

At the time that Rural Hill was built it was not common to have porches on front or back. Many years later the house was improved by adding single-story porches with round, concrete-covered brick columns on both the north and south sides and by bringing light into the garret by extending the roof line to make it a peaked roof with windows in the gable ends. Many of these improvements were made in 1848–49.

An entry in Brevard Davidson's farm journal for 14 October 1849 reads, "Finished raising my porch to the north side of my house to day, and putting the rafters up." Brevard also wrote that the previous August he had made about 34,000 bricks, and in November he bought 15,000 shingles in Cheraw. In September 1849 he hired three hands "to cover & repair my house."

A grandson of Major John's who lived in Florida visited Rural Hill in 1853 and wrote to his wife that the house had been much improved, including the gabled roof. He had last visited Rural Hill in 1838.[19]

When Rural Hill burned in November 1886, the John Springs Davidson family lived in the house, and all were in Charlotte at a fair. It should be noted that the newspaper article about the burning of the house does not call it Rural Hill. Rather it is called "the old Davidson house, in Hopewell." This article also shows that John Springs Davidson was commonly known as "Springs."

Long before his death in 1832 Major John wrote two wills plus a deed of trust, all of which are important in understanding how he distributed his property among his children. The first will was dated 6 September 1823. This will was never probated, was not recorded in the county will book and a copy has not been found. Perhaps someday it may be discovered in the papers of the descendants of William B. Alexander or of William Lee Davidson. Until then some details of the distribution of his property will remain a mystery.

Three months after that first will, on 22 December 1823, he wrote a deed of trust. He wrote that (at the age of 88) he had decided to "break up house keeping ... & to retire from the [illeg] of the world & spend the reminder of my days with my Children." Feeling, from "age and infirmity," incapable of personally handling the disposal of his assets, he appointed his son-in-law William Lee Davidson as his trustee. Lee was the youngest son of General William Lee Davidson, born shortly after the general's death at the Battle of Cowan's Ford during the Revolution. He and Major John's youngest daughter, Elizabeth, had been married in 1805.

This deed of trust directed Lee Davidson to distribute Major John's property as recorded in the will of 6 September 1823, saying that the will was "in the hands of W^m. B Alexander for safe keeping & I hereby authorize the s^d. W^m. L Davidson to take a copy of the s^d. Will & to make it his guide in selling off my property as affors^{ed}."[20]

Major John directed William Lee Davidson to dispose at public sale all of his "negroes, horses, cattle, corn, cotton, household furniture, blacksmith tools, a still and vessels," farming equipment and nearly all other

> **An Old Time Residence Burned.**
>
> News reached this city yesterday evening that the old Davidson house, in Hopewell, had been destroyed by fire. We did not learn the origin of the fire. Mr. J. Springs Davidson, the owner, was here at the fair when the messenger arrived. The house was a large and splendid brick building, built in 1778, by Major John Davidson, grandfather of Mr. J. S. Davidson. This splendid mansion was endeared to many in this section by tender memories and recollections of genuine hospitalities, and the loss will cause a pang of sincere regret in this entire section of country.

THE BURNING OF RURAL HILL. The mention of "J. Springs Davidson" is one of the very few places where we can see how people of this era were referred to. Legal records used first and last names and sometimes middle names. We learn that some people went by their middle names or by some nickname only through newspaper articles, journals and personal letters. *Charlotte Daily Chronicle* 5 November 1886.

THE RUINS OF RURAL HILL. This photograph was taken around 1890. The woman in the foreground may be Minnie Caldwell Davidson. Note the two dogs and a sheep. In those days, before the invention of the lawn mower, sheep were often allowed to roam the grounds to keep down the vegetation. The English boxwoods still grow at Rural Hill. The men standing in the doorway of the ruins might be Minnie's husband, John Springs Davidson, and their two oldest sons, Jo Graham and Thomas. Photograph in the collection of the authors, a gift from the May Davidson Estate.

personal property. Lee Davidson was to distribute the proceeds from this sale according to the terms of the will. Major John reserved for his own use two Negro men, a Negro woman with two children, two horses (named), one bed and other furniture, his bedroom in his house (Rural Hill), and a corn crib at Rural Hill.

Lee Davidson was to distribute certain Negroes to legatees as described in the will as well as the land willed to his sons Benjamin and John. Lee was allowed a 5 percent commission on all sales.

Although Major John reserved a room at Rural Hill for himself, along with a corn crib to feed his horses, we know that at the end of his life he was living with Elizabeth and William Lee Davidson at their plantation, Beaver Dam, near present-day Davidson College. It is not known exactly when Major John moved from Rural Hill to Beaver Dam, but it could have

4. The Davidson Children and Rural Hill

been a gradual move. At 88 he was still physically active and loved to ride his horses. It may be that he kept a room at each house and rode back and forth frequently. The two plantations are about 15 miles apart, which was a three-hour ride, and it was usual in those times to stay overnight when visiting someone even just a few miles away. Or it may be that the major found living in a house with ten children—the youngest were one, three, six and eight—was not as relaxing as living with a childless couple. In any case, by the time he died eight years later he was living full time at Beaver Dam.

His deed of trust was entered in the court minutes and recorded in the county deed book, but because he had not died, it was not entered for probate and there are no further court entries regarding it. None of the records of the distribution of the assets have been found so the value of the residue is not known.

Major John wrote a final will in September 1831 at the age of 96; it was probated after his death the following January. This will, nine years after he retired and distributed the bulk of his property, was to accomplish the final settlement of his estate. It is recorded in the county will books, and the probate documents are at the state archives.[21]

This will contains a number of bequests that were probably in his first will and some that may have been executed by William Lee Davidson at that earlier time. To that extent it shows us some of what was in Major John's mind when he wrote the original will, modified by several deaths and perhaps for other reasons as well.

In the intervening nine years, two of his daughters, Rebecca Brevard and Isabella Graham, had died. He stated that he was giving their children nothing, "for I have given them more than I will be able to bequest to the rest of my children." This is not an unusual phrase; it is found many times in the wills of prosperous men who lived into their old age and whose grown children had become prosperous or had married well.

He gave nothing additional to his daughter Mary McLean, except one young Negro and a share of the residue of the estate. He likewise gave nothing additional to his son Robert or to his daughter Sarah Caldwell, except for a share of the residue to each.

He gave his granddaughter Violet Harris, the daughter of Margaret Harris, deceased, only that which he had given her mother previously and no share of the residue. Margaret was the subject of the deed of trust mentioned in Chapter 3 and Appendix F. Presumably Violet had inherited all her mother's property as guaranteed in that document.

He gave his son Jacky the Rural Hill land ("the land on which I formerly

ACCOUNT OF THE AUCTION SALE OF MAJOR JOHN DAVIDSON. This single-sheet vendue list (all the items to be sold at a public sale) is the only item in the estate records of Major John Davidson, deceased. For each item the list shows the buyer and the amount paid. This was registered in Mecklenburg County Court on 29 May 1832 by William Bain Alexander, son-in-law of Major John and executor of his estate. Image courtesy of the State Archives of North Carolina, Raleigh NC, microfilm, Estate Files, Mecklenburg County.

lived where he now resides including the mills, mansion house, and other improvements"). Note the plural "mills," indicating that Major John had at least two mills on his home place. This land was described as being bounded by "the Indian Ford, the canal, the [Catawba] R," giving another hint as to the improvements that had been made to the property. The "Indian Ford" was probably that known as Tool's Ford, whereas the canal sent Catawba River water to power one or more mills. He also gave Jacky a 100-acre tract of land and a share in the residue of the estate.

Major John gave the remainder of his land to the six sons of his son Benjamin Wilson Davidson, deceased, plus one share of the residue to be divided among them. His daughter Elizabeth Davidson received one share of the residue.

Finally, the executors were to sell all of his personal estate, divide the money into seven equal parts and distribute them as he had specified.

The puzzling thing about this final will is that in it he disposes of his land, leaving it to Jacky and the children of his son Benjamin Wilson Davidson. Major John's will of 1823 must have made that distribution, and his trustee, William Lee Davidson, must have distributed the land as ordered. Perhaps in this final will John was just reinforcing the previous provisions. This will describes his plantation in some detail, although it did not specify the acreage of the various plots.

The probate of this estate was recorded in the county court and documented in the state archives. The record contains only one paper, which is an account of the sale of Major John's personal assets. As referenced in the deed of trust dated nine years before, the sale lists two Negro men, one Negro woman with two children, one horse, some furniture and eight named religious books. The buyers were all family members—his son Robert, his son-in-law William Lee and several grandchildren.[22]

CHAPTER 5

Holly Bend: Robin and Peggy Davidson

ROBERT DAVIDSON, known as Robin and born in April 1769, was the oldest son and fourth child of Major John and Violet. Little is known of his childhood and education although he was literate and wrote a fine hand. His mother certainly taught him basic reading, writing and ciphering, and he may have received additional education at Hopewell or another of the academies kept from time to time by the local Presbyterian churches. However, he was six years old when the American Revolution began, and 11 or 12 when it ended, so it is unlikely that he went away from home for any schooling. Certainly he learned farming from his father by working in the fields and supervising the hands. He continued this until the age of 25, when he bargained with his father for a good piece of land and established a farm of his own in 1795.

On 1 January 1801 Robin married Margaret McWhorter Osborne, called Peggy. He was 31 and she was 24. This match may have been foreordained as they were born on the same day—7 April—seven years apart. In their long life together they were to have no children, and the family story is that Peggy had no toes.

Without children of their own they raised or supported a great number of their nieces and nephews, giving them practical instruction in housewifery and farming. They also put a number of them through school and left bequests to many of them in their wills.[1]

Peggy Osborne was the daughter of Colonel Adlai Osborne of Belmont Plantation on the west branch of Rocky River in Iredell County, just north of the Mecklenburg line. Colonel Osborne's parents had been among the earliest settlers of the Carolina Piedmont, and his father was a leader in public life. Adlai attended Crowfield Academy near Centre Church with his cousin, Ephraim Brevard.[2]

It must have been a good education as they both went on to attend the College of New Jersey (later Princeton University). Ephraim became a doctor and was the author of both the Mecklenburg Declaration of Independence and the Mecklenburg Resolves. He served in the war as a regimental surgeon, was captured at the fall of Charleston and died shortly after being released from a British prison ship.

Peggy's father was a successful farmer, lawyer and politician. He served as the clerk of the Rowan County Court, a member of the Rowan Committee of Safety before the Revolution and as colonel of the Rowan Militia during the war. Adlai's parents died in 1776 and, as their only son, Adlai inherited Belmont, the family manor house, and over 8,000 acres of fine farmland to go with it. As the country recovered from the war, he went from strength to strength, increasing in land, wealth and political influence.

Peggy was one of eleven children in this family, and when she married at the age of 24, she was surely accustomed to having the finer things of life. Her move to Holly Bend as a young bride may have been a step down but not very far down. This newly built house was one of the finest in the backcountry at the time.

In contrast to his father and father-in-law, Robin took very little part in public and political life. Instead he concentrated on improving his land and increasing his holdings. In doing so he became perhaps the richest man in the county by the time of his death in 1853 at the age of 84.

The first mention of Robert Davidson in the public record was in court in April 1795, when he was 26 years old. There were other men in the county named Robert Davidson so some of these records may not apply to him, but he did serve actively on juries in the Mecklenburg County Court and in the District Superior Court in Salisbury. Also in these early years he served as a patroller in his local militia district as an overseer of roads in his neighborhood and as an overseer of the Catawba River. All of these were unpaid positions.

Patrollers were appointed for each of the militia districts. They were to patrol the countryside occasionally, after dark, looking for lawbreakers such as men hunting by firelight or enslaved people traveling without a pass from the slave owner. Patrollers were also on the lookout for stray horses and cattle and for houses or barns on fire.

Some family stories refer to Robin as having been a magistrate or justice of the peace. If this were so, all court records would have referred to him as "Esquire." In Mecklenburg County records there are many mentions of Robert Davidson, but only two of these call him Esquire. In the county court session of August 1813: "Saturday 28th Met according to Adjournment, Joab Alexander, Robert Davidson, John Rea, Esquires." In August 1827: "Ordered that Robt. Davidson & Wm. L. Davidson, Esq[rs]., be a Committee."

The first one of these indicate that he presided at the Court of Common Pleas and Quarter Session, and only a justice of the peace could do that. In the second instance the honorific may have referred to William L. Davidson, and not to Robin. The fact that he was not called Esquire in his many other court appearances and that he did not appear at the annual meetings of justices of the peace seem to indicate that he was not one.[3]

ROBIN DAVIDSON OF HOLLY BEND. In 1846, at the age of 77, "Uncle Robin" had this portrait made by Thomas Wrightman as a present for a favorite niece. Starting the year after Robin's death in 1853, six or more of his nieces and nephews had copies made. Almost all remain in private hands. Dr. Douglas Marion, Davidson family genealogist, has tracked and documented the whereabouts of Davidson family papers and artifacts, including these portraits. Image from the private collection of Dr. Douglas Marion.

An overseer of roads was responsible for the upkeep of a particular section of the public road. Overseers were appointed by the county court and served without pay. If a man declined to serve, or failed to do his duty as an overseer, he could be fined by the county court, and these were not minor fines. Appendix I covers the particulars of road and river work.

Once a year, or more often as needed, an overseer organized and led a group of local property owners to clean and maintain his assigned section of road. A road was made by cutting down trees and clearing brush without moving any dirt except to knock down the banks where the road crossed a stream. These were dirt roads without any gravel or other pavement.

The modern method of building roads with a surface of gravel was developed by the Scottish engineer John McAdam in 1816 and introduced in America in about 1830. It was expensive and labor intensive and was used only for major roads in northern cities. A method of covering the surface of the road with tar was developed in 1902 in Europe to keep down the dust caused by that modern invention, the motor car.

In 1797 Robin was appointed overseer of the section of road from "Barry's Bridge to Amos Alexanders." In 1801 he was appointed "Overseer of the Road from the Middle of the Catawba River at Tools ford to Andrew Barrys."[4] This is today Neck Road from Mountain Island Lake past Rural Hill to Beatties Ford Road.

According to county court records, Robin Davidson was one of the original Catawba River keepers.

A number of laws were passed in North Carolina in the colonial period requiring the rivers to be kept open for the free passage of fish. From county records we know that these laws were enforced in the backcountry as well as closer to the coast. The fish these laws were designed to protect and encourage were the American and hickory shad, which migrated upstream to spawn in huge quantities in March and April of each year.

Shad are not found in the Catawba River today because flood control and hydroelectric dams have blocked the spawning runs. Below these dams are active fisheries in the Roanoke, Chowan, Neuse, Tar and Cape Fear rivers in North Carolina and in other rivers such as the Hudson in New York, the St. Johns in Florida and the Delaware River in Pennsylvania and New Jersey. Shad have recently returned to other streams when dams were removed.

From recorded deeds we know that Robin owned at least two fisheries on the Catawba and probably many more. He purchased one in partnership with Samuel Wilson in 1796 when Robin was 26 and another on his own in 1825 when he was 56. That same year he bought several islands in the Catawba, just below Cowan's Ford, upstream from his plantation. These may have been for a fishery. He also owned a number of other tracts on the Catawba where he may have established fisheries.

As various colonial and state laws indicate, and as verified by county court records, it was important to keep the river channel clear of trees and other blockages so that fish could be free to migrate upstream to spawn. One example among many is the law passed in 1787, "An Act to Enable the County Courts to Appoint Commissioners to Keep Open Rivers and

Creeks at Their Several Falls so far as They Think Necessary, for the Passage of fish Up the Same." These commissioners were to examine the rivers to ensure that any dams extended only three-quarters of the way across and that the open one-fourth part was in the deepest water. On smaller streams mill owners were to ensure that their dams included slopes, or fish ladders, which were kept open during the spawning runs.[5] Appendix I covers the particulars of road and river work.

There were at least ten fisheries on the Catawba River mentioned in the county records. When they were bought and sold, they always demanded a good price. Robin's neighbor James Latta owned several of these, as did other leading planters who lived on the river.[6]

A fishery was generally a place where the river narrows and diversion dams can be built on both sides slanting upstream. When the fish are running in their spring migration, they are forced to the gap between the two dams, or weirs, in the middle of the river and can be easily caught in nets. The migrating fish swim into the nets and are lifted out of the water.

Indians had fished in the river using fish traps of woven oak splints to catch individual fish. Early settlers built and used traps such as these to catch fish year-round for the table.

There is no documentary evidence, but it is highly probable that grabbling was widely used to catch fish. This is an ancient form of fishing, still used today, in which a person stands in a river or stream with hands in the water. When a fish swims by the human grabs it and throws it on the bank or into a basket nearby. This is an extremely effective method and is today illegal to use for game fish (bass, trout, etc.) in most states. It is, however, used for nongame fish, especially catfish in the southern states.

Some of the fish were sold fresh in the neighborhood and in villages, but most were salted down in wooden barrels. They were used to feed people on the plantation through the year and sold to local merchants for resale. Large quantities were shipped to markets as far away as Charleston.

From there the fish were shipped to the Sugar Islands and elsewhere. At that time the islands of the Caribbean were referred to as the "Sugar Islands" because England, France, Holland and Spain had claimed them and established sugar cane plantations, which were peopled with African slaves. During the fish runs in February and March the fish made a good "cash crop" and also made productive use of the hands (a slave working in the fields was referred to as a hand, whereas one working in the house was referred to as a servant) during a normally slack time.

Throughout the early history of America there are accounts of great runs of shad up all of the rivers on the eastern seaboard. The American shad spends its life in saltwater but, like the salmon, returns to the freshwaters of its birth to spawn. Some die after spawning, but some, like the Atlantic salmon, live to return to the ocean and come home to spawn again. Shad are in the herring family and, although full of small bones, are delicious, either fresh or salted, and much prized by sportsmen today. The shad runs in colonial times were described as "blackening the rivers" or "a boiling of the waters" and contained millions of fish. In some cases the catch was limited only by the number of barrels and amount of salt available for preserving the fish.[7]

In the July session of 1797, when Robin was 28, the county court named him one of the "Overseers and Commissioners appointed to remove obstructions in the navigation of the Catawba." He was assigned the segment from Dutchman's Creek to Tool's Ford. This was the first instance in the county court records when such river commissioners were appointed. As a commissioner he was entitled to draw labor from those who lived on the river, just as the overseer of a section of road could draw on the residents nearby to keep the road clear. The river was divided into four segments with overseers appointed for each segment:

- From the South Carolina Line to the Mouth of the South Fork River.
- From the Mouth of the South Fork River to the Mouth of Dutchman's Creek.
- From the Mouth of Dutchman's Creek to Tools Ford. [This is at the big bend in the Catawba; the western end of Robin's land.]
- From Tools Ford to Lord Granville's Line. [This is today the Mecklenburg-Iredell County line.]

The commissioners were to work with Peter Forney of Lincoln County, who had been appointed by that county's court. They were to make sure not only that the dams complied with the law but also to remove fallen trees and other snags that blocked the stream and prevented fish from migrating.[8]

Apparently some of the appointed commissioners did not do their job well enough, and eighteen months later, "On a petition of Sundry of the inhabitants of the County of Mecklenburg," the court appointed three commissioners to examine the river and ensure that it was being kept clear for the "free passage of fish up the Catawba River." Robin must have been doing the job well for he was reappointed as one of these commissioners.[9]

In 1812 Robin was appointed one of three commissioners to superintend the entire Catawba River in Mecklenburg County and remove obstructions.

In 1816 three commissioners were again appointed to examine the Catawba to ensure that the dams did not block more than three-fourths of the width of the river. Robin was one of these commissioners.

A search of the transcripts of the court records, using the index entry of "Catawba River," revealed many entries regarding river overseers. All of these listed Robin Davidson. From 1801 to 1820 Robin was the only appointed river keeper for his section, and it is probable that he performed that function on a continuous basis. From 1821 to 1860 there is no mention of river overseers in the county court records.

From the beginning of the settlement of the Carolina backcountry into the 18th and 19th centuries Tool's Ford was an important river crossing and landmark on the Catawba River in Anson, now Mecklenburg and Lincoln counties. Eighteenth-century maps showed only a few fords, such as Nations Ford and the Trading Ford, but by 1808 many more fords and the roads leading to them were shown on the maps. Tool's Ford, along with the road leading to it, was referenced in grants, deeds and county records and was shown on all of these maps. However, sometime between 1882 and 1911 Tool's Ford and the road leading to it disappear from the maps and are never seen again.

Matthew Tool was among the earliest settlers in the Carolina backcountry. He received a land grant in Anson County in 1750, the year that Anson was formed out of Bladen County. In 1754 he entered for and purchased a land grant for 495 acres located "at the south side of a beaver pond." Tool was a great friend of the Catawba Indians located in this area. In August 1754 a conference was held "at the house of Mr. Matthew Tool" between the Royal Province of North Carolina and the Catawba Indians led by King Hagler. Tool both hosted the conference and served as the sworn interpreter for the conference and the treaty that came from it. The speech, or "talk," that King Hagler gave at that conference, as translated by Tool, is recorded in the *North Carolina Colonial Records*.[10]

Another conference was held with Hagler and the Catawbas in Salisbury in May 1756. Tool was again the official interpreter for this conference and translated a talk given by King Hagler. These are the only two speeches of King Hagler that are recorded in the *North Carolina Colonial Records*. Apparently Tool had considerable influence among the Catawbas for in November 1756 Virginia governor Robert Dinwiddie complained to North Carolina governor Arthur Dobbs that a Mr. Osborne and Matthew

Tool gave advice that caused the Catawbas not to support the Royal Army in Virginia during the French and Indian War.

Tool died sometime between 1756 and November 1779, when a deed records the sale of land "Being the plantation that Mathew Toole did live on."[11]

Early maps, starting with the Price Strother map of 1808, show a ford in this area. A later map, the MacRae-Brazier of 1833, gives it the name of Tool's Ford. On these maps a road is shown running due east from Tool's Ford to near the plantation of John McNitt Alexander, called 'Alexandriana Post Office.'" The road runs through land owned by Major John and Robin, and the ford itself is on land owned by Robin.[12]

Tool's Ford was well known and used as a reference to divide the river into sections for maintenance. It was used during the Revolution as a crossing place for several groups of militia that would defeat the Tories at the Battle of Ramseur's Mill near present-day Lincolnton.[13]

In early 1781 as the British Army under General Cornwallis advanced toward the Catawba River, Tool's Ford was fortified with fallen trees, a ditch and parapet and defended by 70 men. That may have influenced the British decision to force a crossing at Cowan's Ford, just north of Tool's, which was not fortified and was defended by only 25 men under a lieutenant. This gives some indication of the relative importance of Tool's as a river crossing.[14]

The Kerr-Cain map of 1882 shows the same road and ford location. In 1911 Mecklenburg County issued a map produced by C. A. and J. B. Spratt, surveyors. Tool's Ford and the road leading to it are not shown on that map.

Today Neck Road runs from Beatties Ford Road to Rural Hill, crossing McDowell Creek just before reaching the plantation. A short stretch of this road runs due east and west, south of the ruins of Rural Hill and north of the Davidson Family Burying Ground. At the end of that stretch Allison's Ferry Road branches off to the north. Neck Road jogs south and passes to the south of the Holly Bend Plantation House.

If Neck Road is extended due west at its junction with Allison's Ferry Road, it passes only a few yards north of Holly Bend. The public entrance for this house was on its north face, while the south face, with its wide porch, hosted the family entrance. Electric power lines follow Neck Road to Allison's Ferry Road and then continue due west past Holly Bend to the Cowan's Ford Wildlife Refuge. Visual examinations of the ground have failed to find any other evidence of the road.[15]

Tool's Ford today lies under the waters of Mountain Island Lake, which supplies drinking water to the city of Charlotte. This lake was created in 1924, as a flood control and power generation lake, shortly after the Great Catawba River Flood of 1916. The land is low and swampy on both sides of the lake near where Tool's Ford may have been located, and there is no evidence to be found of the ford on the banks of the river.

It is not known how Tool's Ford came to be abandoned. Moore's Ferry, which crossed the river just north of Tool's Ford, was established as early as 1859. Later in the 19th century Alison's Ferry was located there. Today Alison's Ferry Road runs from Neck Road north to the river, where there is a small settlement. After Moore's Ferry was established, Tool's Ford was probably used less and less and only for very local traffic such as an occasional herd of cattle. Eventually the road fell into disuse and was abandoned. The construction of Mountain Island Dam flooded the land and put a final end to Tool's Ford.

In October 1798 Robin served on a jury to determine the mental condition of the Rev. Alexander Caldwell, who had married Robin's sister Sarah four years before. Alexander Caldwell had been the pastor of Rocky River Church and was dismissed from the pastorate in 1797 because he had become deranged.

The jury found Caldwell to be in a "state of lunacy" and appointed his brother, the Reverend Samuel C. Caldwell, Alexander's guardian. Sarah and her three children moved back home to Rural Hill. These children, Martha (nicknamed Patsy), John H., and David Alexander, were all under the age of five at that time. Holly Bend was just a short walk away, and it is probable that these children spent considerable time at Holly Bend, not only visiting but living there for extended periods through their childhood. It was the custom at the time that when a man or a couple had no children and expected that they would not have any, they took into their home a male relative, usually a nephew, often an orphan. They raised this boy as their own child and made him heir to their estate.

The youngest of the children of Alexander and Sarah, David Alexander Caldwell, became one of the executors of Robin's will and received from him a bequest of 15 Negroes and 500 to 600 acres of land.

Patsy received 10 shares of stock in the Bank of the State of North Carolina that were worth $1,000 and three Negroes in Robin's will. She may have lived at Holly Bend for some time, learning the arts of spinning and housewifery from her aunt Peggy. At the time of Robin's death Patsy was married to Colonel John H. Davidson and lived in Alabama.

The third child of Alexander and Sarah, John H. Caldwell, is not mentioned in either Robin's or Peggy's will. Examination of the county deed books shows that John owned a great deal of property at that time. He had probably been put out to some other relative to learn the trade of agriculture and made his fortune in the usual way, by working for it.

In 1822 the Reverend Samuel C. Caldwell turned over the guardianship of his brother "Alexander Caldwell, Lunatic," to David Alexander Caldwell (who had just turned 21), John H. Davidson (husband of Patsy), and John H. Caldwell.[16]

In the October court of 1802 Robin and Peggy took in an orphan. "Ordered that Jean Price, an Orphan of John Price, Decd. Now about nine years old, be bound to Robert Davidson until she is of Age, to learn the Art & Mystery of a Spinster and Seamstress, & the Said Davidson is to Comply with the Law."

This is the only instance in the court records of Robin and Peggy's taking an apprentice. They took in a number of their nieces and nephews for varying periods of time and taught them the skills of house and farm but either did not feel the need for a formal agreement or did not register the agreement in court.

The institution of apprenticeship was in full force and widely used at that time. It made provision for situations in which an orphan needed somewhere to live, although most apprenticeships seem to have come from intact families that put the children out to learn a trade. Often the trade they learned was "the art and mystery of a farmer" or of housewifery. To us it sounds oppressive, but in that day it was beneficial to both apprentice and master. The child needed to learn a way to make a living or to become a skilled housewife, and the master made good use of the labor.

There were state laws protecting the rights of an apprentice; these provided that at the end of their apprenticeship they were to receive such things as a suit of clothes, a sum of money, tools of their trade, and so on. There were a number of court cases in which a master had an apprentice taken away from him because he abused the apprentice or was not training or providing properly for them. Also from time to time a master was brought into court and forced to provide the suit of clothes, cash, tools, and the like that the law required.

Robin Davidson first appears in Mecklenburg land records with a state grant for "93 A on the east bank of Catawba R. adjacent Bailey and John Davidson." He filed this grant in 1792 when he was 23 years old. It was surveyed by John McKnitt Alexander the next year and issued in July 1794. The cost of the grant was 30 shillings per 100 acres plus the cost of surveying and registering the grant. This grant claimed all of the vacant land between his father's land, that of his neighbor Francis Bailey and the Catawba River.[17]

The following February Robin and his father executed a pair of deeds in which Robin sold Major John a portion of that state grant for a token sum and received a large piece of property "for love and affection." This is the only land Major John gave away until he dissolved his estate near the end of his life.

These two deeds were executed on the same day, 23 February 1795. Robin sold his father 31 acres of his 93-acre grant. In turn he received 430 acres in three tracts from his father. One witness to that deed was Margaret Davidson, Robin's younger sister, who had just reached the legal age of 18 and could witness the deed.

Robin immediately began to acquire more land. The next year, in partnership with Samuel Wilson, who lived nearby, Robin bought a fishery of 23 acres at Tool's Ford. It was the only time that Robin ever entered into a joint investment.

In the next five years Robin acquired an additional 683 acres of land in that same area. By 1846, near the end of his life, he owned several plantations totaling 2,507 acres, all of it on McDowell Creek or the Catawba River; some of it appears to have been for fisheries. This made Robin one of the largest landowners in Mecklenburg County at the time.

Robin was buying all of this land for his plantation and not for speculation. The only piece of land he ever sold was the 31 acres to his father. However, he did give 40 acres to his brother Jacky "for love and affection" in 1819. This was involved in the complicated land sales and swaps in that year as his father distributed land to Robin's two brothers.

Throughout the federal period each county in North Carolina made an annual tax list to assess local taxes in support of the county government. This was a listing of the heads of household showing for each the amount of land in acres, the number of white polls (heads) and the number of black polls in that household. This tax was called a poll tax, or a head tax.

A white poll was a white man aged 21 to 50. A black poll was a black man or woman aged 12 to 50.

In addition to the number of polls, the entries listed the amount of each property owner's land in acres, the number of cotton gins, stud horses and town lots. Cotton gins were listed as the number of "saws." A cotton gin separated the cotton fiber from the seeds by means of an array of saw blades, much like the blade of a circular saw. Thus the number of saws in a gin was a measure of the ginning capacity of the machine.

Over the years most of these tax lists have been lost, but a handful

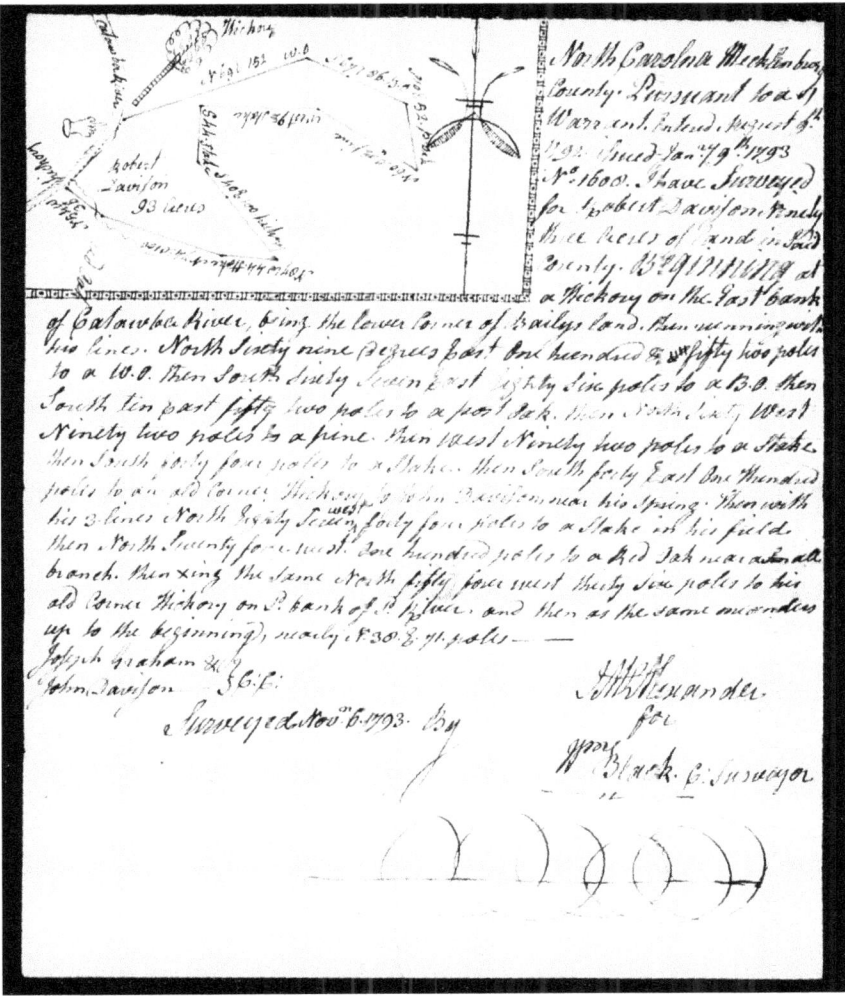

ROBERT DAVIDSON LAND GRANT. This is a "fill-in" grant for unclaimed land surrounded by other plats. It is the claim that began Robin Davidson's land acquisition. The surveyor was John McKnitt Alexander, who surveyed much of the land in north Mecklenburg County. Image courtesy of the State Archives of North Carolina, Raleigh NC, microfilm call # S.108.845 frame 623.

have survived, including five for the period 1797 to 1807. Even these are not complete as some pages are missing. These five tax lists were transcribed by Ralph and Herman Ferguson and give an interesting snapshot of life in Mecklenburg during this brief period.[18]

The listings for Robert Davidson show

1798—500 acres, 1 white poll, 3 black polls

1799—875 acres, 1 white poll, 4 black polls

1806—1,300 acres, 1 white poll, 12 black polls, one 46-saw cotton gin.

These few tax lists document Robin's development as a planter. By 1799, at the age of 30, before he was married, he owned more land than his father, who reported only 600 acres that year.

There is no indication that Robin practiced a craft such as blacksmithing as his father had, nor did he operate as a merchant. He did, however, build and operate a number of grist and lumber mills and at least one cotton gin. The 46 saws shown in his tax list indicate that he owned and operated two, or perhaps three, cotton gins.

With a reliable supply of water power from the Catawba River, he ground grain, sawed lumber and ginned cotton for his neighbors, especially in times of drought when mills on smaller streams were unusable. By law and custom he received a toll of 10 to 15 percent for that service. No records have survived of the income and expenses of his shad fisheries, but considering the amount of money he spent in buying them, they must have presented a considerable source of income, allowing him to buy more land and slaves.[19]

Little is known of the building of the plantation house known today as Holly Bend as no records remain from the time. Fortunately this magnificent manor house still exists today. Additions were built on the north side of the house in the late 19th and early 20th centuries, but the basic fabric of the original house has been very little changed over the years. Today it is owned by Mecklenburg County Parks and Recreation, which maintains and safeguards it.

There are no records indicating whether Robin and Peggy named their house and, if so, what they called it. In 1853 it was referred to as Neck Plantation. In 1933 Dr. Chalmers Davidson called it Hollywood, and 35 years later he called it Holly Bend. Various reports have called it each of these names, as well as "Holly Wood." Today it is known as Holly Bend, referencing holly trees that may have grown in the bend of the Catawba River.

When Robin acquired the property from his father in 1795 at the age of 26, he may have continued to live at home in Rural Hill or in an existing cabin on this property. It generally took two or three years to build a house; tax and census records show that Robin was living on the Holly Bend land as early as 1798. Probably the house was finished before his marriage of 1 January 1801, so the house has been dated as having been built around 1800.

At the time it was built the house was magnificent, although perhaps not as grand as his father's Rural Hill. It remains today one of the finest and best preserved antebellum homes in the area. The Latta Plantation house is nearby and also was built around 1800. While the plan of that house is quite different from Holly Bend's, they share a number of architectural details, and the same craftsmen may have worked on both houses.

Today there is a large porch across the south front of Holly Bend from end to end. Photographs taken in the early 1900s show a similar porch ending just below the outermost windows. When Edwin Osborne visited his aunt Peggy in 1859, he remarked on "the long front porch." Such porches were not common in 1800, but the siding between the these outermost windows is flush rather than lapped. Lapped siding sheds water and is used where there is no roof protection. This indicates that this portion of the original siding was under the porch roof and that the porch itself was part of the original construction rather than a later addition.

After Robin's death in 1853 Peggy continued to live there until her death in 1864. At that time, according to Robin's will, the property went to his nephew Robert F. Davidson, son of Benjamin Wilson Davidson, Robin's brother who had died in 1829.

As in so many other cases, the house and land were sold by the courts during the reconstruction era after the Civil War. At about this time an addition was built on the north side of the house. The house was again sold by the courts during the Great Depression of the 1930s. Finally, in 1970, L. Garner Eakes bought the property as a place to hunt, fish, and entertain his friends. He initially considered pulling the house down but fell in love with it and decided to restore it. Guided and directed by the architect and restorations specialist Jack Boyte, Eakes carefully restored the house. He changed it as little as possible while preserving it from deterioration and making it a comfortable place to spend time. He and his hunting friends enjoyed the house, and his family spent Thanksgiving and Christmas holidays in the old house. This restoration brought heat and plumbing to the 19th-century addition, but the original house received only electricity.[20]

In addition to the decennial U.S. Census and a very few existing tax lists, county court records give us only small amounts of information about enslaved populations. As with the registration of deeds, it was not required that sales of slaves be recorded, although it was usual for the buyer to receive a bill of sale. Except for a few court records of slave sales, the only information we have about the slave population, in addition to the census

HOLLY BEND PLANTATION HOUSE CA. 2010. Except for a late 19th-century extension and the addition of electricity, this house is unchanged from when it was built about 1800. This is where Robin and Peggy lived when they were first married and for the rest of their lives. Today it is part of the Cowan's Ford Wildlife Refuge, and there are plans to open it to the public as an historic site. Photograph by the author.

records, comes from wills and estate papers and a few letters and other original documents that have been preserved. From time to time lists of slaves were kept on some of the larger plantations, but if Robin made any such lists they have not survived, except for the bequests in his will. The 1850 census shows that Robin owned 109 people, making him the largest slave owner in Mecklenburg County. Robin's will two years later named 117 slaves.

The county court records show only two transactions for Robin Davidson regarding slaves. On 1 February 1801 Robin bought two enslaved teenagers, Hannah, 16, and Dilce, 13, from his father-in-law, Adlai Osborne, for $550. This was just one month after Robin's marriage to Peggy. She had been raised in great wealth and may have brought her own slaves into the marriage. Hannah and Dilce may have been particular favorites of hers who were still owned by her father. Perhaps she convinced her new husband to buy them for her.

The other transaction came in 1824, when Robin and his brothers and sisters, the "expected heirs & legatees of Jno. Davidson, Sr.," released to Sarah Caldwell "their interest in the Negro Cyrus." Their sister Sarah had moved to Rural Hill after her husband, the Rev. Alexander Caldwell, was declared a lunatic in 1798. By 1824 she may have gone to live with her married daughter, Patsy, or with one of her sons, both of whom had reached their majority.

The father of Robin and his siblings, Major John, had broken up housekeeping and distributed many of his possessions the previous year. Cyrus appears to have been a gift to Sarah from the other children. Major John's will distributed the land to his children in some way (the documentation has not been found). His personal property, including his slaves, was to be sold by the executors and the proceeds distributed among the heirs. This agreement probably saved Cyrus from the auction block and ensured that he would belong to Sarah.

Chapter 6

Robin and Peggy: Family, Wills and Estates

ROBIN DAVIDSON WROTE HIS WILL on 24 July 1852 at the age of 83. He died eleven months later on 14 June 1853, but his will made almost all of the bequests effective as of the date of the will rather than the date of his death. In this way it was more a retirement distribution than a will. This will is also peculiar in that the usual phrases found at the beginning of wills of this time, such as "being of sound mind and a low state of health," "knowing it is given to man once to die," or "commending my soul to God and my body to the ground," are not present in the will. The will simply states, "Robert Davidson's Will. In the name of God, Amen." It states that this is his last will and testament, gives the date and begins listing the bequests, organized as 26 items over ten pages.[1]

Robin was a very successful planter. In his will he distributed 2,131 acres of land in nine tracts plus one tract of 500 to 600 acres and one tract for which he did not state the acreage. In sixteen bequests he distributed 117 named Negroes in family groups. Twelve of these groups included "and family," indicating an even larger number of Negroes. Since Robin and Peggy had no children of their own, he distributed his fortune among a number of their nieces and nephews after first making provisions for Peggy during her lifetime.

He also disposed of his stock, valued at $100 per share, in the Bank of the State of North Carolina. Robin owned 100 shares of the bank stock, as confirmed by a receipt in his estate papers for a dividend on 100 shares. His will bequeathed 95 of these shares and Peggy's will later indicated that she already owned the final five shares.[2]

6. Robin and Peggy: Family, Wills and Estates

Robin's will gives a unique view of the nature of the real and personal property of a successful planter in 1852, which is not seen in other estates. In many cases the assets of an estate are distributed gradually to the children as the boys reached maturity and as the girls married. These gifts were usually not made part of the public record, and often the deeds were not recorded. In the case of Robin, although the various tracts of land were transferred during his lifetime, none of them were registered in the county deed books at that time. It also appears that many of the tracts of land that Robin bequeathed had not been registered when he acquired them.

In many estates the main piece of property bequeathed is of "the land I now live on" without any further description. This can go from generation to generation without being registered, making it difficult or impossible to determine where the family lived or how much land they owned. Wills seldom mention houses and outbuildings and then only as "the manor house," so it is difficult to determine the size or type of house they lived in.

Over the years Robin and Peggy had taken in many of their nieces and nephews. Some may have spent only a few months, others a number of years, with them. It was usual at the time to send a child to live with a relative to learn a craft or to learn farming or housewifery in exchange for their labors. When a man died, his children were considered orphans even though their mother still lived. Often these orphans went to live with relatives or were put to an apprenticeship because their widowed mother could not support them. These orphans were usually much better off in their new situations: If their mother did not remarry life was hard. If and when she did remarry they were in the position of stepchildren to their mother's new husband without any legal rights or privileges. However, in a wide reading of personal letters, most step-parents referred to their spouse's children as "my children" and treated them as if they were. The words "half" and "step" almost never appear outside of the legal realm. This custom of taking in nieces, nephews and orphans accounts for a large number of Robin's bequests.

◆ ◆ ◆

James Walker Osborne was the son of Edwin J. Osborne, Peggy's brother. After his mother died in 1815, James W. came to live with Robin and Peggy at the age of four. The boy's father soon moved to Alabama and died there.

James inherited land and slaves from Robin and was one of the executors of his will. In that will Peggy received 32 Negroes and their families, who went to Osborne after Peggy's death. Osborne also received 303 acres of land in two tracts.

David Alexander Caldwell was also an executor of Robin's will. He received about 700 acres and 12 Negroes. After Peggy's death he was to receive "the three old servants Cuff, Patt and Dilse and to provide them a Comfortable support during life." He also was to receive Robin's clock and his six-volume set of *Scotts Bible* after Peggy died. David Alexander and his brother and sister had grown up at Rural Hill after his father had been declared a lunatic.[3]

David's older sister Patsy married a man named John Howard Davidson. He was not related by blood to Major John and was known as "Long Headed Jacky" to distinguish him from the other John Davidsons in the area. By the time that Robin wrote his will, Martha and her family had moved to Alabama. She received two Negroes and ten shares of bank stock in the will.

Ben H. Davidson received five Negroes from Robin's estate. He was one of the orphaned sons of Robin's brother Benjamin Wilson Davidson.

A total of 16 nieces, nephews and other extended family members received bequests in Robin's will, as did 19 more mentioned in Peggy's will of 1855. Many may have lived at Holly Bend from time to time, and certainly all of them had visited frequently.

In Robin's provision for Peggy she received 29 percent of his 780 acres and 39 percent of his 117 Negroes. All of the bequests of Negroes included the phrase "and their increase," which avoided any question of ownership of the future children of these enslaved people. Robin's will gave her 46 named Negroes, including five families,

JAMES W. OSBORNE. This miniature portrait was made in 1823 when James was 12. He achieved great success in Charlotte as a lawyer, judge, gold mine owner and supervisor of the U.S. branch mint. Image from the private collection of Dr. Douglas Marion.

and she was to have "complete power of control and ultimate disposal" over these enslaved people. On her death, "in compliance with her expressed wishes," the enslaved people were to go to James W. Osborne for his life and then to his children.

One bequest in Robin's will went to Robert Franklin Davidson. On the date of the will he held clear title to the property but did not possess it until Peggy died. The three parcels of land totaled 780 acres, including "the tract on which I now live" of 430 acres plus a group of 12 named Negroes and one Negro family, Robin's blacksmith tools, cotton gin, machine and press, threshing machine and straw cutter. The mansion house was not named in the will but was included since it was located on "the tract where I now live."

Robert F. was the eldest son of Robin's brother Benjamin Wilson Davidson. Wilson had died in 1829, leaving six sons under the age of eleven. Robert F. was ten years old when his father died. His mother, Betsy Latta Davidson, married Rufus Reed when Robert F. was 16. It is probable that by that time he was living and working at Holly Bend, following the usual custom with orphans. By the time that Robin wrote his will, Robert F. was 33 years old and probably had been running one of Robin's plantations.

Among the Negroes named in Robin's will was Humphrey, who was commended to "the Special Care of my Nephew Robert hoping that by Kindness and attention to his Comfort and happiness he may be in Some degree Rewarded for his faithfulness to me during Many Years Service."

In addition to the property that would go to Robert F. after her death, Robin's will gave Peggy a life interest in those things she would need to have on the plantation: the Negro boy named Charles, household and kitchen furniture, the best wagon and harness, farming tools, five horses or mules, and food for a year for Peggy and her Negroes. In addition she was to select whatever she wanted from Robin's library and to have Robin's clock and his Bible. These last two items were bequeathed to David A. Caldwell on her death.

Benjamin Wilson Davidson's second son, John Ramsey Davidson, received 162 acres of land and a family of seven Negroes in Robin's will. It was probable that he too was raised and trained by Robin. John Ramsey was nine years old when his father died and 14 when his mother remarried. At the time Robin made this will John Ramsey was 30 years old, and he had probably been farming the land that he then received from Robin.

The youngest son of Benjamin Wilson Davidson was Benjamin Howard Davidson, born 10 February 1829, seven months before his father died.

He received a bequest of five Negroes in Robin's will but no land, an indication that he had probably lived with another relative or perhaps was raised by his stepfather, Rufus Reed.

From Robin, James W. Osborne received a very large bequest of Negroes, to be his on Margaret's death. As noted earlier, he was the son of Margaret's brother Edward Jay Osborne. In 1798 Edward was a member of the first graduating class of the University of North Carolina; had married Harriet Walker, daughter of Captain John Walker of Wilmington; studied law and settled in Wilmington. Sometime after 1806 he and Harriet removed to Salisbury.

James's mother died in 1815 when he was four years old, and he was sent to live with Uncle Robin and Aunt Peggy. His father moved to Alabama sometime after 1817 and died soon thereafter. Robin and Peggy raised James Osborne as if he were their own son. They gave him a good education, including sending him to the university; he graduated in 1830 at the age of 18. He studied law in Hillsborough, was admitted to the bar in 1833 and served as Mecklenburg County solicitor for two years. He married Mary Ann Irwin Moore, widow of Thomas J. Moore and daughter of John Irwin, a prominent and prosperous merchant and banker in Charlotte.

Although James Osborne stayed very close to the couple who raised and educated him, he spent the rest of his life in Charlotte. In addition to his law practice, he owned and operated a number of very successful gold mines. He was active in politics and was the supervisor of the Charlotte branch of the U.S. Mint for a number of years.

Starting in 1847 he was a leader of a movement to build a railroad from Charlotte to Columbia, South Carolina, funded entirely with private investments. With the intelligence to understand the issues, the writing and speaking skills to convince people to invest, and the tireless energy to push the issue, he succeeded in raising the required $1 million to build the road. When the Charlotte and South Carolina Railroad opened in 1852, it ushered in an era of commerce and prosperity that caused the population of Charlotte to double by 1860 and ensured the future growth and prosperity of Charlotte and the surrounding area as a transportation hub.

In addition to the Negroes already mentioned, Robin gave James W. Osborne a tract of 303 acres that Peggy had inherited from her father, Adlai Osborne, James's grandfather. Although Osborne had given the land to his daughter Peggy, it had immediately passed to her husband, Robin, and was his to pass on in his will.

Robin also gave bequests to two of the children of James W. Osborne.

He gave Robert Davidson Osborne, age eight at the time, one Negro and a tract of land that Robin had recently purchased to give to the boy. This was the Long Creek Mill tract of unspecified size. Robin's purchase of this land is not registered in the Mecklenburg deed books. The ruins of the Long Creek Mill are a local historic landmark today, on Long Creek near Beatties Ford Road in north Mecklenburg.

Robin left one Negro to Margaret Madeline Osborne, but she died at the age of two, three months after Robin's will was written. Robin did not write a codicil disposing of this person, which left that problem to his executors.

Robert Davidson Alexander was one of the fourteen children of Robin's sister Violet and William Bain Alexander. Robert D. Alexander received a bequest of seven Negroes and the other half of the tract of 500 to 600 acres that was bequeathed to David A. Caldwell.

At the time Robin wrote his will, Robert Davidson Alexander was age 55, a successful planter, justice of the peace, trustee of Davidson College and elder of Hopewell Presbyterian Church. There is no obvious reason that he should have received this bequest. Perhaps Robin wanted to honor one of Violet's children, and he may have picked this man simply because they shared the same name.

Robert Davidson Alexander's plantation house, constructed in 1840, still stands on Eastfield Road in north Mecklenburg. One of his sons was John Brevard Alexander, doctor, historian, author and father of Dr. Annie Lowery Alexander, the first licensed female physician in North Carolina.

Robert Davidson Graham was the grandson of Robin's sister Isabella, and he was nine years old when the will was written. Robin gave him a plantation of 481 acres and a family of six Negroes. As in the case of Robert Davidson Alexander, there is no obvious reason for this bequest except to honor one member of his sister's family and perhaps simply because they shared the same name.

Robert McLean and Dr. William B. McLean were sons of Robin's sister Polly and her husband, Dr. William McLean. Robert received five Negroes and William a family of eight.

Robert and Theodore Brevard were sons of Robin's sister Rebecca. She had married Alexander Brevard, who co-founded and operated the ironworks in Lincoln County. Robert received a family of eight Negroes and Theodore received ten shares of bank stock. Again, there is no obvious reason for these bequests except to honor two members of his sister's family and perhaps was simply because one of them shared his name.

Edward Constantine Davidson received one Negro boy and ten shares of bank stock. He was the son of Robin's brother Jacky who as a lieutenant had led his troops in a significant action in the Mexican War.

Robert D. Whatley of Alabama received one Negro boy. Whatley's relationship to Robin is unknown.

It is interesting to note that there were a total of eight heirs named Robert. Four were Robin's nephews, and four have little known connection to Robin except for the name. This custom of giving bequests to relatives who carry your name is seen in a number of wills and apparently was not unusual at that time.

Robin bequeathed ten shares of his bank stock to Davidson College to be put toward the endowment of a professorship. He left forty shares of bank stock to Hopewell Presbyterian Church under certain doctrinal conditions. See Appendix C for a brief history of the church. Over the years these conditions were to cause the executors a good deal of trouble, which was finally settled in a lawsuit. Robin authorized his executors to use $500 to purchase tombstones for himself and for Peggy. Those stones exist today in the family burying ground located halfway between Holly Bend and Rural Hill.

Robin directed the executors to sell ten shares of bank stock and spend the money ($1,000) to purchase a full suit of clothing for each of Robin's Negroes "of such quality according to the merit of each."

Finally, the executors were to sell the residue of the estate on a credit of 20 months. After settling any outstanding debts they were to pay up to $1,500 (Appendix K. The Value of Money explains why it's difficult to determine how much money that would be today.) to Mary Brumby, the daughter of Robin's sister Rebecca Davidson Brevard. Mary was married to Richard T. Brumby. If the residue was less than that amount, she was to receive all of that residue. If there was a surplus, it was to be divided equally among all the beneficiaries mentioned in the will. The proceeds of the estate greatly exceeded $1,500.

In the July 1853 session of Mecklenburg County Court, Robin's last will and testament was brought to court, recorded and admitted to probate. David A. Caldwell, Warren Moore, and James W. Osborne were appointed executors of the will. Moore, of Lincoln County, was the husband of Isabella, the daughter of Robin's brother Jacky.[4]

Robin Davidson's estate papers at the state Office of Archives and History have been microfilmed and images are available on-line. They consist of 121 images, which we have transcribed. When the will was admitted to probate, the executors announced in the newspapers that all debtors and creditors of Robert Davidson, deceased, should come forward and settle with the estate. These settlements make up the bulk of the documents in the estate file. They range from a bill for $0.75 for shoeing several horses, $2.00 for a tree for a mill shaft (Robin was building a new mill at the time), $66.50 for a nine-month-old doctor's bill and a bill for $13.00 from Dr. Wm. B. Maclean, one of the beneficiaries, for calling on and attending Robin five times, including the day he died.[5]

Other receipts include expenses for settling the estate such as newspaper advertisements, lawyer's fees, selling the bank stock, running the auctions, making a coffin, buying a tombstone, and so on.

The most revealing document in the estate papers is the account of the estate sale, which was held by the executors in August 1853. The listing of the items sold runs eleven pages. For each transaction it lists the buyer, the item, the quantity, and the price. Robin's will had allowed the sale to be held on twenty months' credit, but the executors gave only twelve months' credit.

The detailed inventory gives an interesting view of Robin's plantation and its operation. There were three sales—at the home place, at the Wadle place and at the Long Creek farm—which raised a total of $2,949.00. Most items were sold at the home place with smaller quantities at the other two places.

Peggy bought a number of items at the sale, including Robin's gold

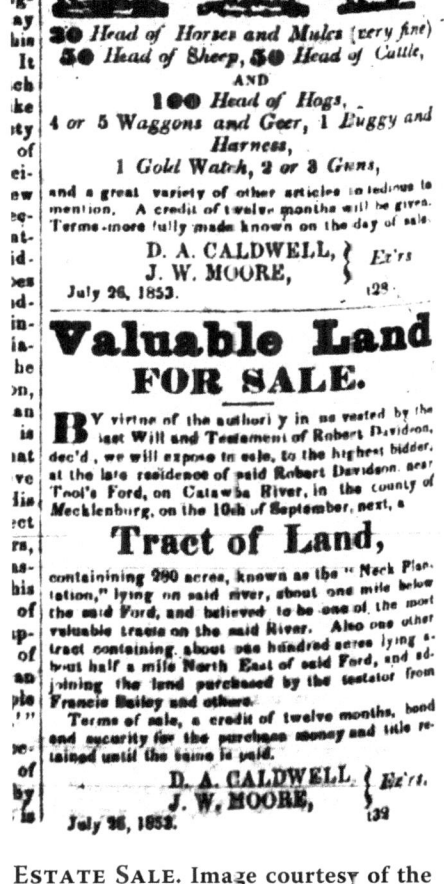

ESTATE SALE. Image courtesy of the Charlotte Mecklenburg Public Library, microfilm of the *NC Whig*.

watch for $75, two bay mares for $65, three shovels, one pair steelyards, a scythe, a cradle and a carryall.[6]

The first page of the estate sale begins:

August 16th 1853
A list of Property Sold by the Executors of
Robert Davidson Dec[d] on a Credit of 12 Months

The three auctions themselves take up nine pages. Page ten is the cash account:

Amt Brot forward		$2949.00
Cash found on hand at the Death of R Davidson	$500.00	
In the hands of D. A. Caldwell	103.41	
Cash Recv[ed] by Moore from S. Steward	30.62	634.03
Doubtful		
One note on Jasper & Larkin Store Due 27 day of October 1852 on Interest from the 27 of April 1852 for $800.00		
Five hundred dollars—July dividend on 100 shares of Bank Stock =		500.00
James W. Osborne }		
Ja[s] W Moore } Execs		
David A. Caldwell }		

The eleventh and final page:

Sept 10th 1853
A list of Sale, [Real Estate] by the Executors
of Robert Davidson Dec[d] at 12 & 24 month credit

Ja[s] Williamson	38 Acre Entry @ 15.00 pr acre	570.00
R F Davidson	70¼ " Entry @ 7.10 pr "	498.77½
" " "	280 " Neck Land @ 17—	4760.00

$2380.00 Which is the one half of the purchase of the Neck Land is on a credit of Twenty four months from date of Sale. The balance is all at twelve month credit

    J. W. Moore   }
    James W. Osborne } Execs
    David A. Caldwell }

There were a number of other items in the sale that tell of the operation of the plantations.

6. Robin and Peggy: Family, Wills and Estates

General:
  85½ lbs of sole leather, 1 side of upper leather
  1,788 lbs of Iron
  21 barrels and hogsheads
  Blacksmith Tools
  2 Canoes
  A great deal of cloth
  Medicine, medicine scales in box, salts, lime
  5 wagons, 1 Gig, 1 buggy, 2 carryalls (total 9)
  1 Rifle Gun, 1 Musket
  1 Saddle
  1 Windmill
  1 lot of Timber and 1,011 feet of Lumber at Mantz Mill
  House furniture at the Long Creek place

Tools:
  12 axes and a great number of hand tools, grindstones, etc.
  Many plows, hoes, scythes, etc.
  6 spinning wheels
  2 churns
  2 log chains
  Brick molds
  2 pr Steelyards
  2 Looms
  1 Still and worm
  2 Cotton gins

Livestock:
  68 cattle: Bulls, calves, cows, heifers and steers
  73 Sheep
  29 Mules, mares, fillies, horses and colts
  123 Hogs, sows, pigs, and shoats

Grain and other foodstuffs:
  Large quantities of corn, rye, hay, cotton, cotton seed, straw, wheat, peas and flour
  At Long Creek, "All the Hay in the barn loft"
  A large quantity of bacon [salt pork]

As noted, Robin's will specified that each of his Negroes was to have a full suit of new clothes. D. A. Caldwell bought clothing for 26 slaves from Davidson & Moss totaling $148.26. These purchases ranged from six yards of domestic cloth for Rachael and Martha (42 cents) to a fur hat, blanket coat, pants, shoes and socks for Dick ($10.77). Most of the clothing was in the form of cloth yard goods, pins, and thread plus such things as hats and caps, shoes and socks. "Quality according to the merit of each."

When Robin died, he owned 100 shares of stock in the Bank of the State of North Carolina. He distributed half of this to various beneficiaries, ten shares to Davidson College to endow a professorship and 40 shares to Hopewell church.

By the terms of the will, the bequest to Hopewell Presbyterian Church was contingent and lasted only

> So long as Said Church shall abide by the Confession of faith and the longer and Shorter Catechism of the Westminster assembly & Continue its Connection With the (Old School) General Assembly of the Presbyterian Church of the United States—the proceeds to be annually apportioned by the Church in the support & Extension of the Gospel.
>
> But should Said Church Cease to abide by the aforesaid Confession of Faith and Catechism and Separate itself from the Said assembly then I give and bequeath the Said forty Shares of bank Stock or its proceeds to the trustees of Davidson College for the use and benefit of the College.

The fact that the church did not receive the bank stock itself but rather the dividends meant that the executors were responsible for monitoring the theology practiced at Hopewell Presbyterian Church forever and to transfer the stock to Davidson College if the church failed to abide by the terms of the will. Quite a long-term responsibility.

In 1859 the Bank of the State of North Carolina was dissolved and rechartered as the Bank of North Carolina. The bank redeemed its stock in cash for $100 per share, and this left Robin's executors with the choice of how to reinvest the $4,000 from the Hopewell bequest. They could have bought stock in the new bank but, fortunately for the Hopewell church, they decided to invest it in eight bonds of the Charlotte and South Carolina Railroad Company. The family had a number of connections to this railroad. Robin's principle heir, James W. Osborne, could be said to have been the founder of the company and Robin's nephew Brevard Davidson served on the board. James W. Osborne was appointed a Superior Court Judge in 1859, well after Robin's death in 1853.

The railroad bonds cost $500 each, with interest payable semiannually at the rate of 7 percent per annum. The bank stock had carried a 5 percent dividend. The Bank of North Carolina closed at the end of the Civil War, but the railroad, although damaged during the war, survived and the railroad stock maintained its value and continued to pay regular dividends.

Hopewell Presbyterian Church continued to observe the old-time

6. Robin and Peggy: Family, Wills and Estates

religion and to receive regular dividends. The church used this income to pay the salaries of its ministers and for other expenses. However, by 1869 the church was in financial difficulty. It was without a minister, and members of the congregation felt they needed to purchase land and build a manse in order to attract one. Traditionally ministers had purchased land near the church where they would build a home, but by the end of the war that practice was no longer economically viable. The terms of Robin's will made a land purchase impossible because the church received the income from the bonds but did not have access to the principle.

In the spring court term in 1869 the trustees of Hopewell Presbyterian Church petitioned the court to order Robert Davidson's executors to deliver the railroad bonds to them. These original documents are in the Robert Davidson Estate Papers. They are much faded and torn but are legible enough to give an outline of the suit and its resolution.

John R. Davidson and J. F. Harry, trustees of Hopewell Presbyterian Church, petitioned the court to order the executors to transfer the railroad bonds to them.

James W. Moore, James W. Osborne, and D. A. Caldwell, trustees of the late Robert Davidson, testified that the bonds should be delivered to the church and used to build a parsonage.

The clerk of court, Edwin A. Osborne, investigated the matter to determine the truth of the petition. He held that using the funds for building a parsonage would be in conformity with the will. This was the same Edwin A. Osborne who was a nephew of Peggy's and had walked from Texas to Mecklenburg in 1859 so that she could provide him an education.

The court agreed and so ordered. The court further held that over the years the executors had paid a total of $4,480 in annual installments to the church and that there was a balance left of $271 to be paid. The executors asked for a commission of 2.5 percent on the money paid out, which the court granted. This left $27.00 due to the church.

On 10 May 1869 Justice of the Peace G. W. Logan determined that the clerk had investigated the petition and found no contest as to the facts. He ordered the executors to deliver the eight railroad bonds to the church along with $27 in cash. This was 16 years after Robin's death.

Most of what we know about Robin and Peggy's nieces and nephews comes from family stories, but in one case we have more solid documentation.

After Peggy's nephew Edwin A. Osborne walked from Texas to North Carolina just before the Civil War so that his aunt Peggy could give him an education, he lived briefly at Holly Bend and later visited there while recovering from a number of war wounds. Edwin and James W. Osborne were cousins because their fathers were Peggy's brothers.

After the war Edwin became a lawyer, then an Episcopal priest and finally the founder of Thompson's Orphanage in Charlotte. In 1924 he wrote his autobiography, which includes a description of the time he spent with Aunt Peggy at Holly Bend just before and during the Civil War.

The Osborne family was prominent in early Mecklenburg and Rowan counties. Some members stayed in North Carolina and their descendants live here today. Many, however, joined the great western migration, and Edwin A. Osborne's family was one of those. Edwin was born in Alabama and raised in Texas. He desired an education, which could not be obtained where he lived, so he wrote to his aunt Peggy Osborne Davidson, by then a widow still living at Holly Bend. Aunt Peggy wrote back and promised to give Edwin an education if he could get himself to Mecklenburg. Because he had very little money, Edwin walked most of the way and arrived in March of 1859.

In his autobiography Edwin A. Osborne describes arriving at his aunt Peggy's plantation.

In Sight of Home—My Journey's End

After leaving Shelby, I continued my journey leaving Lincolnton to the left and going through the town of Dallas [NC]. The second day I came within sight of the Catawba River just opposite my Aunt's farm, but the sun was down and it was too late to cross the river. I spent the night at the home of Mr. Fite who lived within a few hundred yards from the river on a ridge that overlooked his farm and afforded a fine view of both the river and my Aunt's field, known as "Penny's Bottom," which is a fine body of valley land in the bend of the river. Mr. Fite and his wife entertained me very kindly and hospitably and the next morning, which was clear and bright, I was sent across the river in a canoe and landed on my Aunt's farm in the Penny's Bottom mentioned above. This was to save time as the distance around the bend of the river by the road ferry is several miles, while the farm was little more than a mile.

I think this was the first part of March, 1859. The overseer of the farm at that time was Mr. Robert Kerns, a hunch-back man of fine sense and a kind heart. He was in the field at the time I landed, directing the laborers who were negro slaves. Some of the hands were plowing while others were doing other kinds of work.

I introduced myself to Mr. Kerns, who greeted me cordially, and informed me that my aunt had been expecting me and would be glad to see me. He escorted me up to the house and introduced me to my aunt, whom I found sitting near the open fireplace in her living room in the east end of her large, two-story house where, afterwards, I learned she spent her time when at home. My aunt rose from the chair and greeted me with almost the affection of a mother and almost instantly I felt that I was indeed at home in her house.

My aunt, Mrs. Margaret Davidson, was when I met her a well-preserved person of about eighty years of age. She was my father's eldest sister and reminded me of him in many respects, especially in her features and intelligence. She was very low of statue but very robust, with large prominent grey eyes, a short but well shaped nose, a good mouth and chin, good complexion and a fairly good suit of grey hair—almost white—and a smooth, gentle voice, slightly feeble from age.

She was a pious member of the Hopewell Presbyterian congregation. She owned a life interest in the home place, consisting of some fifteen or seventeen hundred acres of land, well stocked with negro slaves, mules, and horses and farming implements. She was ... known and called by all alike, "Aunt Peggy." ... I was not at home when my aunt died. I was in the army at that time.... Her remains were buried near the grave of her deceased husband Mr. Robert Davidson, in the family graveyard on the east of the residence, not far from the lane leading from the said residence to that of the late Brevard Davidson. There was a strong brick wall around the graveyard at the time which I am sorry to hear has since been removed, but the marble tombstone is still there to mark the place ...

When I first reached my aunt's residence I met there a number of her late husband's young relatives who according to the custom of the country at that time, had come to spend the day. I do not now remember them all, but I do remember Miss Sally Moore, daughter of the late Warren Moore, and I think her brother James was there.... I think Miss Sallie Caldwell, afterwards Mrs. White, was there also and her brother Ed Caldwell. She is still living and was the daughter of the late Alexander Caldwell. John Springs Davidson son of the late Brevard Davidson was there and perhaps a few others.[7]

After remaining and conversing with my aunt for some time I went out on the long front porch with the young people who were present and soon someone proposed that we should have some physical exercise in the yard. We agreed to see which one of the young men could jump the farthest.

A line was drawn on the bare ground and the young men, one after the other, "toed the mark" and made one jump. When all had jumped, I, who must have presented

MARGARET (AUNT PEGGY) OSBORNE DAVIDSON. Robert Davidson and Margaret McWhorter Osborne were born on the same date seven years apart and married on 1 January 1800. They had no children, and the family story, repeated down through the ages, is that Peggy had no toes. In their long life together they took in and raised a large number of nieces and nephews. In 1823, when Peggy was 47, they had miniature portraits made of themselves and their favorite nephew, James Walker Osborne. Image from the private collection of Dr. Douglas Marion.

rather a sorry appearance, for I was rather thin and had on my traveling apparel—not having a fresh suit with me—was invited to try my skill. I "toed the mark" and made a spring and outdistanced them all. After several trials it was proposed to try a running start and make a single leap. In this I also surpassed them all.

We then tried several other methods as "half-hammond," three successive leaps, in all of which I proved quite a match for the best and soon all reserve was thrown off and we were all on easy and familiar terms and the day passed very pleasantly. A splendid dinner was served and in the afternoon the young people departed for their homes and I was glad to be left alone with my dear aged aunt, whose kind and motherly treatment completely won my heart.

I was made to feel perfectly at home, which feeling remained with me during her life.

First Trip to Charlotte—Cousin James and Mary Ann Osborne

After one or two day's rest, I went with my aunt in a carriage driven by the faithful negro coachman Ben and purchased some much needed clothing. We spent part of the day with the family of my cousin James Walker Osborne a son of my father's brother Edwin Jay Osborne. Here I had the great pleasure of meeting my said cousin and his noble wife who was a most splendid woman and daughter of Mr. John Irwin, a man of large wealth (and the father of the late Mr. James Patton Irwin of Charlotte).

My cousin the Hon. James W. Osborne was a judge of the Superior Court and a man of splendid ability, a lawyer of distinction and a noted orator. Judge Osborne and his wife Mrs. Mary Ann Osborne received me kindly and we dined with them that day. The Judge was the adopted son of the late Mr. Robert Davidson and my Aunt Peggy and sole legatee of the remainder of the estate (in fee simple) on which they lived....

After a short period of rest with my Aunt, I was sent to visit a number of her neighbors and friends and some relatives of ours. Then I began to prepare for school. Those whom I met during this time—or about this time I shall mention a few and shall probably mention them again in the course of this narrative.

I also met Mr. and Mrs. Alexander Caldwell the parent of Mrs. Sallie White and her brother Ed. Mr. A. Brevard Davidson, wife and family.... Mr. and Mrs. Constantine Davidson one of their sons Dr. J. Z. S. Davidson, now lives on Tenth Avenue, Charlotte, a practicing physician. Mr. and Mrs. Warren McLean and Dr. William McLean who lived across the river in Gaston County. Miss Jennie McLean, his daughter.... A very striking figure in the community was "Uncle Jackie" Davidson (the father of Brevard and Constantine and also Mrs. Warren Moore). He was then very old but quite active in looking after his farm. He was the only surviving brother of Uncle Robert Davidson my aunt's deceased husband.[8]

Aunt Peggy Davidson took Edwin into her home and enrolled him at the Statesville military school, starting the next fall. Also that fall Peggy wrote a codicil to her will that left Edwin a bequest of $500.

When the Civil War broke out, Edwin, along with most of his classmates and professors, enlisted. He was at first a lieutenant but was soon appointed captain and eventually attained the rank of colonel. He commanded troops in a number of important battles in the eastern theater and was wounded three times, coming back to his duty each time after recovering from his wounds. While he was recovering from these wounds, he stayed at Holly Bend rather than making the long trek to Texas. In fact, his autobiography does not indicate that he ever returned to Texas, even for a short visit. Finally, after he had several fingers shot off, he petitioned to be returned to duty in some capacity rather than be discharged; he was given the command of a court-martial.

In 1862, during one of those periods of recuperation, he met his second cousin Fannie Swann Moore, who lived at Rosedale Plantation near present-day Croft, north of Charlotte.[9] When he visited again during another recuperation, they became engaged, and married in March 1865. About the first of April he set out on foot to return to duty. When he arrived in Greensboro, he learned of the defeat of the Confederate army, turned about and walked back to Charlotte.[10]

After the war Osborne taught school in Statesville and then in Charlotte while reading law. When he had passed the bar he sought and received an appointment as clerk of the Superior Court in Charlotte. All of his income came from legal fees so at first he had to work at a number of other jobs to make ends meet, but as the economy recovered so did the courts, and in the end he was quite busy. He held this position for ten years and managed to accumulate some assets.

Born a Presbyterian but never very religious, Osborne converted to the faith of his wife and was confirmed in the Episcopalian Church by 1869. He continued to study religion and was ordained a deacon in 1877. He intended to continue his law work and serve the church at the same time, but soon after his ordination he was asked to take work in the mountains, where there was much need of ministers. Resigning as county clerk, he began preaching in remote mountain churches and soon was ordained an Episcopal priest.

In 1884 Edwin Osborne returned to Charlotte, preaching at a number of country churches and selling life insurance to support his family. Thinking back on his experiences as county clerk, he remembered the plight of the poor orphans who, by state law, were bound by the court as apprentices "every male to some Tradesman, Merchant, Mariner, or other person approved by the Court, until he shall attain the Age of Twenty-one Years, and every Female to some Suitable Employment, til her Age of Eighteen Years." Most orphans were apprenticed to learn "the art and mystery of farming" or "the art and mystery of housewifery." Another alternative was to be sent to be a factory hand at a wage of 12.5 cents per week.[11]

The new state constitution, adopted at the end of the Civil War in 1868, provided for one or more state orphan houses to care for and educate destitute orphans, but no state funds were made available and none of these was built. Instead the state looked to religious organizations to fill this need.

Edwin Osborne wanted to establish an orphanage in Charlotte to be supported by the Episcopal Church, but he had neither land nor funds to accomplish this.

Soon after returning to Charlotte, he approached his friend the Reverend Benjamin Bronson, rector of St. Peter's Episcopal Church in Charlotte, who held in trust some land on Little Sugar Creek. The land had been donated to the church, and to Bronson, by the widow of Lewis Thompson some years before. Lewis Thompson, 1808–1867, was a planter in Bertie County, NC and in Louisiana. He was a politician, served in the NC Assembly, Senate, and NC Constitutional Convention of 1865. He and his wife knew the Rev. Benjamin Bronson when he was in Bertie County.

Bronson had founded a boys' school on the site, but it had failed after only a few years.

What was left of the school was two buildings and 61 acres of land on the outskirts of Charlotte. Bronson agreed to donate the land, with the provisions that the name Thompson be preserved and that the Reverend Edwin Osborne would be responsible for setting up the orphanage and would serve as superintendent.[12]

At that time there were three other orphanages in North Carolina. The Masons built one and the Baptists built two—one for Negro children and one for whites.

When Osborne began Thompson's Orphanage and Training Institute in 1886, all he had was an abandoned classroom building, which had recently been damaged by an earthquake; a brick residence; 61 acres of land along Little Sugar Creek and not a dime to start with. He went door-to-door to raise money for the orphanage, starting in Charlotte. Then he went all over the state to ask for contributions of clothing, furniture and, most important, money. He raised enough money to repair and extend the school building, then called Thompson Hall, and to furnish it. He also found the first matron, Miss Elizabeth Mackay, who was hired for $15 per month.

Thompson Orphanage and Training Institution officially opened on 7 May 1887, with two children. Within the month there were six more, and within a year the building was filled with 30 children. By 1889 there were 39 children living in the one hall in crowded conditions. Thompson's took in orphans from across North Carolina, not only those whose parent had died but also those whose parents could not care for them because of poverty or illness. The little boys and girls worked the farm, growing vegetables, milking cows, delivering that milk to homes in Charlotte and growing in wisdom and stature.

Although Thompson Orphanage was funded and supported by Episcopalian churches, they admitted children without any consideration of religious orientation. Nonetheless the orphanage emphasized religious along with secular and practical instruction. Osborne petitioned the Diocesan Convention every year for the funds to build a separate chapel, as services were being held in one of the classrooms.

In 1889 Judge William Bynum, an old friend of Osborne's from the days when Bynum was a lawyer and Osborne was county clerk, gave $2,500 to build a chapel in memory of his late wife, Eliza, and his daughter, Mary. In 1891 construction began on the chapel with bricks made on the site from clay gathered from the banks of Little Sugar Creek. The chapel was in use by the end of 1892 and was formally consecrated in May 1895 as the Memorial Chapel of St. Mary the Virgin.

Osborne continued to run, build and expand the institution until he took an indefinite leave of absence to enlist in the Spanish American War as chaplain of the Second Regiment of North Carolina Volunteers. After the war he held a number of important positions in the Episcopal Church, concentrating on missionary activities, and never returned to manage the orphanage.

In 1924 he wrote his unpublished autobiography, which gives us a feeling for what it meant to be a poor boy related to Robin and Peggy Davidson.

The organization now known as Thompson's Child and Family Focus offers education, counseling and other social services in Charlotte. It moved from the Sugar Creek location to Matthews (Charlotte area) ca 1950. A portion of the orphanage land became home to a shopping mall and then the land along Little Sugar Creek became a Mecklenburg County Greenway Park. Only one building from the orphanage, Saint Mary's Chapel, built in 1892 still stands on its original site in that park.

As interesting as the story of Edwin Osborne's life is, the way it came to the authors' attention is equally interesting and provides a case study of historical investigation. One of us is an officer of the Mecklenburg Historical Association and it received a letter from an irate woman in Texas, a Mrs. Osborne. Her late husband was a great-great-nephew of Edwin Osborne and was very proud of his lineage. She had joined him in his pride and continued to do so after his death. Shortly before she wrote this letter she had gone east on a business trip and made a special effort on her return trip to spend an afternoon in Charlotte before flying out to Texas. She wanted to see what remained of the orphanage her husband's ancestor had founded.

She had done her homework and knew that St. Mary's Chapel was still in existence, was owned by Mecklenburg County Park and Recreation and was open on Friday afternoons. When she found the chapel, a small but beautiful space, and went in, she met several young women who were there to take reservations for weddings and musical concerts. When she started talking about Edwin Osborne, she met only blank stares. Not only had they never heard the name before but there was no information in the chapel about him.

Flying home, greatly upset at the insult to her deceased husband's ancestor, she decided to send a strong letter to someone.

Jim Williams wrote her a long letter in return. He explained that Edwin's aunt Peggy was familiar to us, but we knew little about her branch of the Osborne family. He promised that we would research it, and that the MHA would take steps to have an information plaque erected on the site so that future visitors would be able to learn about this extraordinary man. Mrs. Osborne was somewhat mollified and several letters passed back and forth when one day, in the MHA's postal box there was a note saying that a package was being held for us. We were greatly surprised to receive a full transcription of Edwin Osborne's autobiography. The original manuscript is in the Southern Collection at Chapel hill with other Osborne papers. It had been transcribed by an Osborne descendant in Charlotte in 1947 and retyped in Texas by this Mrs. Osborne in 1994. In her letters she made clear that she was sending us this document for us to use in researching the Reverend Osborne and we were welcome to make copies of it, but that she considered it a private paper, not to be distributed further.

As a result of the efforts of several organizations in the local history community, Edwin Osborne now has the recognition he deserves. In December 2018 a memorial sculpture depicting him with several children was unveiled on the grounds of St. Mary's Chapel on the Trail of History along the Little Sugar Creek Greenway near uptown Charlotte.

Aunt Peggy wrote her will in February 1855, a year and a half after her husband's death. However, she lived another nine years, until January 1864. She wrote a codicil to her will in 1859 and another in 1863, because in the interim several of her beneficiaries had died. In these documents she gave her name as M. M. Davidson or Margaret M. Davidson. Her full name was Margaret McWhorter Osborne Davidson.[13]

Her executors were her nephews James W. Osborne and John Augustus Young. John Young was the son of Peggy's younger sister Mary Lloyd Osborne Sharp Young. He was raised in Iredell County and in May 1840 had married Malvina Sophia Graham, the daughter of General Joseph Graham of the Lincoln County ironworks. In 1844 they moved to Charlotte, where he built and operated the Rock Island Manufacturing Company, a woolens mill, on the Catawba River near Charlotte and served in the North Carolina House of Representatives.[14]

Peggy's will gave most of her enslaved people, listed in family groups, to her nephew James W. Osborne. Of those 31 people, 18 are on the list bequeathed to her in Robin's will, to be given to Osborne on Peggy's death. She also left Osborne her ten shares of stock in the Bank of the State of North Carolina, worth $1,000. The slaves and bank stock were for his use and benefit, but he was to use them to pay eight pecuniary bequests totaling $4,500.

One of these was for "one thousand dollars, to my Sister Cecelia Byars." Nancy Cecelia Osborne Byars was another of Peggy's younger sisters. She was married to James Smith Byars and lived in Iredell County near Centre Church. In the 1859 codicil Peggy stated, "As since the making of the will referred to in which I give to my sister Cecelia Byars One thousand Dollars. She has died. I direct the legacy intended for her to be equally divided between her two Daughters Mary and Julia."

Another bequest was "to my Niece Jane Johnston five Hundred Dollars." This was another daughter of Cecelia Byars's; Jane had married James H. Johnston of Lincoln County. In the codicil of 1863 Peggy stated, "Whereas my Niece J Johnston daughter of my Sister Cecelia Byars has died since the execution of my last will and testament it is my will and desire that the legacy of four Hundred dollars which I have given to her shall go to her Son Adlai O. Johnston." Presumably her executors were able to resolve this $100 difference.

A third bequest said, "To my sister Lemira Houston wife of D. Houston of Ala. Six Hundred Dollars." Panthea Lemira Houston was another younger sister of Peggy's, and she lived in Marengo County in west central Alabama. The codicil of 1859 adds, "I also give to Sister Panthea L Houston two hundred dollars in addition to the Eight Hundred Dollars I have given her in my will." Another error for the executors to resolve. Apparently Peggy was relying on her memory in writing these codicils rather than referring to the original will.

The next bequest was "to my Brother Ephraim B. Osborne Five Hundred Dollars." He was Peggy's younger brother, a doctor who served in the

War of 1812 and moved west, eventually settling in Texas. He was the father of Edwin A. Osborne, who was raised in Texas and walked to North Carolina on Peggy's promise of an education.

Another bequest was "to my Niece Harriet C. Moore wife of D. Moore of Wilmington N.C. Five Hundred Dollars." She was the daughter of Peggy's brother Edwin Jay Osborne and sister of James Walker Osborne, who had lived with Robin and Peggy after his mother died when he was four.

Also she left "to my Nephew John A. Young Five Hundred Dollars." John A. Young lived in Charlotte and was the son of Peggy's youngest sister, Mary Osborne Sharpe Young, by her second husband.

At the end of her will, as an afterthought, Peggy had made a bequest to John's daughter Mary E. Young. The bequest was the "Negroe Girl Amy, Daughter of Caroline given to J. W. Osborne in the first part of this my will." Peggy reversed this bequest in the 1863 codicil in which she once more gave Amy to James W. Osborne and replaced her with Eliza. Amy must have been someone special.

The final two pecuniary bequests were "to my Niece Adeline Hale, Five Hundred dollars. to her sole and separate use during her life and after her death to her children. This legacy to be managed for the benefit of my Niece by her Brother T. A. Sharpe" and "to my Nephew T. A. Sharpe four Hundred Dollars." These two were children of Peggy's sister Mary by her first husband.

For each pecuniary bequest to a female beneficiary, Peggy added the words "to her Sole and Separate use and to be disposed of as she thinks proper." These words were not legally binding since by law all property belonged to their husbands the instant they received it, but her hope was that the husbands would take these words into consideration.

Next, she divided up her furniture with specific bequests to her sisters Cecelia and Lemira, nieces M. A. Caldwell and Isabella Moore and to Salley E. Caldwell. The balance of the household and table furniture was to be divided equally between the two sisters.

M. A. Caldwell was the wife of D. A. Caldwell, the son of the Rev. Alexander Caldwell, the lunatic. Isabella Moore was the daughter of Robin's brother Jacky; she was married to Warren Moore, one of the executors of Robin's will.

Peggy also gave specific pieces of furniture to James W. Osborne and J. Edward Caldwell, the son of D. A. Caldwell.

The next bequests were of four enslaved people, whom Peggy named: one to niece M. A. Osborne, wife of James W. Osborne; and one to each of M. A. Osborne's three sons, Robert, John, and Francis.

The balance of the estate went to Peggy's nephew James W. Osborne: "All the residue of my property consisting of stock of all kinds farming utensils crops on hand and all other unwilled property I give to my Nephew James W Osborne, to be applied by him to the payment of my debts and towards that discharge of the pecuniary legacies before mentioned."

Finally, she appointed James W. Osborne and her nephew John A. Young her executors. The witnesses to this will were Adam Brevard Davidson and A. E. King.

In her 1859 codicil she wrote that if other beneficiaries were to predecease her, their bequests were to be divided between their children or, if there were no children, between their siblings. In April 1863 Peggy wrote the final codicil, making a few minor changes in her bequests.

Margaret McWhorter Osborne Davidson, Aunt Peggy, died on 9 January 1864.

In all, Peggy's will left James W. Osborne 31 slaves, $1,000 in bank stock and the residue of the plantation property. When Peggy died, he was well established in Charlotte as a Superior Court judge. In the ordinary course of events the sale of the real and personal property would have provided more than enough to pay the $4,500 in monetary bequests. But these were not ordinary times.

After the Bank of the State of North Carolina was rechartered as the Bank of North Carolina in 1859, Peggy probably had reinvested the money she received for her shares in the successor institution. That bank would close a year after her death, and the stock became worthless.

By 1864, the year of Peggy's death, Confederate and state currencies were rapidly depreciating and there was little or no hard money in circulation. At the end of the war the slaves were freed, eliminating almost all of Peggy's estate. If an attempt was made to settle the estate before the end of the war, it would have been nearly impossible to hold the auction. If the pecuniary bequests were paid in North Carolina or Confederate currency, they would have soon become worthless.

Peggy's estate file contains only one paper. It is dated 16 April 1864 and binds Jas. W. Osborne, S. Nye Hutcheson and W. M. Mathews in the sum of $4,000. The condition of this bond is that James W. Osborne, as an executor of the late Margaret M. Davidson, will administer the will and make an accounting to the Mecklenburg County Court. No record of this accounting has been found. The fortune that Robin and Peggy had accumulated in their lifetime was gone.[15]

CHAPTER 7

The Second Generation at Rural Hill: Jacky and Sallie Davidson

MAJOR JOHN'S SECOND SON AND NAMESAKE was called Jacky to distinguish him from his father and other John Davidsons in the area. He was the seventh of Major John and Violet's 10 children. Little is known of his childhood and education, although he was literate and wrote a fine hand. His mother certainly taught him basic reading, writing and ciphering, and he probably received additional education. Groups of neighbors sometimes jointly hired a tutor for their children, or he might have attended a common school or an academy taught in one of the local Presbyterian churches. Hopewell had several of these from time to time.

Jacky lived his entire life on the Rural Hill plantation, farming it first with his father, then on his own and finally with his son Brevard. Jacky was born at Rural Retreat and lived there to the age of nine, when his father built the Rural Hill manor house and moved the family from Rural Retreat.

On 11 November 1800, just one day short of his 21st birthday, Jacky married Sarah "Sallie" Harper Brevard, the daughter of Adam and Mary Winslow Brevard. The Davidson and Brevard families were very close, going back several generations to Pennsylvania. Sallie's uncle Alexander Brevard was married to Jacky's oldest sister, Rebecca. Both of Sallie's uncles and her father had served during the American Revolution. Sallie's aunt Mary Brevard Davidson was the widow of General William Lee Davidson.[1]

It was unusual at the time for a man to marry as young as 21. Members

7. The Second Generation at Rural Hill: Jacky and Sallie Davidson

of the planter class customarily established themselves first and were fully capable of supporting a wife and family before entering into marriage. Both of Jacky's brothers married at the age of 31. Robin, 10 years Jacky's senior, married six weeks after Jacky's nuptials.

Sallie had just turned 20 when she and Jacky were married. She was a bit younger than most brides of the time, who tended to marry between 21 and 25. The young couple set up housekeeping at Rural Retreat. All ten of Jacky and Sallie's children were born at Rural Retreat, just as all ten of Major John's had been in the generation before.

Jacky continued to farm in partnership with his father. In 1823 at the age of 88 Major John "broke up housekeeping" and moved out of Rural Hill to the home of his daughter Betsy and her husband, William Lee Davidson, Jr. By breaking up housekeeping he was turning over the ownership and management of the home and farm to Jacky. In modern terms he had retired. By then Major John's children were grown. Jacky and Sallie moved into the Rural Hill manor house and remained there until 1837 when they moved back to Rural Retreat.

Jacky and Sallie's son Brevard married in April of 1836, and the young couple moved into Rural Hill with his parents. At that time 15-year-old Sarah was the only one of Jacky's children still at home. Augustus was at West Point, William at Davidson College, and Constantine at the Sugar Creek Academy. All of the others were married and lived elsewhere.

When it became obvious that Brevard and his young wife were expecting their first child, Jacky and Sallie may have decided that living their golden years in a house full of small children did not suit them.

As recorded in Brevard's farm journal, a week after the first of his children arrived in February of 1837, he "raised kitchen & smoke house at Rural Retreat." On 9 June he wrote, "Mary & A. B. Davidson went to hous keeping on to day. Father & Mother moved down to Rural Retreat on the 8th." When Mary and Brevard "went to housekeeping," they did not go anywhere. The phrase means that they were now in charge of Rural Hill because his parents had moved to Rural Retreat.

Sallie died in 1864, and Jacky in 1870. They probably spent their final years at Rural Retreat, although Jacky, as an elderly widower, may have moved back in with Brevard. Both Jacky and Sallie now lie in the Rural Hill Burying Ground.

Jacky left very few records from the first thirty years of his married life; most records concerning him are from 1829 and after when Brevard reached his majority and became a full partner in the operation of Rural Hill. Records from this time are primarily receipts and promissory notes for goods bought and sold, money borrowed, and various other transactions. Brevard and Jacky seemed to do most of their business together. The majority of the promissory notes state that on a certain date "we or either of us promise to pay" a designated person, and these are signed by both of them. Only a few of the notes specify the nature of the business; most simply say "for value received." There are a few notes stating, "I promise to pay" that are signed by only Jacky or only Brevard.

Several records from 1839 to 1841 exist of their accounts with the merchant Leroy Springs. Each had a separate account in addition to their joint account during those years. In almost all of these business records their names are written as John Davidson or as A. B. Davidson. Only occasionally did Brevard sign his name as Adam Brevard or Brevard. Letters and other family papers tell us they were called Jacky and Brevard by friends and family.[2]

These merchant accounts are for a miscellany of household goods: the Davidsons appear to have been living well but not extravagantly. They bought hats, shoes, sugar, coffee, wine, tools and hardware plus a great deal of cloth, thread, lace, trimmings, and silk handkerchiefs. Their wives may have been the primary shoppers. They bought shoes, blankets, and other goods for their slaves. Some few entries list items bought for a specific child, slave, or family member.

There are few records of income aside from promissory notes paid to them. Itemized receipts for the sale of cotton exist only for the years 1830 and 1841. In 1830 Brevard sold twelve bales of cotton averaging 325 pounds each for a total of $366.95, or 10.6 cents per pound. He bought homespun cloth, potatoes, molasses, and a few other things from the cotton broker, paid his wagoner $31.55, and came home with $325.99. Brevard was 22 years old and had just begun to farm with his father as an equal.

Although Brevard took the cotton to market and sold it, the crop belonged to them jointly. In 1841 Jacky and Brevard together sold 64 bales of cotton, most weighing 315 to 350 pounds. The total weight was 21,197 pounds, and it earned them $2,146.17, or 10.1 cents per pound. Again they shopped, paid off a previous debt on their account, and pocketed $1,856.03.

The Davidsons operated one or more cotton gins and ginned cotton for their neighbors, keeping 10 to 15 percent as their "toll." The cotton crop was often sold piecemeal, part of it in the late winter and the rest in the spring. These two recorded sales might not have represented the entire harvests of 1830 and 1841.[3]

Brevard kept an extensive farm journal for many years that records

7. The Second Generation at Rural Hill: Jacky and Sallie Davidson

additional cotton sales, although it is not always clear if the sales were for him and his father together or for him alone. The journal also contains detailed information about farming and seasonal activities, as well as lists of slaves and descriptions of many of their responsibilities.[4]

It was commonplace for fathers and sons to form business partnerships. No document has been found describing such a partnership between Major John and Jacky or between Jacky and Brevard in the next generation. These may have existed and been lost, or more likely the men had informal verbal understandings.

In Mecklenburg County the majority of farmers did not own any slaves. Many of these yeoman farmers raised cotton with their own labor and that of their families. The corn, wheat, vegetables and hogs they raised fed the family while the cotton crop paid their taxes and provided necessities and small luxuries for the family.

Of those who did own slaves, most owned three or fewer. Since half of the enslaved adults were women and about one-third were children, a man who owned three slaves would have had one "full hand" who worked with his master in the field. In addition to raising the children, cooking and doing housework, the enslaved women and girls helped out at harvest time. They were considered "half hands."

For a family of fewer than five or six slaves, it was not economical to build a separate house or keep a separate kitchen, so the slaves most probably slept in the same house and ate the same food as the master and his family.

Farmers who owned larger numbers of slaves generally spent from sun up to sun down in the fields working with and supervising their hands. Only when a man had 40 or 50 slaves would the work of supervising their labor take all of his time. Growing cotton could be very profitable but required a major investment to buy the slaves needed to do the manual labor.

In this era, according to the 1850 census, the counties of Mecklenburg, North Carolina, and York, South Carolina, were by far the largest slave-owning counties in the Carolina backcountry. Even in these two counties very few farmers owned a large number of slaves. In 1840 only 800 people, or 35 percent of the farmers in Mecklenburg, owned any slaves at all. Of these 800 slave owners, only seven owned more than 40 people.

According to U.S. Census records, Jacky owned 12 slaves in 1810, 11 in 1820, 25 in 1830, 17 in 1840, and 22 in 1850; this last number consisted of 8 men and boys and 14 women and girls. As far as we know, Jacky did not keep a list of his slaves' names or a record of their activities. Brevard had 15 slaves at Rural Hill in 1840 and 26 in 1850.[5] Since Jacky and Brevard farmed together, these census numbers reflect the combined workforce of those years.

Although cotton was the cash crop, the labor required to grow it was only a small portion of the farming necessary to support those who raised it. Jacky, like all farmers of the time, raised a great deal of corn to feed both people and animals. He also raised wheat, peas, oats, vegetables and other food crops, as well as cows, horses, mules, poultry, and numerous hogs. He lived on the river, and fish were plentiful throughout the year. Like his brother Robin, he may have operated a fishery during the annual shad run as a supplemental cash crop.

There is a family story concerning Jacky that, although undocumented, bears telling. Jacky is said to have been called "Silver Headed Jacky" because a silver plate had been implanted in his skull. According to historian Chalmers Davidson, "Jacky was struck by a falling tree which broke his skull and left part of his brain sticking to the limb. His nephew, Dr. John Davidson MacLean, performed a delicate operation and evidently inserted a silver plate over the fracture."

There is no information about when this accident happened. MacLean was born in 1794 so the event probably occurred after 1820. Another account states that Jacky acquired the silver plate as a result of a trepanning (sometimes spelled trephining) operation. This does not contradict the family story. Trepanning, or the removal of a small section of skull, was an ancient operation done to relieve pressure on the brain resulting from disease or injury.

Jacky and Sallie had ten children, all of whom were born at Rural Retreat and all of whom lived to maturity. Three of the six boys were called by their middle names: Matthew, Brevard and Constantine.[6]

Jacky educated some, and perhaps all, of his children. A newspaper notice dated 20 February 1821 announced that Hopewell Academy was seeking students and that Robin and Jacky Davidson were two of its four sponsors.

In 1827 Jacky and his brother Benjamin Wilson were among fourteen subscribers who pooled their resources to hire Robert A. Sadler to teach their children. Sadler asked his subscribers to provide him with board, washing, firewood when required, and a house to teach in. This was one of a number of independent schools not affiliated with a church. Sadler's classes included orthography, reading, writing, arithmetic, English grammar, geography, and surveying. The fee was $2 per scholar. Jacky paid $7.

7. The Second Generation at Rural Hill: Jacky and Sallie Davidson

Orthography is the study of words and their correct spelling; it is a myth that our ancestors were indifferent to spelling. Several of Jacky's children were the right age to have attended Sadler's school.[7]

A receipt from 1833 states that in January Jacky paid John Madison McKnitt Caldwell "$23.40 in full for the tuition of his children during the year of 1832." Caldwell was related to Jacky by marriage and later became a minister at Sugar Creek Presbyterian Church.[8]

There are no records of which of Jacky's children attended any of those schools.

The Rev. John Williamson was minister at Hopewell from 1818 to 1842. His wife, Sarah, taught at a common school for younger children during many of those years. Jacky's children were probably among her students.

Jacky's son John Matthew became a doctor. There is no record of his education, and he was too old to have taken advantage of the schools just discussed. Schooling for boys was available in the village of Charlotte, and there may have been a school at Hopewell prior to 1818. Many doctors at that time obtained their medical training by apprenticeship.

Jacky's son Robert was probably a lawyer, having read law under the tutelage of an established lawyer. In a letter written in 1838 Robert mentioned his clients and the court schedule.

Augustus was a cadet at West Point when he died there in 1837.

None of Jacky's daughters appears to have attended the Salem Female Boarding School, a North Carolina institution popular with a number of area families. The girls may have attended the common school at Hopewell, and there were schools for girls in Charlotte at the time.

A number of Jacky's receipts confirm that both William and Constantine attended Davidson College. William began his studies when the college opened its doors in 1837. In 1843 he entered the Medical College at Charleston.

In 1837 Constantine was a student at the Sugar Creek Academy and boarded with Dr. David Thomas Caldwell, who lived nearby. Constantine and other boarding students wrote their names all over the walls in a bedroom of the Caldwell home. One bit of that graffiti reads: "E. Constantine Davidson, A Rascal, 1837." Caldwell's home is now a historic site, Historic Rosedale, near the middle of Charlotte, on North Tryon Street just south of Sugaw Creek Presbyterian Church. The scribblings of Constantine and other students can be seen there today in an upstairs bedroom and hall.[9]

Constantine's Davidson College receipt is dated 1839. On 15 August 1841 his brother Brevard wrote, "Brother Constantine started to Cambriage Coleage, Masachusets, started with two hundred & fifteen dollars &

50/100." This was Harvard, where Constantine studied law and was admitted to the practice of law in 1844.

Three of Jacky and Sarah's 10 children moved to Florida. These were their oldest child, John Matthew Winslow Davidson; third child, Violet Wilson Davidson; and fifth child, Robert Hamilton McWhorter Davidson.

Great Britain had acquired East Florida and West Florida from Spain at the end of the French and Indian War in 1763. They were returned to Spain at the end of the American Revolution in 1783. The United States acquired the two Floridas from Spain in 1819. In 1822 East Florida and a portion of West Florida were established as the Territory of Florida. Nearly all of the new territory's non–Indian residents lived near Pensacola or St. Augustine. It was decided to locate a territorial capital about halfway between those centers of population. A rise of land near Lake Tallahassee was chosen "near the ruins of Old Tallahassee, the village which the Indians had abandoned at the time (six years previously) when Jackson was sweeping through Eastern Florida."[10]

In 1823 Gadsden County was established just west of Tallahassee, with Quincy as the county seat. It was named for James Gadsden, who had served in the army under General Andrew Jackson and was at that time a planter, member of the territorial legislature, and a commissioner involved in resettling the Seminole Indians. Many years later, as minister to Mexico, he negotiated the Gadsden Purchase, which is now part of southern Arizona and southwestern New Mexico.

In 1825 a land office was opened in Tallahassee to attract settlers to scantily populated north-central Florida. Quarter sections (a quarter of a square mile, or 160 acres) were placed on the market at $1.25 per acre.

> The selection of Tallahassee as the capital of the territory and the opening of the lands in central Florida to settlement and private ownership soon attracted a large and constant stream of residents—men and women of means, and representatives of old families from Virginia, Tennessee and the Carolinas. They brought with them many slaves and established large and beautiful homesteads and plantations of cotton and corn.... Tallahassee [became] the political, social and educational center of Florida. It is estimated that by 1830 ... 16,000 or two-thirds of the population of Florida, were in ... that section of Florida between the Apalachicola and Suwannee rivers. Although in central Florida the Negroes outnumbered the white two to one, the personnel of the latter numbered a majority of the cultural and wealthy men of the territory.[11]

The territory of Florida became a state in 1845.

This is the area in Florida where Jacky's children decided to settle. Dr. John Matthew Davidson, called Matthew, married Mary Jerusha Sylvester on 4 April 1826. The following October Mary's brother Joseph

7. The Second Generation at Rural Hill: Jacky and Sallie Davidson

Howard Sylvester married Matthew's sister Violet Wilson Davidson. The two couples moved to Florida in 1828. Prior to that, one or both of the men probably traveled to Florida to judge its suitability for settlement. Matthew and Mary had 12 children. The family genealogy states that all of them were born in Quincy in central Florida. However, the 1828 moving date suggests that the oldest was born at Rural Hill. One of Brevard's letters supports the 1828 date, and a letter Matthew wrote to his wife in 1853 confirms it.

Matthew's medical practice covered a wide territory. His letters from Florida say it was not unusual for him to travel 20 or more miles a day to visit his patients. Matthew was a farmer as well as a doctor. In a letter in 1835 he reported having harvested 60,000 pounds of cotton (20,000 pounds after ginning) and planned to plant 75 acres in cotton the following year. He also grew tobacco.[12]

He is said to have employed an overseer and to have owned as many as 30 slaves at one time. In 1860 he owned 18 slaves, according to the census that year. Matthew kept a physician's journal, which is in the Florida State Archives. Matthew and his wife died in Quincy, as did several of their 12, including two who died in infancy.

Brevard wrote in his Rural Hill farm journal in 1838: "Brother Matthew arrived in this country Oct 24 after an absence of 9 years 11 months." On 30 October Brevard listed furniture bought in Charlotte: a folding table for $9, a small bedstead for $7, a washstand for $3, and a clothes press for $7. These were probably gifts for Matthew to take back to Florida. Six weeks later Brevard joined his brother on the return trip to Florida, writing, "December 5 Started to florida & arrived their on the 15th. Left Florida on 4th Jan 1839 & reached home on the 11th not quite 7 days on the road."

Brevard's wife, Mary, had a two-year-old child and a four-month-old baby, yet they may well have gone along to Florida. Brevard does not tell of the route they took, but in those days before the Charlotte and South Carolina Railroad, they probably went by coach to Charleston, by boat to St. Augustine and by coach to Quincy. Brevard probably arranged for the furniture to be shipped separately. Unfortunately he tells us nothing about that Christmas spent with his Florida siblings.

Joseph and Violet Davidson Sylvester had seven children, all of whom were born and died in Quincy, except for one son who died in the Civil War. Letters from Florida state that Joseph was a farmer, primarily growing tobacco.

Robert H. M. Davidson moved to Florida with his siblings in 1828 or joined them there shortly after. He was 18 at the time, and the 1830 census two years later does not show him at Rural Hill. He never married but not from lack of effort. Several of his letters to Brevard mention ladies who had caught his affection. He wanted his brother's honest opinion of the young ladies, for he was most anxious to have a wife. Robert died in Quincy in 1841 at the age of 31. Brevard wrote in his journal, "DEATH 17th [Oct] Brother Robert died in Florida with conjestive fever with six days sickness."

Jacky and Sallie probably brought Robert's body home since he is said to be buried at Rural Hill. His name does not appear on any of the stones, but there are a few unmarked graves in the family burying ground, and several stones are engraved simply "Davidson."

Mary Winslow Davidson married George W. Doby in February 1831 and died slightly less than two years later. No birth or death dates have been found for George Doby, nor do we know where he came from or what happened to him after Mary died. The family story is that they had no children.

However, the appearance of another Doby in the public records may mean that they had a son. The 1850 census lists Joseph Doby, age 19, living in Jacky's household and states that he was a student. Nineteen would be the right age for a son of Mary's born during her brief marriage. In 1850 Brevard paid William Reid for boarding Joseph Doby for two months, and the following year he paid James Ross $62.20 for boarding Doby for ten months. An account with the merchant Leroy Springs states that on 16 August 1841 Brevard bought "1 cap for James Doby" for 87.5 cents, but Springs may have misunderstood the first name. The family story is that Mary Davidson Doby is buried at Rural Hill, but she does not have a stone marker there.

Isabella Sophia Graham Davidson married James Warren Moore on 11 February 1835 at Rural Hill. He had been born in York County, South Carolina, and they probably lived most or all of their married lives in Lincoln County, where he became an elder at Unity Presbyterian Church, and they may have been buried there. Several of the letters to Brevard from his brothers in Florida inquire about "Isabella and Mr. Moore."

Augustus W. Davidson became a cadet at West Point. He died there in 1837 at the age of 22. His brother Robert, who was living in Florida, visited West Point the following year and wrote to their brother Brevard, "I left West Point this morning, visited the monument of our deceased brother A. This was truly painful—it is a just consolation to know that every attention was rendered him in his last hours, that he was beloved by all his acquaintances & they have as a testimony of their great regard erected [illegible word] & I presume the most costly monument that has been erected to any of their deceased cadets."[13]

William Speight MacLean Davidson attended Davidson College in the first class in 1837 and graduated in 1840. In December 1842 he married Jane Elizabeth Torrance, daughter of James Torrance of Cedar Grove. Both families were members and strong supporters of Hopewell Presbyterian Church, and Jane's brother William Torrance was a college classmate and close companion of William Davidson's.

William and Jane had one son, James "Jimmy" Torrance Davidson, born 21 October 1843. In late November of that year William enrolled in the Medical College of Charleston. He had been there two weeks when he wrote to his father-in-law, describing his exciting and heady new experiences, then without pause he almost frantically inquired: "I have written two letters to Jane and have received no word from her yet. I have anxiously expected a letter by every mail for the last week: but have been disappointed every time I go to the [post] office. What can be the cause I know not. You will please write me as soon as you can & let me know for I am very anxious to hear."

Jane, with a month-old infant, probably had little time to write and may have been sickly. She died 3 December 1844 when little Jimmy was fourteen months old. It isn't known if William finished medical school. He probably didn't stay in Charleston long because of Jane's poor health. It's worth noting, at that time licenses were not required to practice medicine. Students attended school as long as they could, or until they felt confident of their skills. Many followed with an apprenticeship to become a practicing physician.

After Jane's death, William had two more wives, Rebecca Reid and Mary Johnston, but no more children. He built Ingleside, a beautiful plantation home, in the 1850s or 60s. It is privately owned and still stands on Bud Henderson Road, several miles northeast of Rural Hill. William died in December of 1873, and his son Jimmy died a year later at age 30, having never married. William, Jane and Jimmy, along with William's second wife, Rebecca, are buried together at Hopewell.[14]

Edward Constantine Davidson may have attended a common school at the Hopewell church and may have been a student of John M. M. Caldwell's in 1832. As mentioned previously, he is known to have been a student at the Sugar Creek Academy in 1837. He also attended Davidson College and Harvard, where he studied law. He volunteered as a first lieutenant in the U.S. Army Third Dragoons and served with distinction in the Mexican War. According to Brevard's journal, Constantine left for Mexico in July of 1847 and returned home in August of 1848.

After the war he gave up the practice of law to concentrate on farming. In February 1858 he married Jane Violet Henderson and in that same year built a home he called Waverly at his farm on Beatties Ford Road. He later served as a major in the Confederate army in the Civil War.

Constantine and Jane had eight children, five of whom lived to maturity. Constantine drowned in the Catawba River at Moore's Ferry in May of 1892 at the age of 72. He and Jane are buried at Rural Hill along with seven of their children.

Jacky and Sallie's youngest child was named either Sarah Rebecca Davidson or Sarah H. Brevard Davidson; both names appear in the family genealogies. She died in February of 1841, three months shy of her 19th birthday, and is said to be buried at Rural Hill, although none of the marked stones bears her name.

Chapter 8

The Third Generation at Rural Hill: Brevard and Mary Davidson

BREVARD WAS JACKY'S FOURTH CHILD AND SECOND SON, born on 13 March 1808. There is no record of his schooling, but his farm journals and other documents written in his hand indicate that he was educated. He probably attended classes taught at Hopewell over the years, and he may also have studied elsewhere. Documents from the 1820s and 1830s concerning the education of Jacky's children apply to the younger ones; Brevard and his older siblings were probably similarly schooled. His journal shows that by his mid-twenties he was farming Rural Hill alongside his father, and Brevard seemed to be confident in his skills and competent in the business.

Brevard and Jacky farmed and did business together for many years. They may have had a written contract detailing each man's responsibilities and assets or perhaps their agreement was entirely verbal. There seemed to be a clear understanding between them of which property belonged to each man, and when crops were sold, each person's portion was often noted.

On 20 April 1836 Brevard married Mary Laura Springs of York County, South Carolina. Mary's father, John Springs III, was a member of a large, prosperous extended family; a number of his kin had close ties to Major John Davidson. Springs's plantation, called Springfield, was in York County near present-day Fort Mill. John Springs owned additional properties in South Carolina, some in Mecklenburg and Lincoln counties in

North Carolina, and perhaps more elsewhere. He had business interests in Charlotte, and his son Leroy became a Charlotte merchant. Descendants of the Springs family are still numerous in York County. The family's legacy includes Springs Mills and Springs Industries, Springmaid sheets and linens, and the beautiful Anne Springs Close Greenway. Katherine Wooten Springs wrote an excellent history of this important family, *The Squires of Springfield*, and we have relied on that source for much of the information about that family.[1]

It is difficult to piece together the everyday lives of 18th- and 19th-century plantation women, except when letters and diaries survive. Women rarely appear in public records. Married women had virtually no legal rights and typically filled their lives with raising children and tending to the domestic needs of their families and their slaves. Most had active social lives through church and visits to family and friends. Weddings and gala occasions often meant visits of several days or even a week. Such events will be noted here when they can be documented.

Mary attended the Salem Female Academy in 1828 and 1829, and in the fall of 1830 she began a year at Mrs. Sarazin's school in Philadelphia. Her uncle Eli accompanied her on this trip, and soon after her arrival she wrote a chatty letter to her parents describing the experience. They traveled by stagecoach to Salem, North Carolina, where she met several former teachers who "seemed delighted and pleased with the idea of my coming to school again. When they found I was for Philadelphia, they laughed, saying they supposed I was going to get the polish."

BREVARD DAVIDSON, CA. 1880. In 1872 Brevard sold off his property, moved to Charlotte and made a second fortune in real estate. This photograph reflects a newly prosperous gentleman proudly displaying his watch fob. The authors have been unable to identify its meaning and wonder what accomplishments it represented. A copy of this photograph is in the collection of the author.

8. The Third Generation at Rural Hill: Brevard and Mary Davidson

Another stop on their journey was for a tour of Washington, which included the grounds of the president's residence (not yet then known as the White House); they toured the U.S. Capitol and its many works of art. Next, the stage took them as far as Baltimore; from there they went by steamboat and barge across Chesapeake Bay, through the Delaware and Chesapeake Canal, and up the Delaware River to the port of Philadelphia. When she reached the school, Mary's friends Camilla Torrance and Mary Ann Irwin had already arrived. The girls were natural companions, being so far from home together. Camilla was raised on a large plantation near the Hopewell church; Mary Ann's father was a prominent Charlotte merchant. Though they had not been raised in close proximity to one another, their fathers were important in the community, and the girls were well acquainted. This was quite a cosmopolitan adventure for a young lady and a great contrast to her adult life as a plantation mistress and the mother of a large brood of children.[2]

On their wedding day Brevard was 28 and Mary was 22. By then her father was a widower, her mother having died two years earlier. According to *The Squires of Springfield*, the wedding was an elaborate affair held by candlelight at her father's home. Brevard described the marriage in his journal: "Aprile 20 I was married on this day about 50 persons at the weeding and about 75 at the infair." It was commonplace at the time to hold weddings in the bride's home, rather than a church. An infare (reception), as it is properly spelled, was typically held at the home of the groom's family on the day after the wedding—or several days after, if travel was required. Most newly married couples of the time took up residence on or near the groom's family's land. The infare consisted of dining, dancing, and general frivolity to welcome the new bride into the family and to her new home.

The newlyweds moved into Rural Hill with Brevard's parents and had a fine start in life. John Springs gave his daughter an extensive dowry, including the 959.5-acre Dickson Plantation in Lincoln County and 19 slaves. Both the plantation and the slaves are mentioned frequently throughout Brevard's farm journal.

The Dickson Plantation was located several miles northwest of Tuckaseegee Ford near the present-day town of Mount Holly and was about 10 miles from Rural Hill. Joseph Dickson had served in the Revolution as a captain at the Battle of Kings Mountain and as a colonel during the British invasion of North Carolina. He was a prominent lawyer and politician and one of the founders of the University of North Carolina. In 1803 he sold his plantation to John Springs and moved his family to Tennessee.

Of course the moment Brevard and Mary said "I do," her property became his and he referred to it throughout his journals as "my plantation." Although Brevard and Mary married in April, the dowry came to them the following December. The crop year was over at the end of December, at least as far as finances were concerned, and contracts on hired-out slaves expired then, so this was the logical time for John Springs to transfer his property.

Springfield York, D[istrict]. S. C. 8 Dec[r] 1836

D[r] Sir

I have been expecting you and Mary down, but perhaps it is not material, as I have sent up Marys negroes &c to your house, and you can select out such as you wish to keep at home and place the others on the plantation

I think Ann the best cook, but she has a large Family I dont know how you would arrange with them. Peggy has Cooked longer for me than any Negro I own, or at least Mary[s] Mother kept her at it longer, but I never admired her for a Cook and she is getting old and blind. Julia says she has cooked a good deal, but she is likely to have a larger encumbrance of Children. Fanny has no encumbrance of Children and probably wont have, but she has never been put to cooking, and is equal almost to a Man on a Plantation I have an expectation of getting Ann[s] Husband, if so I will take back Wilbert in his place. I will send you up Bill one of my Black smiths, Christmas Holidays, you can hire him out or work him at home. I have had three or four applications could get $250 next year for him without any trouble, but I think I would try it at home. a constant shop always can find a good deal of work any where, and Bill is getting old you ought to learn a young one before he wears out, unless you have a choice boy of your own. you could put Henry, Alek, or Wilbert, at any rate I would learn one of my own and not for another. These however were the reasons I wanted to have seen you before I sent up the negroes to have advised with you. I send you 3 heifers of my improved stock and a pair of little steers, which all you had better keep at Home. I bought 3 fine Young Cows from M[r] Duffy that will all have calves between this and Spring and two yearlings which will be enough to commence with there as forage will be scarce. I send 250[lb] Bacon to feed the negroes on the Plantation. you had better take it in charge and not let them cut on it to waste

I have taken a little cold and feel rather unwell but if nothing happens I will meet you at the Plantation on Monday, till which time you can keep the negroes at home. send Wheeler back on sunday from your House with the little Bay Colt. the pair of Dun Horses the two Fillies, Waggon gear & harness &c I allow you to keep. You can probably go with four Horses to the Plantation, if not you can put one in the place of the Bay Colt as I want Wheeler to return on Sunday

I am inclined to think I would try Alek with Bill if so it would be convenient if Mary would take his Mother for a Cook. I send 3½ bushels salt When the Waggon came up I found one of the Dun match Horses snagged in the shoulder and so swelled he was not fit to go. you must keep the bay Colt till he gets well, and then we can change. send the bay filley by Wheeler

Respectfully yours
John Springs[3]

8. The Third Generation at Rural Hill: Brevard and Mary Davidson

Inventory and valuation of the Property given off to Mary Davidson and charged to her on my Book December 1836

1828 to 1831	To your expenses at Salem & Philadelphia Inventory &c &c	1742
1836 August	1 side saddle	20
	1 cutting box & knives $9 pr wedges 2 Mattocks $4 Grindstone $5	18
Novr 8	1 fine Mahogany bedstead 40. Bureau & dressing glass 45 set Tables 90	175
	2 Beds 3^{pr} sheets 2^{pr} Blankets. quilt, coverlid 3 Counterpains	100
	Table cloths Towels &c &c	10
	2^{pr} Candle sticks snuffers & tray	4
	Silver soup spoon 1 set Table & Tea spoons salt spoons & sugar Tongs	41
	1 full set knives & forks compleat	15
	Bill of Crocking ware bought by Leroy	34
	1 Doz Chairs lost in the steam Boat	15
		2174
Decr 9	3 Cows two yearlings 60. 1 Sow & 4 Shoats from Duffy 15	75
	3 Heifers & 2 Steers from home 60. Stack fodder from Duffy 12	72
	3½ Bushels salt 5 Meal & corn	8
	250^{lb} bacon at 15	38
	New Waggon gear & Harness for five Horses Cover &c	250
	1^{pr} Dunn Horses 4 y old 250 Spotted filly 4 y old 125 Sorrel filly 3 y old 100	485
		928
	Dixon Plantation in Lincoln containing 959½ Acres 11 sold to West 970½	5000
	Bill Black Smith 51 years old	1000
	Ann 42 years old 300. Fanny 21. 450. Wilbert 15. 500	1250
	Rhody 12. 350. Hannah 10. 300 Nancy 7. 250	900
	Humphrey 5. 250. Celia 3. 200	450
	Tom 30. 600. Julia & Child 500. Austin 7. 300	1400

	George 5. 250. Lemuel 2. 200	450
	Burrow 54. 400. Sinai 14. 400	800
	Peggy 50. 200. Henry 18. 500. Alek 15. 500	1200
		7450
Decr 14		
	193 Bushels Corn 145.	
	Cash to furnish Plantation 300	445
	1375^{lb} Bacon at 13	178
		623
		$16175

Drawn off and valued by me this 17 August 1837
   John Springs

   The listing of slaves implies several family groups: Ann and seven children; Tom and Julia and three children; Peggy and two children. Brevard wrote in his farm journal on 12 December 1836, "Moved Mary's negroes down to the Dixon place 18 in number—Burrow, Ann & seven children—Tom, Julia & three children Peggy & two children kept Sina at home." The number written in Brevard's journal entry is clearly 18, but there are only 17 names listed, which is probably the number he meant. Although Burrow and Ann are mentioned together, they were not married, as Springs's letter said he would try to acquire Ann's husband. Sinai (more often spelled *Sina*) is mentioned frequently. The "& child" following Julia's name probably meant "& children," referring to the three listed. Brevard's journal records the birth of four more sons to Julia. Then, in 1847, he notes, "Julia,s first daughter & eights child ... 5th born since I owned her." This confirms that Julia had only three children when he acquired her.

   Although Major John and his son Jacky farmed Rural Hill for many years, neither of them kept records of their work. We can assume they produced crops adequate to feed their families and excess to sell, and used simple farming methods typical of their time.

   Brevard was influenced by the new scientific farming principles that were becoming popular, and at the age of 26 he began keeping a farm journal. He kept this journal in a blank book for 21 years, from 1834 to 1854. His second journal was a book printed for use as a farm journal, and his entries covered only a few months in 1856. Most of the information about farming at Rural Hill comes from those two journals. They complement each other, are a rich source of information and are cited frequently throughout this text. Both journals are in the Davidson Family Papers at

8. The Third Generation at Rural Hill: Brevard and Mary Davidson   105

the University of North Carolina at Charlotte (UNCC) and have been transcribed, annotated, and published as a book edited by one of the authors.[4] See Appendix H. for an account of Brevard's slave inventories.

Brevard opened his first journal with these words: "March 7th 1834. I have made the attempt two or three times to keep an account how we plant our crop and have always failed—I shall now make one more attempt." This time, to our benefit, he was greatly successful; he kept the journal until 1854, making several crisp business-like entries each week, although there are many streams of daily notes. A few gaps exist, one spanning nearly two years, others of days or weeks.

The purpose of the journal was to make him a better farmer by noting when plowing, planting, building and other farm tasks were done, the weather trends from year to year, and how the crops fared under various conditions. He also noted when significant events in the family and the community occurred. He recorded the births of his own children, as well as many births of slaves, horses, and cows, usually naming the mother, and the number, gender, and sometimes the name of the offspring.

His journal for 1856, published in 1852 in Richmond, Virginia, begins with about twenty pages of instructions provided by the publisher on how to manage a farm using the latest scientific principles, such as crop rotation, to achieve the most bountiful crops. There is also advice on treating slaves humanely, policing their activities, and appropriate punishment when necessary. It was intended to be kept by a farm manager, or overseer, for the edification of the farm owner. However, Brevard kept the journal himself. It contains blank pages to record daily activity, including columns for weather data, and pages to list slaves, farm implements, crops, and so on, and instructions for filling in those pages.

His daily record in this journal covers only the period from January through early April of 1856, but the entries are more detailed than in his first journal. Slaves were frequently named in this record, a definite change from his earlier volume, and they are listed by name and occupation. In the same journal he made another slave list in 1864.

The volume also includes a chart for a "Daily Record of Cotton Picked." Brevard filled two pages of the chart that cover the four weeks from September 16 to October 14 of 1856, probably about half of that year's harvest. He listed his slaves' names, the amount each person picked on each day, and the total poundage picked. From this volume we can get a clearer idea of Rural Hill's slave activity, as well as inventories of equipment and livestock.

The 1834–54 journal is written in a blank copybook measuring 12½ by 8 inches and 1 inch thick. The cover boards are wrapped in golden brown marbled paper, and the spine and corners were bound in light brown leather, which is now missing on the corners. All of the writing is in ink that has turned brown with age. Written on the first two right-hand pages are "Farmers Recollection," and "A. B. Davidsons Bought of Daniel Gould, Price $1.50." Brevard then apparently made one of his false starts. Written at the top of the next right-hand page is "February 20th 1834," and nothing more. Then he began in earnest on 7 March 1834 and numbered that page 1. All the pages are numbered; the main journal ends on page 144 with his last entry of 20 September 1854. On page 145 there is one brief entry for 1 January 1867. These pages occupy about half the copybook; the remaining pages are blank.

The commercially printed 1856 farm book measures 10½ by 8½ inches and is half an inch thick. Again, brown marbled papers decorate the cover boards. The spine binding is worn away, and some of the exposed sewing threads are broken. It consists of 127 pages. Fourteen of the "Daily Record" pages were filled in, two of them in the handwriting of someone other than Brevard. Most of the book's pages are blank. Many of the unused pages were for daily records and cotton harvest records. The book also has pages for inventories of livestock, farm equipment, and other items, records of slave births and deaths, doctor's visits, and financial account pages. A few of these are filled in.

Although most of Brevard's journal entries were about farming, he did make note of family and neighborhood events, giving us a peek into his everyday life. He told of his marriage, sawing lumber for building Davidson College, and his parents' move back to Rural Retreat. On 3 February 1837 he wrote, "Mary's & A. B. Davidson first child was born." This was Mary Laura Davidson, the first of their sixteen children. Then, on 25 September, he noted, "Our little daughter Mary Springs is very sick with the huping couf has been down seriously ill for about five weeks we think is a little better." Although Brevard called his daughter "Mary Springs" in this entry, there is no other indication that "Springs" was part of her name. Mary recovered, yet there was a death to report in November: "My Brother Augustus W. Davidson died at West Point Oct 25th 1837. Aged 22 years & 4 monts."

In August of 1838 he wrote, "Birth Monday 6th Our son John Springs was born." This boy was known as John throughout his childhood and in the journals kept by his father and mother. At some point, probably when he reached his maturity, he took the name of Springs or, more formally J.

8. The Third Generation at Rural Hill: Brevard and Mary Davidson

Springs, and appears in newspaper articles as such. In his father's will he was John Spring Davidson.

On 20 July 1840 Brevard wrote: "Our third child second son born ½ after two oclock 1 year, 11 months 14 days after the birth of John Springs our 1th son." This was William Lee Davidson. Subsequent children were generally noted this way by birth order and gender; only occasionally was the child named.

Brevard actively farmed the Dickson Plantation that he received from his father-in-law. The road that ran in front of Rural Hill ended at Tool's Ford on the Catawba. It was easy to cross on horseback, making the river, for the Davidsons, no more than a fat creek. However, there were occasional freshets on the river when heavy rainfall swelled it out of its banks, causing people to stay put for a few days. He wrote about farming and other activities there, all very much like Rural Hill's but on a smaller scale. In August of 1839 he wrote, "Raised my Barn at my Dickson plantation." The first entry of 1840 states: ' Set up a shop at my Dickson Place the firm of Davidson and springs."

Brevard and his partner and father-in-law, John Springs, kept a daybook for this shop, which is also in the Davidson Family Papers at UNCC. It begins on 4 February 1840 and is a financial record of goods bought and sold as well as work done on the plantation. Some of the work was done for, and charged to, others. The business was a partnership, but the farm clearly belonged to Brevard. The plantation produced hogs and other goods in significant quantities, including enough cotton to justify building a gin in September of 1841. Brevard noted in the daybook on September 2, 1841, "Osborn Flanigain commenced working at my ginn at the dickson plantation is to put up the [gin] house, running gear, & screw press for $115.00." In March of 1842 "Mr. Hutchison has about 20 Acres corn planted." Cyrus Hutcheson was the overseer at Dickson for many years.

The unreliable nature of weather was always a bother to Brevard, as it is to any farmer. He wrote incessantly that it was too wet or too dry and the crops were being harmed. He noted weather that was unseasonably hot or cold and occasionally of a fine season and beneficial rain. One notable occurrence was a freshet on 28 May 1840. Freshets on the Catawba were nearly always caused by unusually heavy rainfall, rarely by snowmelt from the mountains. Crops along the riverbank could be severely damaged, and travel across the much-forded Catawba was often curtailed. "A very high freshet in the river said to be the highest in 50 years. I saw one in 1824 about 11 Inches lower & one in 1814 about six inches lower, making this one the highest by 6 Inches I ever saw, about 32 ft past common water in fact water courses all very high & a great deal of rain, more injury done on the river than ever was done."

The detailed May 20 entry was longer than Brevard's average account. His entries on 25 May 1840—"Very wet weather"—and 26 May 1840—"Stopped by rain"—are more typical. The rains continued; on 6 June he wrote, "Have done no ploughing for neare three weeks." In mid–July he wrote again that plowing had been hampered for weeks by rain. He cut his oats but could not get them tied up for six days. Crops were damaged, and many acres were lost. In August an exasperated Brevard wrote, "Finished working our crop or rather quitt it." But of course he didn't quit. By fall he was farming as usual. Crops may have been smaller that year, but they appear to have been satisfactory.

Brevard often reported river flooding as a number of feet "past common water," meaning the distance beyond the normal riverbank. The six inches he referred to in May of 1840 were probably a portion of the 32 feet past common water, rather than a measurement of the water's depth.

This is in contrast to the weather of the previous year. In the fall of 1839 he wrote: "Have about 17000 lb cotton out with out any rain, very dry weather water courses said to be lower than they have ever been by some of our oldest men, our mill is nearly stoped, in fact the crick is nearly stoped running.... Mcdowels crick is stoped running from our Bridge up. Catawba river never known to be as low."

The first few months of 1856 were particularly cold and snowy. On 4 January he wrote, "Commenced snowing about 11 Oclock at night." It continued until one o'clock the following afternoon; eight inches accumulated. It snowed off and on for the rest of the month. He wrote several times that there had been little snowmelt and that the snow remained eight to 12 inches deep in most places. The weather remained cold, once reaching two degrees below zero.

During most of this time the men were chopping and splitting firewood, probably in the barn, and the women were inside spinning. Spinning was rarely mentioned in earlier years as it had nothing to do with making a crop; apparently there was little else to be done with so much snow on the ground. On 26 January the women were still spinning, and he wrote, "Not a furough of ploughing since the new year set in, & no cotton picked out of the field I have about 6000^{lb} in the field."

Finally, in about mid–February the snow had melted enough that he could finish picking cotton and begin plowing his land. Ordinary late fall tasks resumed: killing hogs, and ginning and packing cotton. Plowing continued apace through March. The 1856 journal ends in early April; probably the new cotton crop was planted midmonth. This was indeed an unusual snow. In 1835 he had noted nine or 10 inches of snow, "the deepest I ever saw, and the deepest since the death of Washington" in 1799.

Like the rest of his clan, Brevard and his family were Presbyterians and Hopewell was their church. Presbyterians at the time celebrated the sacrament of communion at least once a year, sometimes more often. To participate in the service each church member was required to appear before the elders, demonstrate an understanding of Presbyterian theology, affirm a sincere belief in Presbyterian teachings, and express sincere remorse for any wrongdoing. Those who met the criteria were given tokens that they presented on communion Sunday to receive the sacrament.[5]

Hopewell's practice was to hold these services in the spring; nearly every year Brevard's journal noted "Hopewell Sacrament" in May or June. In 1841 he wrote, "Our Hopewell sacrament was on the 23 of May. Mary & Myself connected our selves with the church & had our children baptized—Mary, John, and William." It was not unusual for sincerely religious people to regularly engage in worship services yet not become church members. According to Dr. Chalmers Davidson, Brevard was an elder at Hopewell from 1846 to 1875.[6]

Brevard recorded many births and deaths of his slaves and family members. He also noted births and sometimes conceptions of horses and cows. On 26 May 1841: "My little mare Ariel took the horse," and on 1 August "spot cow took the bull." Various livestock births include "two calves Frosty's & Bet's," "My little mare Ariel colted yesterday, the 1st day of April," "Sinet colted at the plantation the last day of March." Many others are recorded; most of them name the mother. His recordings of slave births also named the mother and sometimes included the child's name.

Earlier we mentioned the journal entries for the births of the first three of Brevard's own children. Journal entries relating the births of his other children are as follows: "Our third son was born 15 minutes after three p.m." This was Robert Augustus, who was born on 13 March 1842. On 10 December 1843, "Our fourth son was born to day. Austin Richard." On 16 August 1845, "Our Sixth child & second daughter born"; this was Sarah "Sallie" Harper. On 17 November 1847: "Our third daughter & seventh child Jane [later called Jenny] born." The birth of twins came on 17 June 1849: "Mary gave birth to two daughters this morning about 6 O,clock (9 children)"; and "Sept 29th [1849] to day Isabella Sophia & Amanda Margaret Baptised by the Rev. H. B. Cunningham, Pastor our church."

Next comes a surprise. In recording the birth of Adam Brevard, Jr., he wrote on 20 March 1852, "Our 5th son & 11th child born." Eleventh child? When the twins were born he wrote "9 children." There is a break in the journal from 3 November 1849 to 18 September 1851. Was a child born during this interval? The next birth entry, "12th child & 7 daughter [Blandina] was born October 15th 1853," confirms that there was indeed another child, a daughter, born between the twins and Adam Brevard, Jr. She must have died at or soon after birth; there is no other record of her existence. Altogether Mary and Brevard had 16 children; the last four were born after his journal-keeping days had ended. In June of 1861 Mary gave birth to Fanny Baxter Davidson. Mary was 47 years old, and at last her child-bearing days were spent.

Brevard also noted in the journal the deaths of a number of family members, friends, and slaves. Previously mentioned were the deaths of two of Brevard's brothers. Others deaths include Mary's father, John Springs, in 1853; the death of her aunt Sophia in 1839; and on 14 February 1841, "Sister Sarah died this morning at half past one Oclock." Sarah was Brevard's youngest sister and was 19 years old.

On 3 February 1842 he noted: "Aunt Sarah Caldwell died." Sarah, daughter of Major John, had been married to the Rev. Alexander Caldwell, the minister who was dismissed from Rocky River Presbyterian church in 1797 upon becoming deranged. Very shortly afterward Sarah and her three small children fled back to Rural Hill to live with her parents. Her children lived at Rural Hill, at Holly Bend with their uncle Robin and aunt Peggy, or at Beaver Dam with their uncle William Lee Davidson and aunt Betsy, probably spending time in each of those households. Sarah remained at Rural Hill until her children were grown; she was living with one of them when she died.

A slave named Peter died on 8 November 1851, and on 8 May 1853, a Negro boy named Charles died. Brevard makes a few mentions of infant slave deaths; other slave deaths, which must have occurred, went unreported in the journal.

Brevard's journal tended to be businesslike. Most births, deaths, and happy events were noted with scarcely a hint of emotion. The tribute that follows is an exception, perhaps the most heartfelt words in the entire journal.

> The Rev John Williamson Pasture of our church died the 16th of September 1842 about 7 Oclock in the evening a man of fine judgment, good common sense, and beloved by all of the congregation, & no doubt will be missed very much in the neighborhood & as a good neighbor as well as the Pasture of the Hopewell congregation.

Williamson had been Hopewell's minister since 1818, when Brevard was 10 years old. Williamson was really the only minister Brevard had ever known. The Reverend Hugh B. Cunningham, D.D., became the next minister at Hopewell.

Weddings and other happy occasions were mentioned. On 6 April 1842 Brevard wrote, "Went to James Osborn weding in Charlotte to Mrs Moores & returned to day." James Walker Osborne was the nephew of Brevard's aunt Peggy Davidson; she and Robin had raised James at Holly Bend. James's bride was a young widow, Mary Ann Irwin Moore—the very same Mary Ann Irwin who had been a classmate of Mary's at the boarding school in Philadelphia. Although Brevard doesn't mention that his wife attended with him, surely Mary was present at her dear friend's wedding.

On 8 December he wrote, "Brother W. S. M. Davidson & Jane Torrance were married to day," and on the 9th: "Infair at Fathers to day about 100 persons took dinner & a small dancing party at my house at night." Jane Torrance's sister Camilla was also a classmate of Mary Ann Irwin's and Mary Davidson's. Camilla probably was among the guests at her sister's wedding, but it may be that she missed Mary Ann Irwin's nuptials since the following April Camilla wrote her father: "Mary Ann and Mr. Osborne were down this week ... I was very much pleased to see Mary Ann ... she is very lively and looks quite as well as ever, the Same old Mary Ann and has changed as little as anyone in my knowledge."[7]

In 1840: "July 3 & 4 Attending the great celebration at sals-bury [Salisbury], said to be about ten thousand people."

On 20 May 1844 Brevard wrote, "I attended a meeting in charlotte to day, a monumental meeting." This was a celebration of the Mecklenburg Declaration of Independence of May 20 1775, the earliest such declaration in America. His grandfather, Major John Davidson, had been a participant in the convention that wrote the Declaration and had signed it. This celebration was also to begin fund-raising for the erection of a monument to the memory of those signers of the Declaration.

On 30 March 1844 a meeting had been held in Charlotte "to make arrangement for the celebration of the 20th of May." This was reported in the *Charlotte Journal*, a weekly, of 12 April. Another article in the same issue noted that the Mecklenburg Monumental Association had been incorporated by the assembly for the purpose of raising funds and erecting a monument in the town of Charlotte in commemoration of the Mecklenburg Declaration of Independence.[8]

In the issues of 24 and 31 May 1844 the *Charlotte Journal* reported on the celebration of May 20. The attendance had been less than expected, perhaps due to a lack of publicity but primarily due to the absence of a fife and drum, essential to collecting a crowd. The celebration began at the courthouse in the morning when celebrants fired a cannon and rang a church bell to gather a crowd. At noon a procession formed and marched to the grove of the Presbyterian churchyard. After a prayer by the Reverend Freeman, the Declaration was read by W. R Myers. Then James W. Osborne, the invited speaker, delivered an eloquent and feeling oration that pleased and enchanted the crowd who, according to the paper, only wished it had gone on longer. His address to Major Thomas Alexander, the only Revolutionary War soldier present, brought tears from people in the crowd. The ceremonies concluded with a chorus singing "Old North State" and a return to the courthouse, where the crowd was dismissed.[9]

At 3 o'clock dinner was announced by the ringing of the Baptist church's bell. After a delicious meal, the tablecloth was removed and wine was placed on the table. There were thirteen formal toasts. The first and fifth were greeted with six cheers and a discharge of cannon. Two toasts, those to Ephraim Brevard and George Washington, were drunk in silence. The ninth toast was to the Mecklenburg Monumental Association, greeted with six cheers and a cannon volley. It was followed by a call for a speech from H. C. Jones, which led to a number of contributions to the monument fund. Then James W. Osborne was called to give his speech, which yielded even more contributions. This was followed by toasts to General William Lee Davison and to the memory of the signers, which attendees consumed in silence. The twelfth toast, to North Carolina, after the ladies sang "The Old North State" to six cheers and a cannon volley. This encouraged the women, who gave a concert that was "quite a 'jam.'" They raised another $100, the paper noted.

After the thirteenth formal toast, to "the fair sex," there were 21 more volunteer toasts. A merry time was had by all, and the celebration raised more than $300 for the monument. Whether a monument was built with these funds is not known.

It is quite evident that Brevard and Mary educated all of their children to one extent or another. Mary taught them the alphabet, counting, basic reading and writing, addition and subtraction. Her brief journal, kept from January through mid–March 1843, mentions teaching Mary and John reading and catechism and perhaps other topics, and listening to them recite their lessons. Mary was six, John was five. Their mother may have continued this to advanced reading and drills of writing a "round hand" and memorizing tables of multiplication and division. Once the older children were able, they probably took over this instruction of the younger children.[10]

Only a few records, in letters and journals and scattered receipts, address higher education. Fortunately the Davidsons had a habit through the generations of keeping all sorts of miscellaneous records. Combing through these can reveal more about the type and amount of instruction the children received, and we can piece together an outline of their education.

While there was no universal education at this time, there were a number of schools, such as the academy at Sugar Creek Church, the Moravian girls' school in Salem, North Carolina, and Edgeworth Female Seminary in Greensboro, North Carolina, that operated over periods of many years. However, most schools, sometimes called academies, lasted only as long as a minister served at a church or for however long a young man taught school while he decided what to accomplish in his life. Both boys and girls could be educated, and that education commenced as soon as the children were old enough to be away from home and to walk the distances involved. Since it was unusual to have a school close enough to walk to every day, most schooling required boarding at homes near the school. Dr. D. T. Caldwell of Rosedale boarded a number of boys who attended Sugar Creek Academy, just a half-mile away.

In his journal Brevard mentions the schooling of a few of his children who were of school age during the years he was writing (1834–54). The 1850 census notes that seven of his nine children had "attended school within the year." Mary Laura at 13 was the oldest scholar, and three-year-old Jenny the youngest; the one-year-old twins were the only ones not attending school.

In November of 1846 Brevard wrote, "Mary, John, & William went over the river to Mr Moors to go to school thursday the 12th." Mary was nine; her brothers were eight and six. Mr. Moore was probably Brevard's brother-in-law, married to his sister Isabella. They lived in Lincoln County, where James Moore was an elder in Unity Church. The family papers contain two brief progress reports for John and William from Unity Academy. The following November Brevard wrote that he "brought the children home from school Mary, John, & William, have been there four months." This was a subsequent session, perhaps at the same school or another one.

On 6 April 1848 Brevard "took Mary, John, & William to B. W. Alexander,s to board to go to Rev. H. B. Cunningham school 3^d Inst." This school was held at Hopewell, about three miles away, close enough for the children to come home on weekends.

In July of 1848 "Mr John Springs took my daughter of to Salem 20th of this month." The Salem Female Academy, operated by the Moravian Church, was a very popular institution for daughters of area planters. Mary,

Brevard's wife, had studied there when she was a girl. Salem records show that Mary entered Salem in July 1848 and left the school in May 1852. She was there from ages 11 to 15.

In March 1853 Brevard wrote, "John, William Robert Richard Commenced going to school to W. A. Patton March 29th 1853." This is Brevard's only mention of school for Robert and Richard, who were 11 and 12 that year.

In January 1856 he took John and William to the Ebenezer Academy in Ebenezerville, South Carolina, now a part of Rock Hill. They were 17 and 15. Their tuition and board cost $115.

Only a few of the surviving receipts specify school expenses. Most are written for "value received"; some of those may have been for educational expenses.

On 16 September 1862 Brevard sent his daughter Sallie to Edgeworth Female Seminary in Greensboro, North Carolina. He paid $150 for her tuition. Another receipt from Edgeworth for $100 is dated 1 October of the same year. This might have been an additional expense for Sallie, but it was more likely for her sister Jenny. Sallie was 17 that year; Jenny was 15. That November he paid Salem Academy $200 for the education of his twin daughters, Amanda and Isabella, who were 13 years old.

Dr. Chalmers Davidson states that both Robert and Baxter (Edward Lee Baxter Davidson) attended Davidson College, and when Baxter died he became the largest donor in the college's history. A journal kept by Brevard's daughter Sallie confirmed that her brother Baxter was at Davidson College in 1877.[11]

Brevard had many interests besides farming. He was one of the group of local men who bought stock in the Charlotte and South Carolina Railroad to support its construction. The railroad's board of directors was formed in 1847, and Brevard was one of its founding members.[12]

The Catawba River was only partially navigable and then only when conditions were right. Before 1852 Brevard and his neighbors had to pay men to drive wagons loaded with cotton to Cheraw or Camden, South Carolina, where the rivers (Catawba and Pee Dee, respectively) became navigable. Or sometimes when there was shopping to be done, they drove their crops all the way to Charleston. The high cost of this transportation meant that cotton was the only major crop profitable enough to be sent to market. Even then, cotton grown in the Carolina backcountry was less profitable than that grown closer to river or rail transportation.

The original plan for the C&SC Railroad was to build it to Charlotte from either Camden or Columbia, both of which were already terminals

8. The Third Generation at Rural Hill: Brevard and Mary Davidson

on the South Carolina Railroad. Since almost all of the track would be in South Carolina and the terminus would be in North Carolina, it was believed, correctly, that no aid or assistance could be expected from either state. The entire construction cost of $3 million had to be raised by selling stock to citizens living in the area served by the railroad.

Beginning in June 1847, potential investors could subscribe for stock in a line from Camden or for one from Columbia. A third type of stock was available for a line from either of these terminals, as decided by the board of directors. As much more was subscribed for stock for the line coming from Columbia, the Camden subscribers got their deposits back, and construction began from Columbia, crossing the Catawba River and terminating in Charlotte.

The Charlotte and South Carolina Railroad was completed in October of 1852 when the first train arrived in Charlotte. With this connection to Columbia, Charleston, and the world Piedmont farmers had, for the first time, reliable and inexpensive farm-to-market transportation.

Brevard went to many railroad meetings, which were often held in Columbia. In March of 1848 he wrote, "Returned from Columbia, from a meeting of the board of directors of the Charlotte & S. Carolina R. Road, also took a ride on the Cars [railroad cars] to Charleston on 16th & returned to Columbia on 17th & home on the 20th Inst ... very cold hard freeze. I saw Ice & Ice sickles plenty between Branchville & Charleston as large a walking cane." This jaunt was surely planned to whet the appetite of the railroad's investors and potential investors. It was probably a first train ride for many of them. Roaring across the countryside being pulled by a smoky noisy "iron horse" at the breathtaking speed of 12 miles per hour was certainly a heady experience. It took one day to go the 120 miles from Charleston to Columbia by railroad and three days to make the 100 miles from Columbia to Rural Hill on horseback.

In May of 1852 Brevard attended a meeting of the railroad's board of directors at the proposed Ebenezer depot. However, no such depot had materialized when the railroad opened in October. The citizens of Ebenezerville declined to have a depot built in their peaceful little town, believing their town would be spoiled by noisy trains spewing soot and ashes, so depots were built instead in Rock Hill and Fort Mill. Ebenezerville's residents may have regretted their decision; Rock Hill and Fort Mill thrived and grew while Ebenezerville ceased to exist and was absorbed into Rock Hill. Brevard remained on the board of directors after the railroad opened. He wrote of attending a meeting in 1856, and the historian Chalmers Davidson said Brevard served on the board until his death.[13]

Brevard was a member of the Mecklenburg Agricultural Society and became its president about 1845. He was an advocate of the latest improvements in farming methods, including crop rotation, deep plowing and improving livestock by selective breeding. In his journal he mentioned his attendance at many Agricultural Society meetings.

As we will discuss in Chapter 10, an enormous amount of work took place at Rural Hill: plowing, planting, cultivating and harvesting, as well as building cotton gins, mills, farm roads, fences, and other structures. Brevard's slave population was small for the meatier projects, so he frequently hired others, both white and black, to assist them.

At least once he hired a slave on a yearly basis to work alongside his own people. On 29 December 1835 he hired "Aaron belonging to Estate of B. W. Davidson deces^d @ $98.00 this is three years we have hired him does very well at plantation." Annual contracts for hiring slaves were usually made at the end of December or in early January.

B. W. Davidson, Brevard's uncle Benjamin Wilson Davidson, had died in 1829, leaving a widow and six boys younger than 11. When Brevard arranged to hire a slave from his uncle's estate, these boys were all still minors and the widow, Elizabeth Latta Davidson, had not yet remarried. It is probable that in hiring this slave for at least three years, Brevard was providing ready money to the guardians of his young cousins who were still all under the age of 17. When these boys reached 21, Aaron either would become the property of one of them or perhaps would be sold.

Brevard employed overseers from time to time, and he also had tenant farmers on his land. Again, their contracts were typically made near the beginning of the year. On 4 January 1847 he wrote, "Getting boys to repairing the dwelling house at the mill for James Johnson as overseer." And on 1 January 1849: "Jacob Riley set to work with me on Monday the 8th Inst. @ $10 per month." Note that the hire of an overseer was $120.00 per year while the cost of a rental slave was nearly as much at $98.00 per year.

Cyrus Hutcheson, as we have mentioned, was the overseer of the Dickson Plantation. Having an overseer on his Lincoln County land, some distance from Rural Hill, made perfect business sense. Usually a specific portion of the farm's bounty was reserved for Hutcheson, and it often included several of the hogs that were slaughtered each fall.

In September of 1840 Brevard wrote, "Finished the brick house at the Dickson plantation, to day covering, ten thousand five hundred shingles." This probably was the house occupied by the Dickson family, who had moved to Tennessee when John Springs III bought the plantation in 1803. Neither he nor Brevard used that plantation as their principal residence.

8. The Third Generation at Rural Hill: Brevard and Mary Davidson

This journal entry almost certainly refers to replacing the roof on an existing brick house. There is no mention of making or obtaining bricks or other building materials, and ten thousand shingles implies a substantial structure.[14]

It would have been unusual to build such a grand structure for an overseer, but if the brick house was already there, it made sense to keep it in good repair. Brevard often stayed at Dickson for several days at a time, and his father-in-law may have done the same. They may have had rooms reserved for them in this house.

In September of 1842, while building a mill at Rural Hill, Brevard hired John D. Prim for three and three-quarter days at 75 cents per day; Prim was one of a number of men hired for this project. In May of the following year Brevard planted seven or eight acres of corn "by Prim's little house." Prim lived on the property for a number of years and was a tenant farmer who was hired for specific jobs from time to time.

The 1850 census includes Eliza Prem, age 20, as a member of Brevard's household. The only John Prim in that census was an 11-year-old living in the home of the Duckworth family. Eliza and John may have been orphans of John D. Prim, but there is not enough evidence to be certain. Ibzan Tanner was also a tenant farmer. In November of 1837 Brevard had received "of Ibzan about 70 bsh [bushels] of corn for wrent of upper plantation." John D. Prim and Tanner, and occasionally others, received a portion of the hogs slaughtered and had the cotton they grew ginned by Brevard.

It is unclear how much land Major John Davidson owned and how he divided it among his three sons. Deeds often were not registered, and those of inherited lands rarely were. Jacky's portion of the inheritance eventually came to Brevard. During the years they both actively farmed, Jacky and Brevard had a clear understanding of how the land was divided between them, but they left no documents to reveal that division.

Brevard referred to his various fields as the swamp, the bottoms, the meadows, the upland field, the orchard, the field by the barn door, and so on. His journal often recorded where a crop was grown and, when it was sold, if it was his or his father's crop.

Over the years he purchased a few parcels adjacent to Rural Hill. In October 1841 he bought land from the estate of Richard Barry for $1,031 that Brevard called "my Barry plantation"; he doesn't mention its acreage. One of his neighbors was Miss Jane Barry, a sister of Richard Barry. In April of 1847 Brevard was "making a fence between Miss Jane Barry and mine," which tells us her farm was adjacent to Rural Hill, and she may well have lived with her brother before his death. Brevard mentioned Barry's land early in his journal, but he does not mention Miss Jane Barry prior to the purchase from her brother's estate. In October 1849 he collected rent corn from the Barry place, so a tenant was probably farming a portion of the Barry land Brevard had purchased.

In 1844 Brevard bought 111 acres from Rocinda Wilson for $388.50. It lay on McDowell Creek, the eastern border of Rural Hill, adjacent to Jane Barry, and probably also adjacent to Rural Hill.

In October 1849 Brevard bought 100 acres from Joseph M. Davidson for $1,600. Joseph's father, Benjamin Wilson Davidson, was Brevard's uncle who had died in 1829. When Major John died in 1832, the inheritance intended for Benjamin Wilson Davidson was divided among his six sons. Considering the very high price Brevard paid for this piece of property and that it abutted both McDowell Creek and the Catawba River, it may have been a fishery. It is also possible that Brevard paid more than market price for this land in order to make provision for his cousin Joseph, who was just starting out in life.

In the 1850 census Brevard reported the value of his property as $19,000. This is not a valuation for tax purposes but a self-reported estimate. This census did not ask for a farm's acreage, just for its value. In Brevard's farm journal of 1856 he listed his Rural Hill farm as consisting of 1,982.5 acres valued at $8 per acre for a total value of $15,860. Although Jacky was still alive and active, Rural Hill was considered one farm. This was probably the plantation's maximum acreage. It is doubtful additional tracts were purchased between 1856 and the beginning of the Civil War.

Chapter 9

Brevard and Mary: Mills, Wills and Children

THE DAVIDSONS OF RURAL HILL had owned and operated a variety of mills since colonial days, but the locations of these mills have not been determined. The first mention of milling in Brevard's farm journal was in 1836. In January he began sawing huge quantities of lumber for construction at Davidson College, and later that year he sold 1,300 pounds of flour in Charlotte. In 1842 he began construction of a new mill, which must have been a grand edifice indeed. On 19 August he "commenced digging our mill pit with 6 hands." Over the next week: "Three days at the pit six hands $3.00 ... have had from 6 to ten hands this week 6 days with two mules. $14.00 ... two days with 8 hands & two mules at our mill pit." His workers at the new mill were skilled craftsmen, including Harry Worke, a free black brick mason, and his brothers. Others included day laborers, hired slaves, and Brevard's Rural Hill slaves. All of the hired slaves were paid, and he assigned a value to the work of his own slaves. It was customary to give slaves a portion of the money they had earned. Brevard and the owners of the hired hands may have done so.

On 3 September Brevard began quarrying stone: "John Hiss 6 days splitting & blasting rock for our mill." The blasting was done with black powder; dynamite was not invented until 1867. Work continued at the quarry until late November. Altogether 288 wagonloads of rock were quarried and hauled to the mill site. Again he noted the number of workers: a few day laborers, hired slaves, and his own people, and he listed the cost or value of their services. The rock came from the Cashen Quarry, which was the closest place where the quality and quantity of stone he needed could be found. Today there is a Cashion Road about two miles north of Rural Hill, running from Beatties Ford Road toward the river. As that area was being developed in 2019, the land was found to contain a multitude of rocks up to boulder size, indicating that the Catawba River ran there millennia ago.

On 18 September Harry Worke commenced building the mill wall. Information obtained from a descendant of Harry Worke's tells us that he was a free black who lived in Iredell County and was a skilled brick mason. Worke's wife and one of his children were willed to him by their owner in 1841. By 1850 he and his family had moved to Michigan.[1]

Worke, his brothers, and several hands continued building until 24 November: "Harry finished mill wall today ... 37 days at it." During those 37 days there were often two or three hands "waiting on Harry," or assisting him while others continued working at the quarry. There was apparently little or no work done on the mill through the winter; the days were filled with harvesting cotton and other crops, killing hogs, sowing the winter wheat, and preparing the land for spring planting.

On 23 March 1843, Brevard noted, "Isaac Pain, his Brother, & Brother-in-law came here to build the frame of the mill house." On 3 April "Martin Sigman & his workeman came here to day to commence mill." Five days later: "Raised our plank kill at the mill." In May they "raised the husk fraim of our mill Ten hands—in 4 hours" and "raised our mill house the fraim." The husk is a building's outer shell, or exterior walls, which are nailed to the support structure or frame.

Early in August Brevard recorded in his journal: "Commenced digging our mill race. Dug 1 day & half with 11 hands, men. Dug 2 days with 17 men, boys & women." Over the next several weeks they dug the heel race with "12 hands, two hired ones," and the head race with 16 hands. In the craft of milling and in relation to a water-driven mill the water source can be a river or a pond. The ditch and wooden trough that brings the water from that source to the mill is the head race. The ditch that takes the water from the mill and returns it to the stream or river is the tail race.

On 7 September he wrote, "Still at our mill"; the race was not yet complete. Then a bit of frustration: "Started our new mill the corn stones, not a good head grinds about 3 bushels in 40 minutes." Stones used to grind corn or wheat were grooved differently, and the corn stone was probably not grooved well enough. Two grinding mills could be built and the power shifted from one to the other, or a mill's stones could be switched to suit the task. On 3 October Brevard noted, "Started our wheet mill," indicating that two sets of mill stones had been installed. And finally on 7 November

1843, he wrote, "Finished our mill dam & races cost of our own labour about $320." There was one more improvement to be made. On 7 September 1844 Brevard noted that they had "finished burning brick four days and knights, burnt about 43 or 4 loads of wood." Early in October: "Halling Brick & sand for mill house chimney built by Edwin Lundergain $12.00."

Mills of course needed upkeep. On 16 October 1852 Brevard wrote, "Finished my mill race after a siege of six weeks, with 17 hands & three hired ones, blasting rock. I think it cost six hundred dollars. 18th Started the mill today, after being stopped near two months."

Slaves were the millers at Rural Hill. Unfortunately the farm journal of 1834–54 gives us little indication of which slaves were doing which jobs and no mention of who the millers were. In Brevard's journal of 1856 he lists the occupations of his slaves, and Thomas was the miller. Several times in that brief journal he stated that Tom was at the mill, once assisted by George. In all of these instances the mill was "out of fix," and the men were working on the problem.

According to the 1830 census there were 25 slaves at Rural Hill, all in Jacky's household. This was a smaller workforce than one might imagine, considering their ages. Nine of them were younger than 10, and another ten were aged 10 to 23. Three men and one woman were between 24 and 35 years of age, and one man and one woman were older than 36. Brevard was 22 and was listed as a member of his father's household with no indication of which slaves belonged to him.

When Brevard began his journal in 1834, he had not yet married and was very active as one of the two farmers. As in 1830, Rural Hill was worked with the labor of Jacky, Brevard and 25 slaves. During the journal's first three months, March through May, they planted 125 acres in corn, 70 acres in cotton, and set out 900 tobacco plants. The only mention of how the labor was used in this period was in planting 14 acres of corn with five hands on 22 March, and 18 acres with five hands several days later. Prior to planting, a great deal of work was done to prepare the soil. After planting there was nearly constant plowing, hoeing and harrowing until the plants were well established. Then followed the harvest, hog killing, cotton ginning, baling, and such until it was time to begin anew in the spring. In addition there were other farm tasks: cutting trees, hauling and splitting wood, raking and hauling manure, building and repairing fences, and so on. This was an enormous amount of work for a force of twenty-five, about half of whom (and perhaps fewer) were barely out of childhood.

Brevard's family often visited Springfield, the South Carolina home of Mary's father. On 11 April 1840 Brevard noted that "my self & family went down to Mʳ John Springs on a visit & returned on Tuesday 14th." In June of 1842 Brevard went to Springfield to retrieve Mary and the children, who had been there for three weeks.

John Springs's first wife and the mother of his children was his first cousin Mary. They had been married for 18 years when she died in 1834, two years before the marriage of their daughter Mary Laura to Brevard Davidson. Family letters indicate that John grieved deeply for Mary and was not enamored of the single life. In May of 1837 he married a young widow, who died within six weeks of the wedding. In August of 1849 at the age of 67 he married the widow Elizabeth Hill from Waterbury, Connecticut. During his later years he loved to travel. In the fall of 1853 John and Elizabeth Springs were in Connecticut.[2]

John Springs was every bit as devoted to scientific farming as was Brevard, and in 1853 he was eager to attend the Georgia State Fair, which was held in Augusta. He and Elizabeth traveled by boat from Connecticut to Charleston, then by train to Augusta, where they joined several other family members. He spent the first day there, October 18, visiting with many old friends who were also in town for the fair. That evening he was unusually exhausted and sent for a doctor. The next day he was much worse; the doctor visited again and left medicine, but this effort was futile. Springs died several days later at the age of 71. Brevard wrote on 1 November: "Mʳ John Springs died in Augusta Georgia October 21th 1853 on Friday." His body was taken by train to Columbia, South Carolina, where it was put on the recently completed Charlotte and South Carolina Railroad. This was fitting, as John Springs, along with Brevard, had been instrumental in seeing that the rail line was built. Springs died on the first anniversary of the railroad's maiden run. He was buried in Charlotte's Settler's Cemetery and thirty years later was reinterred at Elmwood. Apparently his son Baxter wanted a place where family members could be buried together. Baxter's sons, who died in 1881 and 1882, were the first to be buried at Elmwood; this was probably when John Springs was reinterred.

The Civil War was hard on Brevard and Mary and their family, both financially and emotionally. Three of their sons served in the Confederate army. Robert was captured and spent a year and a half in the severely overcrowded prison camp at Elmira, New York. At the end of the war he was released and returned home but died soon after. Brevard continued to work his farm throughout the war, but it became increasingly difficult when labor was scarce, and after the war the freedmen had to be paid.

Bearing and raising children had absorbed much of Mary's life. Over the first 25 years of her marriage she bore 16 children. The last one was born in 1861 when Mary was 47 years old and still had at least eight children at home. Her oldest daughter was married. Only two children had died, a son at the age of 17 and the unnamed daughter about 1851. However, in 1869 another son died at 17, and her last child was a daughter who lived only two years.

In 1872 Brevard gave up farming and moved his family to Charlotte, where business prospects were more promising. Mary died there that same year, at the age of 58. Four years later, at age 68, Brevard married again, this time to Cornelia Elmore. She was the daughter of the banker and late former U.S. senator Franklin H. Elmore of South Carolina; she was 41 and had not been married before.

Brevard died on 4 July 1896, at the age of 88. He and Cornelia had no children. Brevard and Mary are buried in the Rural Hill Burying Ground. Cornelia is buried in Columbia, South Carolina.

Transcriptions of his will were published in the *Charlotte Observer* of 14 July 1896 and in the *Charlotte Democrat* of 16 July. In what was perhaps a Davidson family tradition, the will was very businesslike and practical, without any of the customary phrases about his mental and physical health and with no mention of God or the life hereafter.

It seems that Brevard had already settled most of his affairs, and this will was to confirm the payments and transfers already made and to distribute the residue among his children.

He gave to his "beloved wife Cornelia" all of the property he had acquired by his marriage to her and some furniture, including "a secretary in my sitting room." This is probably the Brevard Davidson secretary now owned by Davidson College. It came to the college as a gift from Brevard's son Baxter. Perhaps Cornelia had no use for the secretary and gave it to Baxter or left it to Baxter in her will.

Brevard had previously entered into an agreement with Cornelia in which he transferred to her a good deal of property and stated that the agreement was "in the possession of Mr. R M Oates, Sr."

In an unusual bequest regarding his son John Springs Davidson, Brevard stated that he had already given 300 acres to John Springs's wife, Margaret A. Davidson, and their children. Brevard had also given 300 acres to John Springs's son Joseph Graham Davidson. Further, Brevard had given 100 acres to his brother-in-law W. R. Myers to satisfy a judgment against John Springs. Finally, Brevard stated that he had given John Springs "largely in excess of what I am able to give my other children" and specifically stated, "I make no devise of real estate to him, the said John Springs Davidson."

In another peculiar bequest Brevard gave his son E. L. Baxter Davidson the Bank Building at 5 East Trade Street. Baxter was to hold it in trust for his older brother Leroy, collect the rents and profits, and pay them over to Leroy after deducting all taxes, repairs and mortgage payments. Brevard had already transferred real estate to his six daughters and to his son Baxter and had registered those deeds in Mecklenburg and Cabarrus counties.

Brevard's will included the usual gifts of furniture and other personal possessions, and he specifically relieved his children and sons-in-law of any and all advancements, debts, obligations, notes, accounts and judgments. These were all to be canceled "as I do not wish the same collected from them or any of them."

The residue of the estate was to be converted to money and distributed among his children. The executors were his son E. L. Baxter Davidson and his friend John. E. Oates.

The sixteen children of Brevard and Mary have been mentioned at various places in this and the previous chapter. There are a number of interesting family stories told from generation to generation about these children.

Brevard and Mary's firstborn child was Mary Laura. She was called Mary as a small child, but later took the name Laura. She had attended Salem Academy, and on 15 September 1854 Brevard wrote, "Returned from the North with my Daughter Laura. I was absent from home 5 weeks." Laura was 17. This may have been a journey to broaden her horizons or perhaps he was retrieving her from a northern boarding school like the one her mother had attended many years before.[3]

On 10 August 1858 she married the Rev. Alexander McLean Sinclair, who was the minister of the First Presbyterian Church in Charlotte. He was born in Scotland and served a number of churches in America over the years. In Brevard's 1864 list of slaves he noted that he had given Harrison and Susan to M. Laura Sinclair. She died at the age of 65; both Mary and Alexander are buried in Charlotte.

Brevard and Mary's second child was John Springs Davidson. He served in the Confederate army and on 31 May 1864 married Margaret "Minnie" Abigail Caldwell, daughter of Harriet and Dr. David Thomas Caldwell of Rosedale Plantation. John and Minnie had six children, one of whom died in infancy.[4]

Their son Baxter Craighead "Craig" Davidson spent much of his childhood in Charlotte at Rosedale with his mother's brother and sister, Uncle Baxter and Aunt Alice, neither of whom ever married. When Uncle

Bax died, he left Rosedale to Craig, who became the father of Rosedale's last two residents, Mary Louise Davidson and Alice Davidson Abel, neither of whom had children. Today the 1815 Historic Rosedale Plantation is a historic site near downtown Charlotte.[5]

John Springs, Minnie and their children were living at Rural Hill in 1886 when the mansion house burned to the ground. After the fire they moved into the old family home of Rural Retreat. This is probably when they sent their son Craig to live with his aunt and uncle. There was much work to do to make Rural Retreat livable again. Craig was 11, old enough not to need constant supervision but not quite old enough to take on the heavy labor of rebuilding.

Rural Retreat burned 12 years later, in 1898; Minnie died in July of that year—whether before or after the fire is not known. John Springs and the children who were still under his roof moved into what had once been a log kitchen at Rural Hill. It had been much improved by the addition of several rooms, a second story, and beadboard siding. John Springs died the following year; he is buried at Rural Hill along with Minnie; their oldest sons, Thomas and Jo Graham; and John Springs, Jr., who died in infancy.

Robert Augustus Davidson served in the Confederacy during the war and was taken prisoner in September of 1863 at Jack's Shops, Virginia. He was taken to Point Lookout, Maryland, and then transferred to Elmira, New York. At that point in the war prisoners were no longer being exchanged, and all prisons on both sides were drastically short of food, medicine, blankets and guards. The prisons were severely overcrowded with men and their yet-to-be-buried comrades. Elmira was no exception.

Several surviving documents tell of the attempts by Robert's family to free him from prison. On 17 November 1864 a passport was given to the Rev. Alexander Sinclair of Charlotte by the Confederate States of America War Department in Richmond. It states: "Permission is granted Rev. A. Sinclair, wife, sister and two children to pass our lines to the United States, subject to the discretion of the Military Commander. By order Secy. of War, J. A. Campbell, Asst. Secy. of War." The Reverend Sinclair was married to Robert's oldest sister, Mary Laura. They had two small children at the time; Sinclair's sister was not identified. They left Charlotte and had arrived in Philadelphia by early January. Whether the sole purpose of this journey was to retrieve Robert from prison or the Reverend Sinclair had other business to attend to is not known.

On 7 January 1865 Mary Laura wrote the following poignant letter to Abraham Lincoln:

To his Excellency,
President Abraham Lincoln,

    Amid the onorous duties of your very responsible position, it might seem like presumption on my part to intrude a letter upon your notice. I am impelled, however, by the yearning affection of an anxious sister's heart, to address you in behalf of a beloved brother, who has been a prisoner at Elmira, N. Y. for the past sixteen months (my brother is R. A. Davidson, private in the 5th N. C. Cavalry). My earnest desire is to get him paroled upon his word of honor not to take up arms against the U. S. until regularly exchanged by the proper authorities.... He would certainly do no injury to the U. S. Government, and would relieve it of some expense. I have thus stated the case to your Excellency. Earnestly hoping that it may meet with your notice and approbation.

                               I have the honor to be,
                               Your obedient servant,
                               M. L. Sinclair

Whether Lincoln himself saw her letter is not known. Two weeks later the office of the Commissary General of Prisoners replied and rejected her plea.[6]

    According to the family story, after receiving this rejection the Sinclairs visited the White House to present their petition in person and later received a letter from President Lincoln stating that Robert was being released. If so, the letter has been lost or is in private hands. If the Sinclairs received such a letter, it probably reached them after they returned to Charlotte.

    Another sister of Robert's, Amanda "Maude" Davidson Beall, who was 16 at the time, passed along the following account to her children. Robert was released from prison and returned to Charlotte, almost certainly by train. There he secured a horse for the 15-mile journey to Rural Hill. He was in such deplorable health, having nearly starved to death in prison, that he fell from his horse upon arriving home and died about two weeks later. There have been other reports of war prisoners' being released as they approached death's door. This was probably done for several reasons: The man was too ill to reenter combat, he would no longer drain the prison's resources, his body would not have to buried or shipped home, and there was the meager chance that he could live long enough to rejoin his family.

    Robert's sister Sarah "Sallie" Harper Davidson wrote her memories of him in her journal on 1 March 1868: "I've felt particularly sad at the approach of it [March] as it brings to my mind very forcibly the sad recollection of the death-bed scene of my darling brother Robert who died the 31st this mo. three years ago." Robert was 23. He was unmarried and is buried at Rural Hill.[7]

Sallie Davidson never married but lived quite an adventurous life. She kept a short travel journal in which she told of a wonderful sojourn in Philadelphia in 1868 and a "Centennial Trip" in 1877 to many eastern U.S. cities. She wrote that she longed to travel to Europe and later did go there as well as to Japan, South America, Egypt, South Africa and other exotic places. Her traveling companion on many of these ventures was her younger sister Blandina. Sallie was a wealthy eccentric, dressing as she pleased regardless of style and frequently entertaining in her Charlotte home. Family stories about Sallie bear repeating. They were passed down in the family and recorded by Doug Marion, a family genealogist.[8]

Once while in New York she went to Tiffany's to buy a piece of jewelry. She made her selection and paid with a check. The clerk was skeptical of this woman's unfashionably drab attire; long black dresses were her usual garb, and she was sometimes mistaken for a beggar. The clerk gave the check to the store manager, who telephoned Sallie's banker in Charlotte. He was told, "You can sell her the whole store if you want. She has lots of money."

On another occasion she was planning a trip to Europe and was asked if she was buying a new wardrobe for her trip. She replied, "Why should I, no one over there knows me." Her friend then said, "Oh, you're going to buy new clothes overseas to bring home?" Sallie answered, "Of course not; everyone here knows me."

At the age of 83 she was still spry enough to take a four-month tour of South America and South Africa with stops in Europe. During one of their trips Sallie and Blandina flew from Brussels to London, quite the adventure for ladies of a certain age during the Roaring Twenties.

Sallie died in Charlotte at the age of 89 and is buried at Rural Hill.

Leroy Springs Davidson never married. He died in Charlotte at the age of 60 and is buried at Rural Hill. In Brevard's will of 1896 he left Leroy the income from an office building in Charlotte but not the property itself. That was to be managed by Leroy's younger brother Baxter and the net income given to Leroy. Leroy was 41 at the time of this bequest.[9]

Edward Lee Baxter Davidson, Brevard's youngest son, was apparently the son whom Brevard most trusted with financial matters. He deeded property to him, left him "the Bank Building" to manage for Leroy, and made him executor of his estate.[10]

As an adult Baxter lived in Charlotte and was devoted to his civic duty in many forms. He contributed a great deal of money to a number of worthy causes. He expended time and money on researching the history of his family and erected historical markers documenting the Davidson family history, especially that of his great grandfather Major John

E. L. Baxter Davidson, Esq. Baxter with one of his stone walls and a plaque to his great grandfather, Major John. The mix of light and dark stones, all said to be from the Catawba River, is characteristic of his walls. Many can still be seen in northern Mecklenburg County. Photograph from the book by Chalmers Gaston Davidson, *Major John Davidson of "Rural Hill"* (Charlotte, NC: Lassiter Press, 1943).

Among his passions was building stone walls to set off important places. His legacy survives in the restoration of the Rural Hill Burying Ground and in the stone wall he built around it in 1923. The interior brick wall had been built much earlier. Baxter also built the wall on both sides of Beatties Ford Road in front of the Hopewell church and may have erected a number of similar walls that still survive in northern Mecklenburg County.

Baxter was a bachelor until he married the widow Sarah Williams Vosburgh (1883–1973) in 1935. Baxter was 76 on his wedding day; his bride was 52. According to a Charlotte newspaper article, Baxter had been severely injured in an automobile accident near Lincolnton that occurred while he was traveling to Charlotte from Asheville, where he had just celebrated his birthday. The car was driven by Sarah Vosburgh of Charlotte, a trained nurse, who sustained a broken collarbone.

The article is undated, and the accident probably happened a year or two before they married. Baxter died at 85 and Sarah at 90. Their graves are the ones closest to the entrance of the Rural Hill Burying Ground, just inside Baxter's beautiful wall. Buried with them is David W. Vosburgh, Sarah's son from her first marriage.

CHAPTER 10

Scientific Farming at Rural Hill

SINCE THE BEGINNING OF RECORDED TIME humans have bred their animals and selected their seeds to produce a desired outcome. Larger, tastier and hardier meats and produce were often the goal. Animals bred to perform specific tasks or plants adapted for difficult climates were also useful. There are 18th-century records of farm management and experimentation at Washington's Mount Vernon. Jefferson kept a farm journal and brought plant species from France to try at Monticello. The original *Encyclopaedia Britannica*, published in Scotland in 1771, contains a 30-page section on agriculture.[1]

By the 1830s, as farms grew into plantations, agrarian production in the South became an enormous factor in the national economy. The practice that became known as scientific farming had a great influence on planters. It included the intensive preparation of fields, proper soil nutrition, crop rotation, and letting fields lie fallow. Methods to control animal breeding were also being introduced.

On 7 March 1834 Brevard Davidson began his first farm journal: "I have made the attempt two or three times to keep an account how we plant our crop and have always failed—I shall now make one more attempt." This time he succeeded. The purpose of the journal was to record what was planted in which fields and how the crop fared. Weather was always an important factor and was generally noted. With this information he strove to make himself a better farmer. He kept this journal in a blank copybook for over twenty years, until 1854.[2]

Brevard kept a second journal for only a few months in early 1856. This was a printed book titled *Plantation and Farm: Instruction, Regula-*

tion, Record, Inventory, and Account Book, written by "A Southern Planter." This book contains instructions for managing a farm, with specifics about various crops and livestock. Pages were provided for the farmer to enter such things as lists of slaves, livestock, farm implements, carpenter's tools, and blacksmiths' tools. This is followed by the "Manager's Journal or Daily Record." These pages are formatted, one page per week, for the farmer to enter the weather and farming activities for each day. Brevard kept this journal for a little over three months but kept it available and entered some information in later years, such as a slave list in 1864.[3]

Mecklenburg County had a very active agricultural society, and Brevard was a member for many years. He often served on its board of directors and was president for at least one term about 1845. His journal is replete with accounts of his attendance at the society's meetings and fairs. Local newspapers noted when these were held and who received awards in various categories. They published some of the speeches given at these meetings, and detailed articles with instructions on how to better manage land and livestock were regular features in these newspapers. These agricultural fairs were the predecessors of the county and state fairs that became so popular in the 20th century.

Brevard attended the agricultural fair that was held in Charlotte in November of 1847. The November 11 issue of the *Charlotte Journal* covered the event. It printed a long address given by Brevard's cousin, David A. Caldwell, who had been raised at Rural Hill and Holly Bend. Certainly the advice he gave was familiar to Brevard.

After stating that the society was devoted to the advancement of agriculture, Caldwell told his fellow farmers that their task was Herculean. He encouraged horizontal plowing as plowing up hill and down allowed the crop to be damaged by erosion. Once the nutrients had been washed from the soil, and the soil itself washed downhill, the land was difficult to reclaim. He talked about the importance of manuring with green manure (barnyard waste enhanced by the addition of plant material and minerals often derived from limestone). He suggested using weeds and coarse grasses cut from field margins along fences and adding swamp earth, leached ashes, and barnyard manure. The mixture, he said, produces an excellent compost and should be liberally applied.

The plowing under of cowpea vines was recommended; farmers then were unaware that cowpeas fix nitrogen in the soil, but the excellent crop yields were obvious. Caldwell said that an acre of land so improved could produce 40 bushels of corn, 1,000 pounds of seed cotton (meaning cotton weighed before ginning), or 20 bushels of wheat. He believed that 125 acres of improved land would yield as much as 300 acres left in its natural state. Eight hands and five horses should be sufficient to work 90 acres of properly nurtured land. This may explain how a plantation as large and profitable as Rural Hill was maintained by a relatively small workforce.

Brevard's journals attest to his adoption of these scientific methods. In late winter he cleared his fields of the previous year's stubble and cleared any new land he planned to use. During the time he kept his journals, farmers gave increasing attention to crop rotation, fallow fields, and the cultivation of new land.

As noted in Chapter 8, he named all of his fields. The names are generally based on location, and their meaning is often obvious. The black jack field was named for a type of oak tree, but the meaning of "pint field" is a mystery. He named the fields to help him identify exactly where he planted each year's crops.

The preparation of the fields was a lengthy process. Cotton and corn were the most important crops and were the first to be tended to each year; fields for both crops received the same treatment. As soon as the land could be worked in late winter, the fields were cleared, and the land was broken up by plowing. Two to four plowings were commonplace, each one biting into a deeper layer of soil and plowing under more nutrients. Plowing may have been more intense in the Carolina Piedmont than elsewhere because the red clay soil compacts so readily.

When plowed sufficiently, rows were formed by making a furrow on either side of a raised bed, hill, or ridge. The words were used interchangeably. The cross section of a row resembled a *W* with the center point—the bed—a bit higher than the outer points that represent the surrounding land. The *V* shapes between the points were the furrows. This arrangement drained the soil well while keeping the roots moist and allowed for weeding and cultivation in a way less likely to damage the crops' roots. The center ridge, or bed, was where the seeds were planted. A person would walk along each row and poke holes with a stick, another person dropped in the seeds, and a third person covered the seeds with soil.

Corn was planted from late March through April; cotton was planted during the last half of April. After the seeds were in the ground, plowing, harrowing, and hoeing were done for weed control. Plows turned under the weeds, which kept the soil loose and nourished. A harrow has spikes or discs that root out the weeds vertically and break up the soil without turning it over. Hoeing was done by hand when a delicate touch was needed to avoid harming the crop.

Throughout the summer this work continued, and crops were thinned and replanted if damaged by weather. When the crops were well established, they were "laid by," which means they were given a final thorough hoeing. Then attention could be turned elsewhere until harvest time. Both cotton and corn were laid by in July. Brevard does not mention laying by other crops.

The term "green manure" is not in the journals, but this was obviously how he nurtured his fields. He frequently applied multiple wagonloads of manure to particular crops, and he wrote of mixing vegetative matter with barnyard manure. He also used marl, which was a mixture that contained mineral matter, probably limestone. In October of 1846 he harvested 110 bushels of peas to feed people and animals. Then the vines were plowed into the soil. He made use of everything. Stems, stalks, and vines became compost, mulch for his fields, or fodder for his animals; some items, such as wheat straw and corn husks, became bedding in the barns.

In 1793 Eli Whitney invented an improved cotton gin that transformed the American economy, particularly in the South. Old World cotton, such as that grown in India, has hard black seeds that adhere loosely to the fiber. It could be ginned readily by being passed between a pair of smooth rollers. This did not work for America's upland cotton with its soft sticky seed firmly attached to the fibers. Small amounts of this cotton were grown for home use; most of it probably became quilt batting. A worker could clean only about a pound of cotton a day by picking out the seeds by hand. Even with slave labor cotton was not a profitable crop. This was a great frustration for 18th-century farmers; people knew that cotton had potential, if only they could figure out a better way to remove the seeds.

Whitney's gin changed everything, and by 1810 upland cotton was on its way to becoming a lucrative crop on many southern farms. This gin was simple but counterintuitive: instead of removing the seeds from the fiber, as roller gins did, it removed the fiber from the seeds. Whitney obtained one of the first U.S. patents, but once seen this style of gin could be easily made, and cotton gins sprouted across the South like mushrooms. After several years, when Whitney had received his patent and litigated it in state courts, he and his partner negotiated with each southern state for royalties. In North Carolina farmers were taxed on the basis of the number of saws in their gins. This money was passed on to Whitney as his royalty. He became very rich and invested his money in the invention of interchangeable parts and milling machines, which revolutionized manufacturing in America and Europe.[4]

Brevard generally planted 70 to 100 acres of cotton each year. In the journal he often noted either the name of the field or the number of acres planted on a given day but rarely both. Therefore the acreage of the total crop is difficult to determine. The crop was carefully tended early in the season; as plants matured, they were more often cultivated with hoes. Brevard noted in his journal when the first cotton blossom was seen and when the first boll opened.

Two-thirds of the weight of mature cotton bolls is seeds. Therefore 1,000 pounds of cotton picked from the field would yield about 330 pounds of ginned cotton. The journal mentions "seed cotton"; this meant cotton containing seeds, not cotton to be used for its seeds, although he did save seeds to plant for the next year's crop. He occasionally mentions specific cotton varieties, all of them forms of upland cotton.

COTTON PLANT IN SEPTEMBER. This cotton plant is just coming into bloom. The buds are called squares after their shape. The flowers start out white and quickly turn to pink. At this point the plant has attained its full growth. The blooming starts at the top and progresses down the plant throughout the season. Illustration from D. A. Tompkins, *History of Mecklenburg County* (Charlotte, NC: Observer Printing House, 1903).

In 1843 he harvested 32,000 pounds of cotton at Dickson and 53,070 pounds at Rural Hill. This was seed cotton and appears to have been that year's total crop. The weight of the crop after ginning would have been about 28,000 pounds. Brevard's neighbor James Torrance sold his cotton for 7.5 cents per pound that year; the same price would have netted Brevard $2,100.

The bolls began to ripen in late August. Harvest began in September and lasted about two months. Each field was picked over several times as new bolls ripened. Picking a boll meant reaching into a boll and cupping the cotton fiber with one's fingertips to avoid the bracts; however, neighboring bracts were hard to avoid. The prickly bracts, the varying height of the bolls, the weight of the bag of accumulating seedy cotton, and the relentless hot sun made for a brutal job, yet planters expected their slaves to pick a complete and timely harvest.

Frost stopped the plants from producing, but ripened bolls did not spoil in the field. When cold weather or snow interrupted the harvest, the last bit of cotton was gathered in late winter to allow for the preparation of land for the next crop.

Brevard had a cotton gin at Rural Hill and another at Dickson; this was typical on large farms. Some small farmers had their cotton ginned by one of their neighbors; Brevard occasionally ginned other people's cotton and kept 10 percent of the ginned fiber as his toll.

The gin, short for engine, operated by feeding seed cotton into a slotted hopper next to a roller fitted with rows of sawtooth blades. When the roller was turned, the blades passed through the slots and grabbed the fibers, leaving behind the soft sticky seeds. These were too large to pass through the slots and dropped out at the rear of the gin. Another roller fitted with brushes turned in the opposite direction from the saw blades. It brushed the now seedless fiber

COTTON PLANT IN NOVEMBER. The flowers develop into bolls that ripen and burst open. By November most of the bolls have matured. The plants are killed in the first frost but the ripe bolls can be harvested throughout the winter until it is time to pull up the plants and prepare the soil for the new crop. Modern cotton plants have been hybridized to grow to a shorter, uniform size and to mature all at once so that the bolls can be harvested by machine. Illustration from D. A. Tompkins, *History of Mecklenburg County* (Charlotte, NC: Observer Printing House, 1903).

COTTON GIN AND PRESS. The gin is located on the upper floor of the gin house. In the space below, mules turned the mechanism that rotated the saw blades that removed the cotton fiber from the seeds. Next to the gin is the cotton press, which also used mule power to compress the ginned cotton into bales. Illustration from D. A. Tompkins, *History of Mecklenburg County* (Charlotte, NC: Observer Printing House, 1903).

into a container at the front of the gin. Any bits of bracts or other waste material fell between the two rollers. Ginning could be done in a gin house with a mule-driven gin. However, someone with only a small amount of cotton to process might have used a gin with a hand crank. In 1856 Brevard noted that "Logan, at the ginn, Jerry & Jo, driving the mules." If the gin itself was under roof, ginning was rarely stopped by rain.

The ginned fiber was then pressed into bales, a job Brevard sometimes called "packing bags." A cotton press consists of a box about four feet on a side and as tall as 10 feet, open at the top, with removable sides. Bagging cloth is draped inside the box, and the box is filled with ginned cotton. A heavy mule-driven screw presses a platform down onto the cotton to compress it. The screw is backed out, and more cotton is added and pressed. This continues until the box is nearly full. The bagging cloth is sewn tightly across the top of the resulting bale, the sides of the box are let down, and the bale is wrapped tightly with ropes.

Bagging cloth and ropes had to be especially sturdy to keep the com-

THE COTTON GIN MECHANISM. Operating the gin required only one man, while several others drove the mules, brought the cotton to the gin, removed the clean cotton and the seeds, and operated the press. Illustration from D. A. Tompkins, *History of Mecklenburg County* (Charlotte, NC: Observer Printing House, 1903).

pressed bale from bursting open; farmers often noted where they bought their bagging and how much they paid for it. Pressing and baling were outdoor chores because the press, screw, and mule race take up a fair amount of space. Unlike ginning, baling was a job that rain could halt. Each cotton bale was weighed individually; the average bale weighed 300 to 350 pounds.

The baled cotton that left Rural Hill and other Carolina Piedmont plantations generally was carried to the Port of Charleston. From there it could be shipped across the Atlantic to England or north to New England. Much of it was shipped to cotton brokers in New England, then transshipped to British cotton mills. There it was spun and woven in the mills once used for cotton from India. The spinning and weaving mills in New England had previously processed Sea Island cotton or local wool. Mill employees were mostly young women from poor families; the labor they provided was a small step above slavery yet highly preferable to laboring in the fields.

Cotton was not just king in the 19th century, it was a tyrant. Its botany and life cycle were demanding, its desirability was seductive, and its labor intensity played right into the perpetuation of slavery. Cotton grows across the entire American South, unlike rice and sugarcane, which tolerate only a tiny microclimate. The ultimate irony is the North's participation in the system: The New England shipping lines that had brought slaves into America since the 17th century carried away the cotton grown by slave labor in the 19th century. The entire U.S. economy was addicted to this bounty.

By 1860 cotton comprised 60 percent of all American exports, 80 percent of England's imports of fiber for British weaving mills, and two-thirds of the entire world's supply of cotton fiber. Prior to Eli Whitney's 1793 invention of the cotton gin, the world's cotton was primarily grown in India. America's upland cotton is softer and finer, and the coarser Indian cotton fell from favor. In 1830 America produced 50 percent of the world's cotton. By 1860 the world had come to depend on American slave-grown cotton, a fact not lost on the North. It certainly perpetuated the attitude about slavery held by some in Northern states: "just not in my back yard." However, with the election of President Abraham Lincoln the high moral road of the abolitionist movement prevailed in the North, and war was soon to follow.

Although cotton was the cash crop, corn was the largest crop as it fed the workforce. Field corn, also called Indian corn, was dried to feed animals and ground into cornmeal and grits to feed people. Hugh quantities were used to fatten the hogs. Pork was the meat staple of the 19th-century diet in the South for black and white alike.

Corn was planted from March through April, and the harvest began in September. Field corn has a low water content, can be easily dried for grinding, and keeps well for animal feed. The sweet corn we enjoy today has a very high water content and will rot before it dries. It was grown in kitchen gardens in small amounts for the table. As with cotton, determining the acreage Brevard planted in corn is difficult; he seems to have planted at least 100 acres most years. In December of 1839 he wrote, "Finished putting up our corn 40 loads & 10 before, making for this year <u>50 loads about 2500 bsh</u> without the roton [rotten] corn."

After harvest the corn was cleaned, or husked, then stored in a crib. Brevard sometimes counted the bushels of "sound" corn, and "nubbins," which were small ears that were stunted or undeveloped. Rotten corn had spoiled in the field or in storage before husking. The husks were saved for stuffing mattresses or for animal bedding. They were also braided into horse collars, which protected the animals' necks and shoulders from being rubbed and abraded by harnesses and gearing.

After corn and cotton, wheat was the next most important crop. The few times Brevard listed the yearly total acreage sown in wheat, it was 25 to 60 acres. It was sown at the rate of three and a half bushels of seed per acre. Yearly yields of harvested, threshed, and cleaned wheat range from 130 to 340 bushels per acre. As with other crops, he most often listed the acreage and yield of individual fields and rarely the entire year's crop. Wheat was ground at his mill. He sold a fair amount of flour in Charlotte, including 1,300 pounds in 1836 for $4.50 per hundred pounds. Wheat was sown between October and January and cut in June.

Oats were sown every year, usually in March, and cut in July. Brevard planted about 40 acres in 1837, 60 in 1839, and 70 in 1844. Another year he sowed 80 acres with 84 bushels of seed. He planted common oats and ruffled oats, which were mostly used to feed his horses. Also in March he sometimes sowed rye, barley, and clover. In April and May he planted Irish potatoes, usually several acres, and harvested about 100 to 125 bushels per acre. He also planted sweet potatoes; in 1835 he sold 55 bushels of sweet potatoes for 50 cents per bushel. Most years he planted turnips, pumpkins, hay, and various grasses. In March of 1840 he "sowed nearly a peck of timothy at the lower end of the Meadow." Several times he planted tobacco, unusual in Piedmont North Carolina. In May of 1834 he set out about 900 plants, and in 1841 he planted tobacco again. As a cash crop, tobacco can be very labor intensive; these plants probably were for his own use or simply an experiment.

There was some fruit grown at Rural Hill. Watermelons were planted several times; in the spring of 1848 Brevard planted them on an island in the river. Mary noted that she had strawberry beds in her kitchen garden. In February of 1847 there were "three Ohio men grafting apple trees…. Mr Taylor finished grafting trees between three & four hundred grafts." Brevard must have learned the process: the next month he "grafted 146 apple trees." He doesn't mention an apple harvest; the trees were probably not yet mature by the time the first journal ended in 1854, and the brief 1856 journal was not kept during the apple-picking season.

In the 1856 journal he briefly mentions peach trees and plum bushes. This may have been a new venture, much as apple trees had been in 1847. There may have been other small crops that he didn't write about. His purpose was to record the information that could be used to make him a better farmer, and his primary need was for accurate records of his cash crop and the crops that fed his slaves and animals.

In 1838 Brevard wrote that he had "finished paling in our garden, have been about two weeks at it done by Ibzan Taner @ 75 cts per day." This was certainly the kitchen garden where herbs and summer produce were raised. Mary kept a brief diary during January and February in 1843. On February 14 she wrote that she had gone into her garden for the first time that year and "had our onions planted and also some shrubbery replanted likewise burnt over my strawberry beds to benifit the vines. I received note from Cousin Martha Caldwell answered it promptly and complied with her request of garden seed." A week later she wrote, "Gardening continued sowed all the seed that I can plant now with safety.... Cabbage, lettuce, tongue grass, Mustard ribs kale radishes turnips lambs quarter, parsnips, beets." She trimmed and replanted various hedges and "changed the form of one of the flower beds."

Brevard wrote that Mary planted a few rows of corn in her garden; it was probably sweet corn for the table. Kitchen gardens also grew English or sweet peas, cucumbers, okra, green beans, greens for cooking and salads, and other table vegetables in addition to culinary and healing herbs. She engaged her female slaves for tending the garden. A kitchen garden was a woman's responsibility and not part of Brevard's workday, so he saw little need to mention it in the journal. In general it took an acre of kitchen garden to feed a family of 10. Slaves were often permitted to keep their own kitchen gardens and to raise a few chickens and gather eggs for their tables. Brevard's slaves may have done so.

Some of the crops planted in the 19th century would not be recognizable today. Brevard mentioned several varieties of wheat; he frequently planted May wheat, which might have been a specific variety or simply a term for spring wheat. Several times he planted Mogule or Magule wheat, a popular variety at the time that is not widely grown today. Modern wheat has been hybridized to produce more bushels per acre and to be harvested mechanically. Old wheat varieties have tall straw useful for fodder, thatch, and animal bedding and deep roots to hold the tall plants firmly in the soil. Those roots would not have hindered Brevard in cutting his wheat with a scythe. Both characteristics are problematic for modern mechanical harvesters.

The journal also mentions several types of cotton that were planted at Rural Hill, including Petted Gulf cotton seeds sent by a friend from South Carolina; all were types of upland cotton. Cotton plants of the 19th century grew up to five feet high, and had squares, or buds, blossoms, newly formed bolls, ripening bolls, and fully open bolls all at the same time. None of these characteristics can be handled by mechanical harvesters. Modern upland cotton has been hybridized to be low growing, only about two feet high, and to ripen all at once.⁵

It wasn't until the early 20th century that another problem arose: the boll weevil. Various cotton pests have always been with us, but this particular weevil was especially virulent. It marched up from Mexico, then across the American South from west to east, destroying nearly every cotton field in its path. The journey took two or three decades for the weevil to nearly eliminate cotton farming in the area. The fact that this process culminated during the Great Depression made its economic impact especially harsh.⁶

Today it is illegal to grow heritage cotton varieties without extremely careful monitoring. Modern cotton has been hybridized to be boll weevil resistant. However, this resistance is far from total. Today's historic farm sites often have small patches of heritage cotton for interpretive purposes. Each patch must contain a boll weevil trap, a device that gives off female weevil pheromones to attract the males. The traps are inspected regularly by the state departments of agriculture, and if a single weevil is found in a trap, the entire cotton patch is burned. The boll weevil is still taken very seriously.

Pork was the main source of protein in the antebellum Piedmont diet. At Rural Hill hog farming was somewhat affected by scientific methods, yet retained many of its 18th-century roots. Hogs, both male and female, were mature animals, and pigs were the babies. Shoats were juveniles, although Brevard never used this term in his 1834–54 journal. He adhered strictly to these definitions and never used the words "pig" and "hog" interchangeably. Hogs did not need to be kept in pens and fed during the summer so adult animals and their piglets were let loose in the spring to forage. In March or April Brevard "spayed and marked' his pigs prior to setting them loose. Marking was making a distinctive notch in the pigs' ears; each farmer had his own mark.

In October Brevard gathered his hogs from the woods to be fattened for slaughter. It was probably not difficult to keep them penned when they were being fed generously with corn. Today spaying means to neuter a female animal; however, he used the word to mean neutering any animal. He needed only a few boars to maintain his swine population, and neutered male hogs were more docile and produced tastier, more tender meat, just as a steer makes finer meat that does a bull.

Brevard nearly always wrote of marking and spaying pigs—never hogs—so it must have been done when the animals were small. One exception was in April of 1847 when he marked and spayed a number of pigs and "three old sows." He must have had a good reason; neutering a female is a complicated procedure and in itself does not make economic sense.

Only once did he write of losing pigs during this process; in March of 1847 he "marked & spayed 24 pigs 2 died." Brevard probably never pastured his hogs. Hogs that were pastured usually had a piece of gristle cut off from the front of their snout. This prevented them from rooting and tearing apart their pastureland. Brevard does not mention this, another indication that all his swine fed themselves in the woods.

Only hogs, never pigs, were kept in fattening pens until they had plumped up sufficiently and the weather was cold enough for slaughter, usually between November and January. Brevard kept careful records of his slaughtering: how many hogs were killed, their total weight, their average weight, and often the weights of individual hogs. He also recorded the destination of the meat from the various hogs: how many were his father's; how many went to overseers, tenants, or others; how many were sold and how many remained at home. These statistics were often recorded for both Rural Hill and the Dickson Plantation. Of the hogs' average weight he sometimes gives a number and so many pounds "over." This is a remainder from division. For example: "Killed 20 hogs at home average weight 216 lb & 4 lb over whole amount 4324 lb." 4324 divided by 20 equals 216 with a remainder of 4. Several times he mentioned how much lard was rendered.

Hogs are large creatures, and it would have been impossible to safely gut and clean them, salt down the meat, prepare it for the smokehouse, and render the lard in warm weather before the meat spoiled. Mary wrote in her brief diary that she rendered lard herself and that she and her enslaved women Ann, Polly, and Julia worked together to make sausage and liverwurst. Journals of the period frequently imply that blacks and whites worked together at various chores; Mary's journal is one of the few places where such activity is explicitly stated. Brevard did not mention sausage but would not have wasted any bits and pieces of pork; this was kitchen work done by women, not farm work done on the land, and therefore not within his purview.

The only inventory Brevard made of his swine was in January in the 1856 journal. He had 1 boar, 6 sows, 37 pigs, 20 shoats, 57 pork hogs, and 44 mill hogs. The journals often mention mill hogs; this might refer to where they were kept or something else altogether. The mill hogs were much less valuable than the others but at slaughter weighed the same as the other hogs.

He didn't mention where the swine that were not slaughtered were kept during the winter. He didn't note whether the sows and boars were kept separately; they may well have been allowed to breed at will. Yet he did make one mention that implies that some breeding was controlled. In May of 1845 he said he had "eight Berkshire pigs of a nepoliton sow"; the rest of his pigs were of a common sow. He did give a few hints about his swine, and we can draw tentative conclusions. Several times he told how old the hogs were at slaughter. In February of 1848 he killed nine hogs that were 13 months old, which means they were born in January. Some hogs killed in January of 1849 had been born in July, others in November.

Brevard did not refer to any animals as shoats even though in the 1856 inventory the word appeared on a printed form he filled out. The swine that he called pigs must have been immature animals of assorted ages, including shoats. Those gathered into the fattening pens in October were all hogs, which implies they had matured enough during the previous six months in the woods to be ready to fatten for the slaughter. The pigs that were gathered from the woods were not mature enough to be slaughtered and were probably kept in the barn along with the brood sows. Some sows gave birth while the other hogs were fattening. By March or April those pigs born in the fall and winter were released to the woods along with all the others.

In the 1856 journal Brevard inventoried his livestock and noted their value. This was the inventory for Rural Hill and did not include the livestock at Dickson.

The inventory of cattle, with the total value of each group was:

- 2 bulls ($250)
- 9 cows ($440)
- 6 calves, 1 year old ($150)
- 2 heifers, 3 years old ($100)
- 7 beeves ($210)
- 5 calves ($85)
- 2 calves, 2 years old ($50)

The beeves were steers, which were raised for meat. The cows, his dairy herd, produced milk, some of which was churned to butter. Most of the calves were born in the summertime. He usually named the mother cow, noted how many times she had calved, and whether the calf was a heifer or a bull. In March of 1840 he wrote, "Marys Heffers first calf to day, three years old last fall." This was probably one of the three heifers from the dowry; if so it would have been only a few months old when it came to Rural Hill.

A calf's father was named if it was his Durham bull, so obviously the breeding was controlled and the cattle were pastured. In June of 1842

Brevard noted that "Spot calved heffer 11th To Durham Bull 4th calf." In other words, Spot had her fourth calf, a heifer. It was the 11th offspring of his Durham bull.

Although the words are businesslike and matter of fact, it must have been a sad day in January of 1846 when Brevard wrote, "Killed my Durham Bull 1376^{lb} including hair and tallow." We can assume the bull was old and perhaps in poor health.

Brevard rarely mentioned his cattle in any context other than their births and the occasional sale of their meat. The cows were milked, and he did write of butter once or twice. This may have been considered women's work managed by his wife. Or, since milking was done every day and was unaffected by weather, perhaps there was no need to keep a record of it.

There were no oxen in the 1856 inventory of Rural Hill, yet in 1839 Brevard had "tied up two steers for oxen, Bender & Youles." They were never mentioned again so this may have been an experiment that failed. In 1853 Brevard bought two ox yokes at his uncle's estate sale. Oxen could be valuable work animals. They were powerful but slow and required careful training and management. They were used on 18th-century farms but by the 19th-century began to disappear from the Carolina Piedmont. Horses and mules were more agile, worked much faster, and were better adapted to hot weather.

Here is Brevard's 1856 inventory of horses at Rural Hill, with the value of each group:

- 4 work horses ($300)
- 2 brood mares ($115)
- 1 mule colt, 2 years old ($125)
- 5 work mules ($680)
- 1 mule colt, 1 year old ($50)
- 1 jennet, 3 years old ($30)

There may have been a similar assortment of animals at Dickson. Note that mules were nearly twice as valuable as horses. Mules were a farm's most useful work animals. A mule is a cross between a mare and a jackass or occasionally a stallion and a jennet; all mules are sterile. Today jackasses and jennets are more frequently called donkeys. Mules are stronger, more surefooted, and can work harder than horses. Their well-deserved reputation for stubbornness may exasperate the farmer, but it serves the mule well. A horse can be worked to death; a mule will quit working when he is exhausted or extremely thirsty. In 1841 Brevard "bought a Giny @ McRee sale for $114." This was probably a jennet, often called a jenny. A jenny was valuable because she could produce a jackass to father a mule. In 1844 "Jany colted jack colt"; Jany was probably McRee's jennet.

Horses were used for farm work as well as transportation. They could be ridden for only about twenty miles at a stretch before needing to rest. When returning from a railroad meeting in Columbia, Brevard wrote that he rode 20 miles on Thursday evening, sixty-four miles on Wednesday, and fifteen miles on Thursday. He doesn't tell us how he managed Wednesday's long journey, but other people's journals offer insight. He probably started before dawn, rode 15 miles or so before breakfast, then rested and watered his horse while he ate. He may have broken his ride again for dinner, perhaps a third time before supper, and completed the journey between supper and bedtime. A long day for both horse and man, but one that, with care, could be accomplished without damage to the animal.

The horses and colts were all named. They were stabled and pastured in fenced areas. He mentions pastures and never wrote of marking or branding a horse. As with the cattle, he notes when colts were born, and if they were horse or mule colts, but not who the sire was. He obviously cared about his horses. He sometimes advertised in the local papers that he had horses that could be bred to improve the bloodlines of other men's stock and stated the stud fee.

Brevard raised sheep. He appeared to have about 50 at any given time. They were almost never mentioned except for sheering their wool. During the extremely cold winter of 1856, the slave women spent many days spinning, but Brevard doesn't say if they were spinning cotton or wool. He does list Julia as a weaver in his 1856 slave list. Probably most of the spinning and weaving was done with wool for the slaves' winter clothing. Horse blankets and other utilitarian items may also have been woven at home. At some plantations slaves were given permission to glean cotton from the fields after the harvest and to use it for their own clothing. This may have happened at Rural Hill.

There is no mention in the journals of chickens or any other poultry, but their eggs were a mainstay of the diet of the time. Again, since feeding chickens and gathering eggs was a daily chore, there was no need to keep a record of it.

The purpose of the farm was to grow crops, but that could not be done without numerous farm buildings, such as stables, barns, gin houses, blacksmith shops, mills, and so on. Many were already in place when Brevard began his journals, since the land had been farmed by his father and grandfather for many years. Those built by Brevard replaced or supplemented existing structures. Several months before his parents moved back to Rural Retreat in 1837, Brevard "raised kitchen & smoke house" there.

The original smokehouse and kitchen at Rural Retreat may have fallen into disrepair or burned; kitchen fires were not uncommon.

In August of 1842 Brevard began building a new mill. This project went on for a bit over a year, which we have described in some detail. There was at least one mill previously on the property; whether this new mill was a supplement or a replacement is unclear.

On 24 August 1847 he wrote, "Moved my Barn." The next day he wrote, "Commenced fraiming my barn shed," so he was obviously moving the barn's location by erecting a new barn, not moving the physical building.

Throughout the journal Brevard makes note of the building of fences. They were composed of panels and were erected to enclose fields or placed along property lines. Whether the panels were made in a workshop, then taken to the fencerow, or made on site is not clear. The building of multiple fences during this time reflects the scientific principles of pasturing and field rotation.

Various building projects employed stocks. An old definition of "stock" is a long log or block of wood that could be sawn into boards. Stocks were also the framework, or primary support timbers, of a building. Brevard used both meanings. He hauled stocks to the mill for sawing and hauled stocks to buildings that were under construction. He also used the spelling "stalks," as in cornstalks.

Chapter 11

Rural Hill: The Last Three Generations

THE FOURTH GENERATION to live at Rural Hill was the family of John Springs Davidson, Brevard's oldest son. He was twenty-three when the Civil War began, and like most of his contemporaries he enlisted in the Confederate army, as did his younger brothers, Robert and Richard. On 31 May 1864, probably while home on leave, John Springs married Margaret "Minnie" Abigail Caldwell, daughter of Harriet and Dr. David Thomas Caldwell of Rosedale Plantation. Minnie's childhood home, Rosedale, was a fine family home. Her father was a farmer as well as a physician who had done very well for himself. Yet Rural Hill with its stately elegance must have seemed quite the mansion when she moved there as a young bride. It was also a bustling household; Brevard and Mary were still in residence, along with many of their brood, ranging in ages from about six to late teens. Richard, and probably Minnie's husband, John Springs, were still off to war. Robert remained imprisoned at Elmira, New York. Four of the daughters who had enrolled in boarding school two years before—two at the Edgeworth Academy and two at Salem Academy—returned home that summer.[1]

Eight years later, in 1872, Brevard and Mary moved to Charlotte. Three of Minnie's children, Thomas, Jo Graham and Harriet, had been born by then, and Minnie and John Springs were finally in charge of Rural Hill and able "to go to housekeeping." Their other three children, Baxter Craighead; John Springs, Jr., who died in infancy; and Mary Laura soon also were born at Rural Hill.

In 1886 Rural Hill burned to the ground. John Springs, Minnie and the children were in Charlotte that day to attend a fair and visit her family at Rosedale. There are conflicting stories about how the fire started, but in any event it quickly got out of control. Probably only the servants and farmworkers were at home. As the fire raged, one of them leapt onto a horse and rode into Charlotte to report the blaze to the family. It must have been a devastating blow.

The *Charlotte Observer* reported on 5 November 1886:

> The old Davidson residence, the finest country house in Mecklenburg County, and one around which an interesting train of historical reminiscences were clustered, was destroyed by fire yesterday. The news was brought to the city about six o'clock in the afternoon, and the Davidson boys at once secured a hack and drove to the scene to learn the particulars of the disaster. The house was an historical structure. It was built in the year 1788, by Major John Davidson and was occupied at the time of its destruction by Mr. John Springs Davidson. The house was built of brick and was considered to have been the finest country residence in all this section of the state. It had already been arranged by the Davidson connection to hold a centennial celebration within its walls sometime during 1888, but the unlooked for and sudden destruction of the old house will thwart these plans. No particulars of the fire were received in the city yesterday, but from what could be learned, it was very probably the work of an incendiary. Mr. Davidson, it is said, lost nearly all his household possessions. This is one of the most unfortunate fires that has ever occurred in Mecklenburg, and the Davidson family will have the sympathy of all our people in the loss of their treasured homestead.[2]

Contrary to this report, the family tradition is that the fire was started by sparks from an iron. In those days ironing was done with a pair of flatirons heated at a fireplace—one iron heating on the hearth, the other one working. The irons were exchanged as needed, and sparks could easily fly. Others contend the blaze originated in Rural Hill's basement kitchen; ironing may have been done there as well as cooking.[3]

After the fire the family moved into the original Davidson home, Rural Retreat, which may have been empty for several decades. Much work must have been needed to make Rural Retreat livable again, and furnishings had to be acquired or repaired. This is probably when their son Baxter Craighead Davidson, always called Craig, went to live with his aunt and uncle at Rosedale. Craig was 11, old enough to be away from home but not quite old enough to take on the heavy labor of rebuilding. His older brothers, Thomas at 20 and Jo Graham at 18, would have been capable of the job, and Minnie probably wanted to keep her daughters close at hand.

Craig Davidson spent much of his childhood in Charlotte at Rosedale with his mother's siblings, Baxter and Alice Caldwell. They were reputed to be an eccentric pair, and neither ever married. Craig was still living at Rosedale when he married Louise Heagy in 1914. His aunt Alice had died a decade before, but Uncle Bac, as he was called, was very much alive. Craig and Louise had two daughters, Mary Louise was born in 1916 and Alice a decade later. Uncle Bac passed away in 1919; there are photographs of him with Mary Louise as a toddler. Craig inherited the property, then passed it on to his daughters. Mary Louise never married, and Alice married late in life. Neither had children. In 1985 they sold Rosedale and a few remaining acres to Historic Preservation of North Carolina, Inc. Rosedale is now a historic site near downtown Charlotte.[4]

Meanwhile John Springs, Minnie, and the rest of the family had settled into Rural Retreat, which burned 12 years later, in 1898. Minnie died that July; whether before or after the fire is not known. John Springs and the children who were still under his roof moved once more, this time into what had previously been a log kitchen at Rural Hill. It was much improved by the addition of several rooms, a second story, and beadboard siding. Some of these improvements were made by John Springs; some may have been made earlier. John Springs died the following year and is buried at Rural Hill, along with Minnie; their oldest sons, Thomas and Jo Graham; and John Springs, Jr., who had died in infancy.

When John Springs died in 1899, his second son, Jo Graham Davidson, inherited Rural Hill. Jo Graham married Annie May Alexander in 1904, and they raised their family in the much improved and modernized kitchen building. Their five children were an infant son who was born and died in 1906, John Springs Davidson III, born in December 1906; Elizabeth, born in 1911; Jo Graham, Jr., born in 1914; and May, born in May 1919. They were the last generation of Davidsons to live at Rural Hill; none of them ever married.

Jo Graham, Jr., died in World War II. He had trained as a pilot, graduating from an Army Air Corps flying school in Texas in April 1942. He corresponded with his sisters, and his cousins who lived at Rosedale, writing about his enthusiasm for flying school, further training in Florida, and a young woman or two who had caught his eye. However, his piloting experience was as short-lived as it was exhilarating. He was flying to North Africa from Cayenne, French Guyana, when his plane crashed over the South American coast on 27 February 1943. His body was recovered and returned to his family.[5]

His gravestone at the Rural Hill Burying Ground is engraved:

1st Lt. Jo Graham Davidson, Jr.
Son of Jo G. & A. M. A. Davidson
Nov. 12, 1914–Feb. 27, 1943
Died in Plane Crash
Cayenne, French Guiana, S.A.
Reinterred May 1, 1948

Jo Graham posthumously received a Purple Heart for his service.

May Davidson, youngest child of the senior Jo Graham, also led an interesting life. She was a graduate of Greensboro College and went to work for the North Carolina Department of Agriculture. She then went to become a secretary in Washington, D.C., as did so many young women during the war. At the end of her career she was secretary to North Carolina's senator Sam Ervin and was in his employ while he chaired the Watergate Committee hearings in 1973. Senator Sam, as he was called, became recognized as a man of agile mind and appealing country-boy mannerisms. People across the country tuned in to the Watergate hearings on radio and television partly because of the nature of the events as they unfolded, and partly to watch Senator Sam in action. May Davidson saved many personal papers relating to her time as the senator's secretary and many photographs of the two of them together. It must have been a heady experience.[6]

John Springs and Elizabeth, the oldest siblings, chose to remain at Rural Hill. A Davidson family descendant shared some fond memories of them. Elizabeth graduated from Greensboro College and taught math for 43 years at area schools, including Alexander Junior High, where some students were Davidson descendants. Elizabeth Davidson was an efficient, no-nonsense teacher. There was little need for discipline in her classes; respect was assumed and delivered. Yet outside the classroom she was warm and friendly, a delight to be with. This was probably a necessary divide in a rural part of the county where

LIEUTENANT JO GRAHAM DAVIDSON, PILOT, U. S. ARMY AIR CORPS. Photographs such as this were typically taken of men before they went off to war. Note Jo Graham's lieutenant's bars and "wings" badge. Photograph in the collection of the authors, a gift from the May Davidson Estate.

11. Rural Hill: The Last Three Generations

MAY DAVIDSON WITH "SENATOR SAM," 1973. Judging by the number of personal notes written on photographs and articles, Senator Sam greatly valued the work of his fellow North Carolinian. Photograph in the collection of the authors, a gift from the May Davidson Estate.

neighbors were close, and many were kin, descendants of several large, much intermarried families. It was not unusual for a teacher to have relatives in her classroom. Elizabeth was also very active at the Hopewell church, as was her older brother. Later in life Elizabeth moved into a retirement community, where she enjoyed the sociability of many friends and neighbors.[7]

John Springs became the sixth-generation farmer of Rural Hill. He had enlisted in the army in 1942 and fought at the Battle of the Bulge. He became a Duke Power employee but was most notably a gentleman farmer, though not a dapper one. He raised some crops but probably farmed as little as necessary. This was not to say he was a shiftless sort; he thoroughly enjoyed people, and along with Elizabeth considered it their calling to take care of the old folks. A good example had been set for them. Their mother, Annie May Alexander Davidson, was the only one of her siblings to marry. The others devoted themselves to the care of the elderly—their parents, aunts and uncles, and whoever seemed to need attention. John Springs and Elizabeth carried on the tradition. Among their charges was their mother, who died in her late eighties after twenty years of widowhood, and those aunts and uncles who had shown them the way. John Springs's self-assigned community service was also a hedge against loneliness, especially after Elizabeth moved from Rural Hill. Whenever you saw John Springs coming up the walk, you knew you had a nice long visit to look forward to.

At John Springs's graveside service Hopewell's minister, the Reverend Jeff Lowrance, described him as

> a veteran, a Presbyterian deacon, a storyteller, and amateur historian par excellence, a totally unique and memorable character whom we held in great affection. We will remember him also as a peace lover become warrior whose soul was scarred by that terrible war. We recall him as one who was unusually charming, but who could become contentious; one who was usually witty, but sometimes biting, reverent one second, earthy the next; often pithy, but becoming long-winded; generous one moment, but tight the next.[8]

May came back to Mecklenburg in retirement and eventually moved into the same facility where Elizabeth lived. In 1992 the three of them sold a large portion of the remaining Rural Hill property to Mecklenburg County. John Springs died in 1998, Elizabeth in 2004, and May in 2011. All three lie in the Rural Hill Burying Ground along with their parents and brothers. All three were memorialized with graveside services.

Today the house in which they were raised is the Rural Hill Visitors' Center, containing staff offices and several museum rooms filled with family memorabilia. Somewhere within the structure is the log house that was first used as a kitchen. The alterations over the years were done so skillfully that no one today knows exactly which rooms are enclosed by the old logs, nor which of the several kitchens built by earlier generations occupies this spot.

It is interesting to note that the last people to live at Rural Hill and at Rosedale were close-knit first cousins. Only one had married, and none of them had heirs. All of them had a deep knowledge and appreciation of local history and their families' places in it. Both groups made arrangements that allowed their ancestral homes to be used as historic sites. Both archived many of their family papers; Mecklenburg history is richer for their generosity.

Appendices

A. Davidson Family Genealogy

THIS IS A GENEALOGY of Major John Davidson; his wife, Violet; their children and some descendants. The names in bold are those who continued to live at Rural Hill as adults. The commonly used names for those not called by their first names are underlined or in parentheses.

First Generation

Major John Davidson (12/15/1735–1/10/1832) and Violet Wilson (8/13/1742–12/3/1818), married 6/2/1761; 10 children.

> Rebecca (1762–1824) and Captain Alexander Brevard (1755–1829), married 1784; eight children.
>
> Isabella (1764–1808) and General Joseph Graham (1759–1836), married 1787; 10 children.
>
> Mary (Polly) (1766–1862) and Dr. William Maclean (1757–1828), married 6/19/1792; 10 children.
>
> **Robert (Robin) and Margaret (Peggy) Osborne; see second generation.**
>
> Violet (1771–1821) and William Bain Alexander (1764–1844), married 8/25/1791; 14 children.
>
> Sarah (1774–1842) and the Rev. Alexander Caldwell (1769–1841), married 10/9/1794; three children.
>
> Margaret (1777–1830) and James Harris (unknown), married 12/10/1813; one child.

John (Jacky) and Sarah (Sallie) Harper Brevard; see second generation.

Elizabeth (Betsy) (1782–1845) and William Lee Davidson, Jr. (1781–1862), married 10/30/1805; no children.

Benjamin Wilson (1787–1829) and Elizabeth (Betsy) Latta (1797–1838), married 8/1818; six children.

Second Generation

Robert (Robin) Davidson (4/7/1769–6/14/1853) and Margaret (Peggy) Osborne (4/7/1776–1/9/1864), married 1/1/1801; no children.

John (Jacky) Davidson (11/12/1779–4/26/1870) and Sarah (Sallie) Harper Brevard (10/26/1780–1/18/1864), married 11/11/1800; 10 children.

> John Matthew (1801–1879) and Mary Sylvester (1809–1855), married 4/4/1826; 12 children.
>
> Mary Winslow (1803–1832) and George Doby (unknown), married 2/9/1831; possibly one child.
>
> Violet Wilson (1806–1877) and Joseph Sylvester (1807–1875), married 10/26/1826; eight children.
>
> **Adam Brevard and Mary Laura Springs; see third generation.**
>
> Robert H. M. (1810–1841), never married.
>
> Isabella (1813–1888) and James W. Moore (unknown), married 2/11/1835; one child.
>
> Augustus W. (1815–1837), never married.
>
> William S. M. (1817–1873) and Jane E. Torrance (1823–1844), married 12/8/1842; one child. William's second marriage was to Rebecca Reid ; no children; his third marriage was to Mary Johnston; no children.
>
> Edward Constantine (1820–1892) and Jane V. Henderson (1831–1914), married 1858; eight children.
>
> Sarah (1822–1841), died at age 18.

Third Generation

Adam Brevard Davidson (3/13/1808–7/4/1896) and Mary Laura Springs (9/3/1813–10/24/1872), married (4/20/1836); 16 children; Amanda and Isabelle were twins.

> Mary Laura (1837–1902) and the Rev. Alexander Sinclair, married 8/10/1858.
>
> **John Springs and Margaret (Minnie) Caldwell; see fourth generation.**

William (Willie) Lee (1840–1857), died at age 17.

Robert Augustus (1842–1865), never married.

Richard Austin (1843–1892) never married.

Sarah (Sallie) Harper (1845–1935), never married.

Jane (Jenny) Baxter (1847–1879) and Dr. James M. Miller, married 10/22/1873.

Amanda M. (Maude) (1849–1939) and Andrew Jackson Beall, married 10/19/1875.

Isabelle Sophia (1849–1933) and Charles Montgomery, married 9/6/1871.

Unnamed daughter, born and died between late 1850 and September 1851.

Adam Brevard, Jr. (1852–1869), died at age 17.

Blandina R. (1853–1937), never married.

Leroy Springs (1855–1915), never married.

Julia Stockton (1857–1930) and the Rev. Thomas Strcehecker, married 4/17/1883.

Edward Lee Baxter (1858–1944) and Sarah Vosburgh, married 4/20/1935.

Fannie Baxter (1861–1863), died at age two.

Fourth Generation

John Springs Davidson (8/6/1838–8/7/1899) and Margaret (Minnie) Caldwell (1840–7/1/1898), married (5/31/1864); six children.

Thomas Brevard (1866–1936), probably never married.

Jo Graham and Annie May Alexander; see fifth generation.

Harriet Baxter (1871–1933) and Abernathy, married?

Baxter Craighead (Craig) (1875–1947) and Louise Heagy, married 1914.

John Springs, Jr. (1878), died in infancy.

Mary Laura Springs (1879–1936) and Jonas Bost, married ?

Fifth Generation

Jo Graham Davidson (4/17/1868–1/11/1949) and Annie May Alexander (9/30/1881–4/30/1969), married (11/23/1904); five children.

Son born and died January 1, 1906.

John Springs (1906–1998), never married.

Elizabeth (1911–2004), never married.

Jo Graham, Jr. (1914–2/27/1943), died in World War II, never married.

May (5/5/1919–2011), never married.
The fifth generation left no direct descendants.

B. Davidson College

MAJOR JOHN AND HIS FAMILY were deeply involved in the establishment of Davidson College in northern Mecklenburg County. In 1835 the Concord Presbytery formed a committee, led by the Reverend Robert Hall Morrison, to establish a college emphasizing Christian education for local men. The school opened its doors to students in March of 1837 with the Reverend Morrison as its president.

Major John's son-in-law William Lee Davidson, Jr., sold the committee 469 acres of land on the Charlotte-Statesville Road, two miles from his home. He sold it for about half of its 1835 value, less than he had paid for it about 10 years earlier. William Lee was the son of General William Lee Davidson, the Revolutionary War hero for whom the college was to be named.[1]

Work was soon begun to clear the land and build the college. Adam Brevard Davidson, Major John's grandson, provided a great deal of lumber for the new college, as he noted in his farm journal on 13 January 1836:

> Mr. Owens gave me the bill of lumber for the manual labour school to fill between 35 & 40 thousand feet 16000 thousand feet of 1¼ plank 10.000 thousand of 1 In. 10.400 of scantling. We have now about 20 thousand of it sawed.

Here the word "bill" means a bill of material, or a list of items ordered, not an invoice. The inch measurements refer to the thickness of the boards, not their width, which varied according to the logs used. "Feet" refers to a volume measurement of board feet. A volume of one board foot is 12 inches by 12 inches by one inch in thickness. Another entry indicates that the one and one-quarter-inch boards were for flooring. On 9 May Brevard wrote that he had "halled 11 loads of lumber up to the coleage (the Davidson,s Colleage)." On 20 May he reported, "I rode up to the Coleage and remained there about one hour, and then to Uncle W. Lee Davidsons for dinner—and returned home in the evening." Altogether Brevard sent 114 loads of lumber to the college and was paid $1,248 in April of 1838.

The school was initially planned to be a manual labor school where the students would pay part or all of their expenses by growing crops, chopping firewood, tending livestock, and doing other necessary tasks. It became apparent that sons of planters had no interest in such work, and their fathers were willing and able to pay for schooling. The manual labor concept was quickly abandoned.

Robert Hall Morrison, the college's first president, had been the minister at Sugar Creek Presbyterian Church and also was the founding pastor of the Presbyterian Church (later First Presbyterian) in the village of Charlotte and had headed the committee to establish the college. Morrison was married to Mary Graham, a granddaughter of Major John Davidson's.

A number of Major John Davidson's descendants were actively involved with the college. His son Robin and son-in-law William Lee Davidson, Jr., were two of the six men who pledged $1,000 each to establish a professorship. Major John's grandson Adam Brevard Davidson was among its early trustees; two of Jacky's sons were students there. his son William was a member of the first class in 1837, and Constantine became a student a year or two later. Among Major John's many great-grandsons, at least two were Davidson students, Robert and E. L. Baxter Davidson, sons of Adam Brevard Davidson's. E. L. Baxter Davidson died in 1944 and left no heirs. According to the records at Davidson College, he left the school Brevard's handsome secretary desk and an estate valued at $1 million. At that time it was the largest contribution the college had ever received. The secretary, where Brevard probably kept his farm journal, is now on display in the college library.[2]

BREVARD DAVIDSON'S SECRETARY DESK, CA. 1820. This desk was at Rural Hill for many years. This is probably the surface on which he wrote his farm journals. Nearby a small placard reads in part: Davidson Family Plantation Secretary ... made for A. Brevard Davidson of "Rural Hill" plantation, Catawba River, Mecklenburg County by George H. Nichols, Cabinetmaker, Charlotte, N.C. (working 1820s–1830s) (Note his name is on the desk lock). Brevard Davidson was a trustee of Davidson College (1853–1877). The secretary was inherited by his son, E. L. Baxter Davidson (Class of 1881), who willed it, with an estate valued at $1 million, to his Alma Mater.... The secretary is nine and a half feet tall and made of crotch mahogany, directoire in design, and has four secret drawers. Photo by the author.

C. Hopewell Presbyterian Church

EARLY MECKLENBURG COUNTY WAS RURAL, and most of its inhabitants were farmers. Charlotte was the county town where court sessions were held for one week every three months. Between court sessions it was a small sleepy village inhabited by a handful of families who kept inns and taverns, owned a few shops, and practiced various trades. Most citizens of Mecklenburg County lived on their farms, and their lives were centered on the Presbyterian churches in the countryside surrounding the village. Hopewell Presbyterian Church today still stands in the northwest corner of Mecklenburg County on Beatties Ford Road. The Davidsons and most of their friends and relations were members and supporters of Hopewell. The church was established in 1762 and was served in its early years by supply ministers, men who took turns preaching to congregations scattered about the county. The first minister of record was Samuel Craighead Caldwell, who served Hopewell from 1791 to 1806. Caldwell also served Sugar Creek Presbyterian Church during this time.[1]

In the early 1800s there was a schism in the church between "New-Siders" and "Old-Siders." This was more of a difference in style than in theology. The Reverend Caldwell was a proponent of the New Side movement and its boisterous, evangelical, fire-and-brimstone style of preaching. He held frequent revivals during which emotional worshipers spoke in tongues, rolled in the aisles, and barked like dogs until they dropped into stupors of exhaustion. Major John Davidson disapproved of this practice. He preferred the staid and sober services of the Old Side school and strongly opposed midweek revivals. His deep faith had taught him that the Sabbath should be devoted to the Lord, and men should attend to their work during the rest of the week. He removed his attendance and membership to Gilead Presbyterian Church, which was several miles north of Hopewell. Other members of the family seemed to weather the brief schism and remained loyal to Hopewell. Gilead Associate Reformed Presbyterian Church, along with its burying ground, still lies three miles up Beatties Ford Road from Rural Hill.

The Reverend Caldwell left Hopewell in 1806 under a cloud of disapproval. He was not formally dismissed but perhaps realized that his style did not fit the somber congregation at Hopewell. He continued to preach at Sugar Creek Presbyterian Church near Charlotte, where his energetic sermons were appreciated.

The Reverend John Williamson became minister at Hopewell in 1818 and remained until his death in 1842. He is mentioned frequently in Adam Brevard Davidson's farm journal. The Rural Hill Davidsons and their extended families contributed spiritually and financially through the centuries to Hopewell's maintenance.

D. The Lunacy of the Rev. Alexander Caldwell

SARAH, THE FIFTH DAUGHTER and sixth child of Major John and Violet Davidson, was 20 when she married the Reverend Alexander Caldwell in October 1794. The Reverend Caldwell was from a fine religious family and was the pastor of Rocky River Presbyterian Church. His brother, the Reverend Samuel C. Caldwell, was the pastor of both the Hopewell and Sugar Creek Presbyterian churches. His father was a minister, as was his grandfather, the Reverend Alexander Craighead, the first minister called by the Presbyterians of Mecklenburg County and probably the most influential.

In 1797, three years after Sarah and Alexander were married, the Reverend Caldwell was dismissed by the session of Rocky River Presbyterian Church because he had become deranged.

In the Mecklenburg County Court of October 1798 a jury was appointed to determine "the mental situation of Alexander Caldwell ... & whether he may be in a State of Lunacy."

The jury included his father-in-law Major John Davidson; his brother-in-law Robert Davidson; John McKnitt Alexander, who had a number of connections to the Davidson family, and nine others. They reported to the court that they "do believe him in such a State of Lunacy as not to be able to take care of his own property, and further that he has lost property for the want of that capacity, and we recommend it to the court to have a guardian Appointed for him to take Charge of his Property, &c."[1] The court ordered that the Reverend Samuel C. Caldwell be appointed guardian for his brother Alexander Caldwell.

Samuel Caldwell served as his brother's guardian until the youngest of Alexander's three children reached the age of 21 when those three assumed the guardianship.

Evidence from the U.S. Census confirms family stories that Sarah and her three children were living at Rural Hill by 1800. Either her husband was not capable of taking care of them or providing for them or perhaps he was violent or abusive toward her or the children. Sarah and the three children continued to live at Rural Hill until at least 1820.

Sarah's three children were

- Martha "Patsy" Caldwell, born 28 July 1795, eight or nine months after the wedding.
- John Hancock (or John D. in one record) Caldwell. His birth date is not known for certain. In the 1800 census he is shown as younger than 10 years old, so he must have been born after Patsy and before David, probably sometime in 1797.

- David Alexander Caldwell, born 17 January 1799.

Note that John was born about the time his father was dismissed from Rocky River Presbyterian Church and that when the Reverend Alexander Caldwell appeared in court and was declared a lunatic, his wife, Sarah, was in her sixth month of pregnancy with her third child.

The 1800 and 1810 censuses indicate that Sarah and the three children were living at Rural Hill. The 1820 census indicates that John Caldwell, age about 23, was no longer living there. Sarah and her other two children remained in the household.

During the February court session of 1822, when David was 23, the Reverend Samuel C. Caldwell petitioned the court to be released from the guardianship of "his Brother Alexander Caldwell, a Lunatic ... and that he be released from his Guardianship upon his Settlement with a Committee of Court." The court appointed three new guardians for Alexander Caldwell: his son-in-law, Major John H. Davidson, and two sons, John and Alexander Caldwell.[2]

At the same session a committee was appointed to "settle with the Revd. Saml. C. Caldwell as guardian of his Brother Alexander Caldwell, a Lunatic." The committee was to meet with Samuel, review his records and certify to the court that he had satisfactorily performed his duty as guardian. This was in preparation for handing the assets of Alexander Caldwell over to the new guardians.

Major John H. Davidson, known as "Long Headed Jacky," was the husband of Martha "Patsy" Caldwell and son-in-law of Alexander Caldwell. He was not otherwise related to the Davidsons and Caldwells in this story.

When David and John were named guardians for their father, they also became guardians of their own inheritance.

During the May 1822 court session the Reverend Samuel C. Caldwell's guardianship of his brother was declared fully settled. In fact the committee determined that he had overpaid the sum of $10.00.

On 18 January 1824 all of Sarah's brothers and sisters gave her the gift of "a negro Man Named Cyrus" and recorded the gift in the February court records. This was just after Major John broke up housekeeping in the fall of 1823, and Cyrus probably came from the general distribution made by the major.

When Sarah had moved back home to Rural Hill in 1799 or 1800, her three children were all younger than five. It is probable that these three children spent considerable time with her brother Robin and his wife, Peggy, at Holly Bend, not only visiting but living there for extended periods, as was the custom of the time for orphans.

Note that at this time in both law and common usage the term "orphan" was applied to a minor child whose father had died. This term did not reflect whether the child's mother still lived or whether the child lived with her.

In 1853 David Alexander Caldwell was one of the executors of Robin's will and received a bequest of 15 Negroes and 500 to 500 acres of land. When a man had no children and expected that he would not have any, he sometimes took into his home a male relative, usually a nephew. He raised this person as his own child and made him heir to a large part of his estate.

In Robin's will Patsy received 10 shares of stock of the Bank of the State of North Carolina and three Negroes. She was raised at Rural Hill and may have lived at Holly Bend for some time, learning the arts of spinning and housewifery from her aunt Peggy. She had married Colonel John H. Davidson and lived in Alabama at the time of Robin's death.

E. The Story of Plum, Enslaved Man, Freedman, Property Owner

BETWEEN 1778 AND 1800 a Negro man named Plum appears in the Mecklenburg County records several times. His story illuminates the life of an exceptional man who was enslaved and then became a free man and owner of property.

In 1778 Samuel Wilson (Major John's father-in-law) died and left his son John "a negro man Plumb," among other bequests.[1]

In 1795 John Wilson died at the age of 38. Having neither wife nor child, he left his plantation and the bulk of his estate to his half-brother William Jack Wilson, who was 17 at that time. William was the youngest child of Margaret Jack Wilson, Samuel's third wife. He had been born after his father's death and, since his father did not know whether the child would be a boy or a girl, was left only a small inheritance. The rest of the family, and John Wilson in particular, probably felt that they should make more ample provision for the boy.

The will also made a large and exceptional provision: "Except half of the orchard and the two fields ... for the use of my negro Plum during his lifetime, and at his demise s^d lands are to revert to the s^d. William." John Wilson also left Plum "a mare, a plow and tackling, my belled cow and calf, all my everyday clothes," and "which negro I hereby set free from all servitude as a slave & the above articles to be at his own disposal with a red heifer ... a ewe and lamb, six head of hogs ... two pots, and my bed and two blankets ... and I also give to Plum an axe and a hoe."[2]

In July 1795 a motion was made in court to admit the will to probate. John's brother David and others questioned ("caveated") the will and asked the court to order that John Wilson's belongings be collected. One of the executors named in the will, John Davidson, a merchant in Charlotte, was appointed to do this under a £2,000 bond.

While we cannot know David Wilson's motives, he was probably acting on behalf of his half-brother William Jack Wilson. At 17 William was still a minor and, although the primary heir, had no standing in court. This may have been an attempt to disinherit Plum or it might have been an action to establish the legality of this unusual bequest. If the court found in favor of Plum, the court record would protect Plum's interests if someone tried to overturn the will when William Jack reached his majority or at some other time.

In October 1795 the question was put to a jury, which heard witnesses for and against and found "that the deceased had a right to devise" and the will was admitted to probate.[3]

Two years later the court ordered that Plum be set free:

> Whereas John Wilson, Deceased, late of the County of Mecklenburg in the State of North Carolina, did by his last will & Testament emancipate and set free from servitude his Negro man Plumb, and whereas it doth further appear from the representation of sundry respectable persons that the Said Negro man Plumb is a sober, Honest, inoffensive, & Industrious person and that he is worthy of his freedom for Meritorious Services rendered to his late Master. Ordered therefore from the above considerations that the Said Negro man Plumb be emancipated and entitled to such priviledges & immunities as the Law of the State grant to those of Colour in Similar situations, and that the Clerk of the Court give a Certificate under the Seal of the County of Such Emancipation.[4]

Finally, three years later, the court appointed Hugh Torrence as guardian of Plum, "a free Negro liberated by Court at October Session 1797."[5] A guardian was appointed by the court when a person had tangible assets and was judged incapable of managing them or did not have legal standing because of being insane, a minor, a female or, in this case, a free person of color.

F. A Marriage Deed of Trust

IN 1813 MAJOR JOHN'S last remaining single daughter, Margaret, married Major James Harris of Cabarrus County. At the time she was 36, which was quite old for a first marriage, and Major John, being very well off, made provision to protect his daughter's ownership of the property she brought into the marriage. Local histories and genealogies place the wedding date at 10 December 1813 but the legal documents are dated 14 and 15 December and refer to her "Marriage intended to be had & solemnized with Major James Harris," which may indicate that the wedding was actually held sometime after 15 December.

A summary of the terms of this agreement appears in Chapter 3. Below are complete transcriptions of the two agreements as recorded in Mecklenburg Deed Book 20.

Please note that throughout this book the transcriptions of deeds reproduce the spelling, capitalization and punctuation as closely to the original document as possible. In a few cases large blocks of legal language are fully included. Abbreviations with superscripts are transcribed as they appear. Some example are S^d for "said," Exr^s for "executors," Adm^{rs} for "administrators," y^e for "the," Ag^nst for "Against," and the various months. Where we could not identify a word, we have replaced it with a blank space. In some deeds words or phrases had been repeated by the registrar, especially when continuing to the next page. In the original documents periods are seldom used, even at the end of paragraphs. Or, sometimes the dot is so small it is not visible or distinguishable from a random speck.

Mecklenburg Deeds, book 20, page 31

N° 28

This Indenture made the 14th day of December Anno Dom. 1813 Between John Davidson of Mecklenburg County in North Carolina of the one part, and William Bain Alexander & Robert Davidson of the other part. Witnesseth that for & in consideration of the natural love & affection which the said John Davidson hath for his Daughter Margaret Davidson, for the purpose of making a Suitable provision for her on her Marriage intended to be had & solemnized with Major James Harris of the County of Cabarrus, and for the purpose of securing to her the absolute right of disposing of the property hereafter mentioned in the event of her decease without heirs of her Body then living, and further, for & in consideration of the Sum of ten Shillings to him in hand paid at or before the ensealing of these presents, the receipt whereof is hereby acknowledged, He the s^c. John Davidson hath bargained sold & delivered, and by these presents Doth grant bargain sell and deliver unto them the said William Bain Alexander & Robert Davidson & the Survivor of them, the Executors & Administrators of such survivor the following Negro Slaves. To wit—Fanny, Melanda, Bet, Plum, Caroline, Dina, and Vergil and the increase of the female part of said Slaves. To have & to hold the s^d Slaves named Fanny, Melinda, Bet, Plum, Caroline Dinah and Virgil and the future increase of the female part of the said Slaves. To them the s^d. William Bain Alexander & Robert Davidson and the Survivor of them; the Executor or Administrator of such Survivor. to the uses, upon the trust, to and for the intents and purposes & under and subject to the provisos and agreements herein after expressed & declared, of & concerning the same. That is to say, That the said Margaret Davidson, for & during the ~~lives~~ Joint lives of her self & James Harris her intended Husband shall receive and have all the benefit & advantage which may arise from the use, hire or labour of the said Slaves and their future increase. And on the death of the said James Harris, The said Margaret Davidson Surviving—the said Trustees and the Survivor of them, The Executor or Administrator of such Survivors, shall permit the said Margaret to receive—& shall deliver to her all the said Negro slaves, and their future increase. To have & to hold to her the said Margaret, her heirs Executors Administrators & assigns for ever. And on the death of the s^d. Margaret, the said James Harris Surviving; The said Trustees & the Survivor of them;—the Executors or Administrator of such Survivor, shall deliver the s^d. Negro Slaves and their future increase to such person or persons as may be entitled to receive the same under the last Will & Testament of the said Margaret And on the death of said Margaret, her said Husband James Harris Surviving, without leaving any last Will & Testament, then the said Trustees, the Survivors of them, the Executors or Administrators of such survivor, shall deliver to the said James Harris, the one third part in value of the said Negro Slaves and their future increase. To have & to hold to him the s^d James Harris his heirs Exec^{rs}. Admin^{rs} & assigns for ever, and shall deliver the remaining two thirds of said Slaves and their increase to the Brothers & Sisters of the said Margaret then living & to the Children of such brothers & sisters as may be then deceased, an equal share to each. And that in the Event, that the s^d Margaret shall die, leaving issue of her Body, during her Marriage with the s^d James Harris then, notwithstanding any of the provisions, limitations, & uses in this deed of trust, herein before expressed, declared or enacted; The said Trustees shall divide all the said Negro Slaves and their future increase, equally among the Children of the Marriage intended to be had between her the said Margaret Davidson & the said James Harris

In Witness whereof the said John Davidson, William Bain Alexander & Robert Davidson, have hereunto respectively set their hands & affirmed their Seals

	} John Davidson {seal}
the day and year first above written	} W^m. B. Alexander {seal}
	} Robt Davidson {seal}
Signed sealed and delivered in presence of us	}
Wm Davidson, B. W. Davidson	}

Mecklenburg County May Court 1814. This deed was proven & recorded. Test. Isaac Alexander C. M. C. registered June 19, 1814

Mecklenburg Deeds, book 20, page 32

N°. 29

State of North Carolina Mecklenburg County

Know all men by these presents that I James Harris of Cabarrus County in North Carolina am held & firmly bound unto William B. Alexander & Robert Davidson of Mecklenburg County in the penal sum of twenty five hundred Dollars, for the pay of which I bind my self me heirs Executors & Administrators firmly by these presents sealed with my seal & signed & delivered this 15th December Anno Dom 1813—

The Condition of the above Obligation is such That whereas a Mariage is intended to be had and Solemnized between the above bounded James Harris & Margaret Davidson. And whereas a considerable personal estate of the value of twelve Hundred and fifty Dollars, consisting of Cash, Bonds, Notes, Cattle, Horses and furniture is accrued to the said James Harris in consequence of the said intended Marriage.

Now if the said James Harris shall permit the said Margaret his Intended Wife to enjoy the use of that property of the kind by him received on his Marriage of the value aforesaid, for and during their Joint lives. And if the said James Harris shall by his Executors or Administrators, deliver to the said Margaret, in the event of her surviving him, Money or property of the like kind of the value of twelve Hundred & fifty Dollars And if the said James—to the person or persons named in the last Will of the said

Margaret, Money or property to the like kind of the value aforesaid, And if the said James—shall deliver to the Brothers and Sisters surviving the said Margaret, and to the children of her Brothers & Sisters Deceased at the time of her death, on the event of said Margaret dying intestate, an equal share to each two thirds of the said sum of Twelve Hundred & fifty Dollars, in money or property of the like kind. And finally, if the said James—shall secure to the Children of the Marriage intended between him & the said Margaret, money or property of the like kind of the amount and value aforesaid. And finally, if the said James—shall, bonofide perform either of the above conditions, when the event on which the same depends—shall happen in the manner, and to the use proposed in a Deed of Trust for Sundry negroes, of the date of these presents, from John Davidson the father of the said Margaret—to the said William B. Alexander & Robert Davidson. Then the above Obligation to be void Otherwise to remain in full force, virtue & effect—

   Signed Sealed & delivered in presence of   } Jas Harris {seal}
      W. L. Davidson B. W. Davidson   }

Mecklenburg County May Court 1814. This Bond was proven & recorded Test Isaac Alexander C. M. C.
registered June 19 1814

G. Naming Conventions and Other John Davidsons

CHARACTERISTIC NAMING CONVENTIONS can be observed among Scots-Irish Presbyterians in America in the late 18th and early 19th centuries. First of all, up until about 1800 very few had middle names. A few exceptions, such as John McKnitt Alexander, would carry the same middle name for generations because it was a name of great family honor. The middle name McKnitt was such an integral part of Alexander that his name often appears, even in deeds and court records, as "John McKnitt" without the Alexander. Middle names began to appear in the Carolina backcountry in about 1800 as the increased population of the area led to confusions in legal records. Soon the use of middle names was widespread, and many people used their middle name rather than their first name.

A larger confusion, however, came from the naming of both boys and girls after their parents and grandparents. In many cases, although not in all, the firstborn son was named after his paternal grandfather, while the second son was named after his father and the third son was named after his maternal grandfather. After that there were more variations but, except for some imaginative ones such as Sugar Dulin and his brother Salt, Darling Belk, Philemon Morris, and so on, most names were chosen from a handful of old family names, other familiar names or biblical ones. Girls likewise were often given family names, although the naming structure was not as rigid as for boys. On the other hand, there were common nicknames for girls, some of which are not common today, such as Ann called Nancy, Mary called Polly and Martha called Patsy.

Another variation appears in wills and estate papers of the time. In many families the son who was given his grandfather's name tended to inherit directly from that grandfather. The same pattern seems to apply to uncles. In the case of Robert (Robin) Davidson of Holly Bend, who had no children, there are six nephews named Robert mentioned in his will.

The widespread use of a few names can lead to confusion in examining legal records. If there was only one John Davidson publicly active at the time, he generally appeared in court records as John. If there were two or more at the time, then one may have been called John and a modifier added to the others such as Major John or John Senior or John Junior. People were also differentiated by where they lived or their occupation, as in John Davidson (river), John Davidson, merchant, or John Davidson, Black Smith.

However, as soon as there was only one man of the name active in court, the listings in the records tended to revert to just plain John. In some cases a nickname stuck. Jacky Davidson, the son of Major John, was known as "Silver Headed Jacky." "Long Headed Jacky" Davidson was related to him by marriage but not by blood.

This confusion may be the original source for the old southern custom of using imaginative nicknames such as Bubba, Sonny, Skipper and so on. By the third or fourth generation of Major John Davidson's family, there were six or eight Johns and eight or ten Roberts, all cousins, many living in the same neighborhood. When they gathered as a family for church or celebrations, it must have been confusing.

The fact that John Davidson was a very popular name across the Carolina Piedmont during this period adds an additional level of difficulty to the task of trying to figure out who Major John was and what he accomplished. For that reason this account ignores any mention of John Davidson that did not fit in with farming in the Hopewell area during his active lifetime, that is, from 1756 when he turned 21 to 1823 when, at the age of 88, he retired from active farming. Some court records refer to Major John Davidson or to John Davidson Senior or Junior but there is little consistency in these references.

Here are some of the conflicts. None of those listed is Major John Davidson of Rural Hill.

- John Davidson of Chestnut Level, Pennsylvania came to the backcountry about 1752. This was the brother of George Davidson, and they were brothers or perhaps cousins of Major John's father, Robert. This John Davidson settled in Rowan County for a while, then moved

Appendix G. Naming Conventions and Other John Davidsons

to the west, settled and built a fort, later called Davidson's Fort, near where the town of Old Fort is today.

- In 1776 a John Davidson and his wife were killed by Cherokee Indians near Davidson Fort. This may have been the man who built the fort or some other John Davidson.
- In 1780 John Davidson, son of Colonel George Davidson, and his family were butchered by the Cherokee near Old Fort. This may have been a confused reference to the couple who died in 1776, or there may have been two John Davidsons who met the same fate.
- There was a prominent merchant named John Davidson living in Charlotte in 1800 and 1806 and probably before and after those dates. According to court records, he served as executor for Major John's late brother-in-law John Wilson.
- A John Davison, a blacksmith, bought land on Fishing Creek in 1763. There were two prominent Fishing Creeks at the time, both on the west bank of the Catawba River. One was opposite the north part of Mecklenburg County and the other in South Carolina near where Historic Brattonsville is today.
- A John Davidson died in 1778. His executors were James and John Davidson.
- There was a Major John Davidson in the Anson County Militia in 1776 and 1777, while Major John of Rural Hill was serving in the Mecklenburg Militia.
- There was a Captain John Davidson in the Rowan County Militia in 1776 and 1777.
- There was a Captain John Davidson who was the horse wrangler for the Cherokee Campaign of 1776.
- There was a private John Davidson in the North Carolina Line of the Continental Army in 1781.
- A field return of the Southern Army under General Horatio Gates at Camp New Providence, North Carolina, was issued by "John Davidson, B.M." This stands for brigade major, a staff position like aide de camp. The entry is not dated, but Gates was at Camp New Providence only from 23 to 28 November 1780. This was most probably an officer in the Continental Line and not our Major John.[1]
- In 1786 John Davidson was an administrator of the will of James Davidson, along with the widow, Jane Davidson. This was probably the Charlotte merchant since we do not know of a James Davidson connected to Major John's family. This James Davidson had a minor son named John Davidson.

- Major John Davidson, called "Long Headed Jacky," was not related by blood to Major John as far as can be determined. He married Patsy Caldwell, who grew up at Rural Hill after her father became a lunatic. Her parents were the Reverend Alexander Caldwell and Sarah Davidson, daughter of Major John.

H. Brevard's Slave Inventories

INFORMATION ABOUT BREVARD'S SLAVES comes from several sources in addition to the census records. There is the inventory of the slaves given to him in 1836 by his father-in-law that includes their names, ages and family groups. In 1856 he listed the slaves with names, ages and occupations and made a similar list in 1864. In addition, the farm journal narratives mention some people by name, occasionally imply whether they lived at Dickson or Rural Hill and record most births. The fact that he owned plantations in both Mecklenburg and Lincoln counties confuses the issue. The census records up to 1850 list people by household and age group but do not give names or reflect ownership. The records that we have consulted are for Mecklenburg only, and the 1856 and 1865 lists are clearly for Rural Hill and do not include Dickson. It is apparent from the journals that some of the enslaved people moved back and forth between the two properties. One can infer from the sizes of the crops planted at Rural Hill and at Dickson that about half as many enslaved people were at Dickson as were at Rural Hill. Since the Barry plantation, bought in 1841, was contiguous to Rural Hill, both properties were probably worked by the same labor force.

As mentioned previously the 19 slaves Brevard received in December of 1836 were Mary's dowry but belonged to her husband the moment they married. Shortly after taking possession of the slaves, Brevard "moved Marys negroes down to the Dixon Place 18 in number Burrow, Ann & 7 children Tom, Julia & 3 children Peggy & two children kept Sina at home."

Since Brevard and Mary had married in 1836, he was listed as a head of household starting with the 1840 census. In that census Brevard had 13 slaves at Rural Hill, nine men and boys and four women and girls, while his father, Jacky, had 17. The ages and genders indicate that some of those sent to Dickson had probably come back to Rural Hill. The 1850 census shows that Brevard had 26 slaves at Rural Hill, 19 men and boys and seven women and girls. His journal recorded 19 births to enslaved women during the intervening decade. Probably eight births occurred at the Dickson Plantation; of the remaining 11 babies, six were boys, four were girls, and the gender of one was not specified. The 1850 census numbers seem a bit askew when compared to the journal. The census may have some errors, but people moving back and forth between the two farms could account for the discrepancies. Some births were not recorded; for instance, Brevard listed Sina's first and third children but not her second. Very few slave deaths were noted, although some names seem to disappear from the record.

Enslaved people lived in cabins, probably close together in family groups. On 18 April 1840 Brevard wrote that he "raised a double negro house yesterday 15 by 30 feet." Not much room for two families, or perhaps one extended family. He may have permitted his slaves to keep gardens and chickens at their cabins and to eat or sell their bounty. This was fairly customary on plantations during this time. Enslaved people usually prepared and ate breakfast and supper in their cabins. The main meal of the day was a midday dinner. It was prepared communally and carried to the fields or eaten wherever people were working.

On 14 February 1844 Brevard wrote, "Father & My self divided our hands this week." This must have been a legal division, perhaps reflecting the numbers in the 1840 census. Unfortunately Brevard gives no details of how many people were involved or how they were divided. Brevard owned fewer people than most other planters in the county of similar economic status. Even if we include a fair number at his Dickson Plantation, his enslaved workforce is in sharp contrast to that of his uncle Robin, who reported a little less wealth in real estate than Brevard yet owned 109 people.

Brevard's 1856 commercial farm journal has a page for listing slaves along with their ages, occupations and values. He listed 30 people; first men and boys, then women and girls by age and not in family groups. Names in bold in this list also were listed in Mary's dowry of 1836.

Name	Age	Occupation	Value
1. **Thomas**	50	Miller	500
2. Adam	42	Wagoner	900
3. Logan	30	Farm	1000
4. **Alexander**	34	Blk Smith	1200
5. Phil	27	Wagoner	1000
6. Hampton	24	Blk Smith	1200
7. **Umphrey**	24	Farm	1000
8. **George**	24	Farm	1000
9. Alfred	20	Farm	900
10. Jerrie	14	Farm	500
11. Joe	11	Farm	550
12. Harrison	11	Farm	550
13. Moses	8	Farm	400
14. David	9	Farm	400

Name	Age	Occupation	Value
15. John	6	Farm	350
16. Bill	7	Farm	300
17. Rufus	3	Farm	300
18. Jim	1	Farm	200
19. **Ann**	61	H. Hand	300
20. **Julia**	49	Weaver	400
21. **Sina**	33	H. Hand	500
22. Sarah	30	Cook	800
23. **Hannah**	29	Farm	800
24. **Nancy**	26	Farm	800
25. **Celia**	22	Farm	800
26. Poly	17	Farm	800
27. Jincy	15	House Maid	700
28. Susan	12	House Maid	700
29. Amy	6	Child	300
30. Dilsie	3	Child	200

In the same book he made a "New list of ages for 1864." It names 35 enslaved people:

Name	Age	Name	Age
Alexander	42	Davie	17
Phil	35	Jack	14
Hampton	34	Bill	15
Umphrey	34	Rufus	11
Alphred	28	Jim	9
Jerry	22	Jef	—
Joe	19	Monrow	—
Harrison	19	Dick about	49
Mose	16	Green	8
Tom	8	Iby	—
Sina	41	Adam	—
Sarah	40	Adeline	—
Hannah	35	Evaline	—
Celia	30	Liza	8
Susan	20	Bob	6
Ginci	17	Molly	4
Amy	14	Alice	2
Dilsi	11		

Sales receipts confirm that Brevard had bought Phil, Hampton, and Sarah. Evalina, and Dick, who was not on the 1856 list, were also purchased and probably lived at the Dickson Plantation. Two others were purchased in 1856. When Brevard's father-in-law John Springs died in 1853, he left Alphred to his daughter Mary and a girl named Jincy to his grandson and namesake, John Springs Davidson. The births of Jerry, Joe Harrison, David, Rufus, Amy and Dilsie are recorded in the earlier journal; Moses and Jim may have been born at one of the farms but not listed by name at the time. It is not known how Brevard acquired Adam, Logan, John, Polly and Susan.

From various resources we can get glimpses into the lives of the people whom Brevard owned. The slaves known to have been bought were Evalina, Phil, Hampton, Dick, Sarah and two others. Evalina came from the estate sale of Joseph McConaughey on 29 October 1839, when Brevard paid $802 for "a negro girl Evalina about 15 years of Age." She appears to have lived at Dickson, and the journal references to her are few. In 1849 Brevard wrote sideways in the margin, "Evalinas 4 daughter & 4th child born at plantation [Dickson] Feb." Later he wrote, "Evelina's 7th child & 6th daughter born April 1853." On 16 March 1856 Evalina gave birth to twins, Tom and Lizzie, at Dickson. Evaline is on the 1864 list with no age; Liza and Tom are both 8. This is probably the same family.

Phil and Hampton were purchased on the same day. On 24 January 1842 Brevard wrote: "Charlotte Court, I attended four days bought two negrow boys, one at Maj Smiths sale for $606.00 Phil 16 or 17 years old, & one at William Davidson's trust sale for $550. Hampton 13 years old." William Davidson, who was not related to Brevard, was a former state senator whose many investments had gone sour. He had mortgaged his property to settle debts, and most of it was auctioned off. His daughter Sarah kept a journal in 1837 in which she wrote, "After tea attended the instruction of our young servants.... I commenced learning them to read.... [They are] progressing as fast as I can reasonably expect." She enumerated the progress of some of her young charges; eight-year-old Hampton was spelling "in three letters." Brevard evidently thought highly of these young men. In 1856 Phil was a wagoner valued at $1,000 and Hampton a blacksmith was valued at $1,200.[1]

A receipt of 1 January 1847 states that Brevard bought "Dick, about 27 years" from the estate of A. F. Derr for $725. Dick is not on the 1856 list and may have been at Dickson. He may have been "Dick about 49" on the 1864 list.

On 17 February 1854 Brevard paid $800 to R. B. Harry "for a negro girl named Sarah aged about 30 years old which girl I do warrant sound in body & mind with the exception of one Finger." In 1856 Sarah is listed as a cook at Rural Hill.

In the 1856 journal Brevard states he bought Bill from Leroy Springs for $1,300 and someone whose name may have been Mick or Dick or Mack from Miss Jane Barry's sale for $909. This could have been the man named Dick listed in 1864. Both of these purchases were made on the same day, probably 15 February 1856. These entries, written in pencil, are faded and difficult to read. One or both people may have lived at Dickson.

Since Brevard's journal recorded many (but not all) Negro births, and named the mothers and often the children, some of those families can be followed. Tom, Julia, and their three children (Austin, George, and Lemuel) were part of the 1836 dowry. Over the years Julia gave birth to six more children, Jack, Jerry, Joe and another son and two daughters who are not named. All of them appear to have been born at Rural Hill. Tom and Julia, along with their sons George, Jerry and Joe, were at Rural Hill in 1856. Tom, 50, was a miller, and Julia, 49, was a weaver. The three sons were all farmers and valued at considerably more than their aging parents.

Sina, also part of the dowry, was 14 in 1836. In 1856 she was a house hand, meaning she worked inside the plantation home, a job for a favored enslaved person. Sina had at least ten children; those named are Hannah, Harrison, Dave, Dilsie and Andy. A son who was probably named Bob was born in 1847 and died at the age of one. Her fifth son, not named, was born in 1848, and another was born about 1850 during the long break in Brevard's journal. Since Andy, born in 1853, was her seventh son, the child born during the journal's break was a boy. The two unnamed sons were probably Moses and John; their ages in 1856 fit those births. Stephen, her 10th child, was born in 1856 and died at the age of six months. Hannah and Andy, who would have been 13 and two, are not on the 1856 list and may have died or were living at Dickson, although it's hard to imagine a two-year-old living away from his mother. Sina was only 34 when the 1856 journal ended. She may not have been quite finished with childbearing.

In 1836 Ann was 42 and Burrow was 54. Although they are mentioned together in Brevard's journal entry in December that year, they were not married. John Springs's letter that accompanied his daughter's dowry inventory states he hoped to acquire Ann's husband, who could be traded for Wilbert. No husband is ever mentioned, and Wilbert remained Brevard's property. Ann had seven children when she came to Rural Hill: Fanny, 21; Wilbert, 15; Rhody, 12; Hannah, 10; Nancy, 7; Humphrey, 5; and Celia, 3. Wilbert is not on the 1856 list, but that year Brevard bought Wilbert a coat for $3.50, so he was probably at Dickson. Burrow is not mentioned after 1836. Fanny and Rhody must have lived at the Dickson place. Fanny had five or six children, three of whom were daughters. Two children were born at Dickson, and the births of the others were recorded a week or so after the fact, indicating they were probably also born at Dickson. Rhody had three or four children, at least two of whom were boys. Both Fanny and Rhody are mentioned several times as being at Dickson; neither lived at Rural Hill in 1856. The fact that Brevard didn't note their children's names, and was unclear about their exact number, indicates he was not as familiar with them as the people who lived "at home."

Ann's other children, Hannah, Nancy, Humphrey, and Celia, were all at Rural Hill. Hannah grew up to have five children: Amy, Henry, Ann and two other boys. In 1856 Moses was eight and may have been Hannah's son. Henry had disappeared from the record. Ann's daughter Nancy was the mother of Rufus, who was three in 1856. Hannah and Nancy each had a son in 1854; Jim was probably one of them. In March of 1856 Nancy gave birth to Lidia. Nancy died in August of that year, and Lidia died about six weeks later.

There were two enslaved women named Polly; neither is in the dowry. On 27 April 1841 "Polys child born on the 22nd of this month." She was probably at Dickson since the birth was recorded a week after the fact, and the name and gender of the child are not given. The Polly on the 1856 list was born about 1838, so she could not have been the woman giving birth three years later. The Polly who was 17 in 1856 gave birth to Green in June of that year.

In examining the available records for slave births, marriages and deaths, it is necessary to remember that in general in the antebellum period in backcountry North Carolina no formal records were kept of these events for anyone, black or white.

Brevard never noted the fathers of the enslaved children. Surely some of the men he owned were married to the women bearing children. Slave marriages were not legally binding, but they were generally recognized and honored by slave owners. This was partly for religious reasons and partly because of the belief that family life kept slaves contented and productive, which discouraged them from running away and also produced a future generation of laborers.

The scant evidence available about life in the slave cabins indicates that these people had moral codes similar to those of their owners and were often very devout Christians. Regarding marriage customs, some evidence is found of formal marriages in the slave quarters. In a few of these stories this was called "jumping the broom."

Even if the slave owners wanted to recognize the marriages, they could not because the reality was that sometimes families were broken up as a result of sales in bankruptcy or probate. The existence of a recognized marriage might have caused legal difficulties.

Very few slave deaths were recorded in Brevard's journal. We have already mentioned Sina's son and Nancy and her daughter. On 8 May 1853 Brevard noted that "Negrow boy Charles died." There is no other mention of Charles in any of Brevard's records. In November 1851 he wrote, "Peter died to day the 8th." Peter had been brought to Rural Hill from Dickson several times. He was one of the men who helped build the mill. Many enslaved people simply disappear from the records; most likely they died. There are no receipts nor any mention of Brevard's ever selling a slave nor of any running away.

The "Daily Record of Cotton Picked" in Brevard's 1856 journal provides a detailed snapshot of a portion of one cotton harvest. On the chart the names of workers are listed down the left-hand side of each page and days of the week across the top. The chart covers 22 days (Sundays excluded) from 16 September to 10 October, which was the first half of that year's harvest. It is filled in with the number of pounds picked by each person each day. Seventeen names are listed, 13 men and boys and four women; all of them did not work every day. Adam, age 42, and Phil, 27, were both wagoners and worked about half the days. Alec, 34, and Hampton, 24, were blacksmiths; Alec worked only three days, Hampton 14. These men certainly had responsibilities other than picking cotton. The other men and boys worked most days, except Jerry, 14, who picked only one day. He may have been ill. Two others were in their teens. Moses and David were eight and nine.[2]

The four women were Julia, 49, who was a weaver, and Hannah, 29; Celia, 22; and Polly, 17. Julia worked only three days; Polly worked seven. Hannah and Celia were among the most productive enslaved workers; in fact Celia picked the most cotton of all, and Hannah's total was surpassed only by Celia and two of the men. As one would expect, little Moses and David picked the least of those who worked regularly.

There were a couple of light days; it may have rained part of the day, or they may have been picking a relatively unproductive field. Altogether they picked 17,650 pounds of cotton. This was seeded cotton, which yielded about 6,000 pounds after ginning. Four weeks represents only about half a year's cotton harvest. These numbers are on a par with Brevard's typical cotton crops.

We have no concrete evidence of how Brevard treated his slaves. He never mentions punishing a slave or being dissatisfied with anyone's work or behavior. There are several mentions that other men's slaves had run away but none of Brevard's. He seems to have kept families together, valued his slaves' work, and may have felt compassion for them. The journal is businesslike; rarely are Brevard's emotions seen even when recording death or illness within his own family. He had a large farm with many acres under cultivation. In describing the multitudinous farm chores, he obviously expected diligent work from his enslaved people and the same of himself. Hard work was a fact of life.

I. Road and River Work

BY THE LAWS OF THE ROYAL COLONY of North Carolina, the county court appointed overseers, who served without pay, to lay out and maintain roads. All property owners near a road were required to provide labor (their own or that of their "hands") for the maintenance of the road. From time to time the assembly passed laws regulating roads; the laws specified the width and height to be cleared, and kept cleared, for the roads. The assembly also passed laws requiring roads to be built between two villages. The work of laying out the road was the responsibility of the counties through which it passed. Laying out a road consisted of finding the most convenient way for the road to run and clearing the trees and underbrush to the specified dimensions.[1]

In general this work did not make any excavations or move any dirt except where creek banks had to be knocked down to allow a crossing. Maintenance involved clearing fallen limbs and trees, cutting back the undergrowth, and filling in or rerouting a road after a washout. In Mecklenburg County, with its rich red clay, travelers noted that in wet weather the roads were bottomless mudholes, except on the tops of hills, where they were as slick as ice.

These were dirt or mud roads. It was not until 1830 that John McAdam of Scotland invented the process of covering roads with hand-made gravel. And not until the 20th century was tar or asphalt was applied to gravel roads to hold down the dust In Mecklenburg County in the first half of the 19th century, all roads were dirt with the exception of a few plank roads.[2]

Throughout the colonial period the assembly passed a number of laws regarding the clearing of rivers. Just as with roads, supervisors were appointed and made responsible for gathering the landowners along the river and clearing their assigned section of fallen limbs and trees. Although this was important for navigation, the stated purpose of the law was to keep the rivers clear for the passage of fish This included prohibiting any dams that stretched more than three-fourths of the way across the major rivers, including the Catawba. There were several fisheries on the Catawba, and at that time most rivers in the eastern part of the country had massive shad runs each year. There is some evidence that the Catawba yielded hundreds of barrels of salt fish per year and that running a fishery was a profitable enterprise.[3]

J. Iron Making in North Carolina

THE MANUFACTURING OF IRON and steel goods in North Carolina started in a small way just before and during the American Revolution. These furnaces were singled out for destruction by the British Army as it advanced through South Carolina and into North Carolina. William Hill had an active ironworks on Allison Creek, near the Catawba River in South Carolina on the North Carolina border. It was destroyed by a detachment of the British Legion commanded by Tory captain Christian Huck in 1780.[1]

During and after the war the North Carolina Assembly passed a number of laws to encourage the iron-making industry. In the Carolina backcountry the largest and most successful iron-making area was "the Big Ore Bank," a ridge of iron ore running southwest to northeast through Lincoln County. The earliest documented ironworks in this area was built in 1784 by William Hill for John Sloan of Lincoln County.

After the war, iron making started up in a number of places, encouraged by more laws passed by the assembly. A 1788 law granted 3,000 acres of vacant land, free of all state and local fees, and free of all taxes for ten years, to anyone who would build an ironworks. The only requirements were that the land had to be unfit for cultivation and the works had to produce 5,000 pounds of iron within three years.

By 1825 there were at least eight blast furnaces and eight forges in Lincoln County. Iron makers included Major John Davidson, along with his two sons-in-law, Alexander Brevard and General Joseph Graham, and General Peter Forney, John Sloan, James Madison Smith, John Fulenwider and others.

Many of the early settlers in this area were Palatine Germans who settled in Pennsylvania for a generation and then moved to North Carolina. They came from the iron-making region of Germany and may have brought their expertise with them.

Iron making in America in the late 18th and early 19th centuries used charcoal, iron ore and limestone combined in a blast furnace to produce cast-iron goods such as pots and pans, farming tools, wagon parts, firedogs and firebacks plus pig iron.

The blast furnaces built at that time were stone cylinders roughly 30 feet high and 10 feet in diameter. They were sited beside a hill so that the raw materials could be easily loaded at the top and near a water course for power to drive the blast of air. They required nearby deposits of iron ore and limestone plus forest land for making charcoal. Large quantities of these materials were assembled throughout the year, and the furnace was "put into blast" in the late fall or winter and was run continuously for four to six months.

The process of iron making uses iron ore, which is iron oxide with sand and other impurities, charcoal for heat and carbon, plus limestone as a flux. Air was pumped into this mixture to superheat the combustion of charcoal. This melted the iron ore and limestone and produced carbon monoxide. The carbon monoxide combined with the molten iron oxide to form iron and released impurities. The molten limestone combined with these impurities to form slag. Without the limestone, the impurities from the iron ore would not separate and would form solid inclusions in the final iron product.

As these physical and chemical reactions were taking place, the molten iron gathered at the bottom of the furnace. Floating on the iron was a layer of molten slag. Above this was the mixture of charcoal and other ingredients still undergoing reaction.

Near the bottom of the blast furnace were three holes. Highest up was the hole to allow air to be pumped, or blasted, into the furnace by bellows, usually run by a water-driven mill. Below the air inlet was a hole for drawing off the slag. Below that was a hole for drawing off the iron. In front of the furnace was a large bed of sand. Impressions were made in the sand of the items to be cast such as pots and pans, plowshares and wagon parts. A large part of the sand bed was made up of depressions in which the pig iron ingots were cast.

From time to time the ironmaster knocked out a clay plug in the slag hole to allow the slag to run out, cool and solidify so that it could be broken up and hauled away. When the slag had run out, the ironmaster inserted a new clay plug. When sufficient iron had accumulated for a run, he knocked out the clay plug in the bottom hole, allowing the molten iron to run into the impressions in the sand bed. When sufficient iron had been run out, he pushed a new clay plug into the hole.

When the cast-iron pieces had cooled enough to be handled, they were removed to be broken apart and cleaned up while the sand bed was prepared for the next run. During all this time batches of the three ingredients were being dumped into the top of the blast furnace. This process was continuous and ran night and day for the entire season of four to six months. In times of emergency such as war, some furnaces were kept in blast the year around.

The iron ingots that came from the furnace were known as pig iron. The liquid iron ran out of the furnace through a main channel to depressions in the sand arranged in rows on either side of the channel. When the iron was cooled and removed from the sand, the individual pieces of iron looked like pigs lined up to nurse at their mother. When this structure was broken up, the center piece and other scrap were recycled to the top of the furnace.

The fuel source used at this time was charcoal. In England in the early 18th century, as forests there became depleted, the furnaces began to use coal, which was processed into coke by heating in the absence of air. However, in America charcoal continued to be used as long as the forests were available since this was easier and safer work than digging in the earth for coal.

The making of charcoal was hard, hot, dirty work that went on all year long. Trees were felled, the trunks cut into four-foot lengths and split lengthwise. After a period of seasoning they were stacked on end in a mound and covered with turf and mud. A hole was left in the middle of the mound, running up to the top as a chimney and the wood pile, now called a kiln, was set on fire. The fire consumed some of the wood and heated up the rest, driving off and burning volatile gasses and leaving behind only the carbon in the form of charcoal.

The charcoal maker kept watch and adjusted the fire for several days. He opened vent holes around the bottom if the fire was not burning hot enough and closed them if it was too hot. At least once in the process the kiln became hollow, and the charcoal maker had to climb up on the burning pile and jump up and down to collapse it into a more compact form. When the charcoal maker judged that most of the wood had been converted into charcoal, he closed up the vent holes, smothering the fire and letting the charcoal pile cool. After a few days he broke open the pile, broke up the charcoal with a sledge hammer and carted it off to the blast furnace. Then the process started all over again.

Iron ore was dug out of deposits with picks. Shovels were used to lift the ore out of the deposit so that it could be broken up with sledge hammers. Likewise limestone was dug out and broken up. These ingredients, along with the charcoal, were transported to the blast furnace. In Lincoln County the iron ore came from "the Big Ore Bank" where the furnaces were built. The Big Ore Bank was a general area where most of the iron deposits lay. It includes much of present-day Lincoln and Gaston counties. It runs generally south-west to north-east through this area. It is marked by the City of Iron Station, the historic buildings of Vesuvius Furnace and Mt. Tirzah Forge and a NC State Historical Markers for Peter Forney. The NC Highway Marker reads, "Iron Works: Many iron mines and forges were operated within a radius of ten miles of this point between 1790 and 1880."

Limestone was at first transported from a deposit near Kings Mountain. Later, limestone deposits were discovered near the furnaces, reducing effort and labor costs and increasing profit.

There were usually one or more forges (industrial-scale blacksmith shops) near each blast furnace. Air was pumped, usually by water power, into a bed of burning charcoal. Iron pigs were heated in this fire to red hot and then beaten on large anvils with hammers. Often a trip hammer was used: using water power, a heavy iron hammer was lifted up and dropped on the red-hot pig iron, beating it flat. When the iron cooled during this working, it was returned to the furnace to be reheated.

The forging process reduced the amount of carbon in the iron, making it much less brittle and more malleable, or easily worked. It changed the shape of the iron into plates, bars and other shapes. This was then called wrought iron. Other operations at the forge or at blacksmith shops turned this wrought iron into finished goods such as nails, chains and wire.

If the wrought iron was heated and beaten sufficiently, it could be converted to steel. This was a complicated process requiring the expertise of a skilled steel maker.

K. The Value of Money

It is nearly impossible to determine the value of 18th-century expenditures in 21st-century money, but a familiarity with the types of money in circulation at the time can help to understand this in a general way.

In the early colonial period the official money was British pounds, shillings and pence. Twelve pence made a shilling and 20 shillings made a pound. This was "specie," "hard money" or "bullion" of gold and silver. Pennies were made of silver, were very small and very few circulated; halfpennies and farthings (quarter pennies) were made of copper, were good sized and circulated widely in Britain. The value of gold and silver coins lay in the value of the precious metal they contained; there was no royal paper money. There was no official method for distributing coins; they had to be purchased at the Tower of London. As a result there was a chronic shortage of coins of all types in parts of England remote from London.[1]

This money was symbolized as £, s and d. The pound sign (£) is a stylized *L*, which came from the Latin *libra ponde*, a pound by weight. This accounts for the abbreviation lb. for pound weight and the astronomical sign Libra, the scales. The word shilling (s) is from a German word for "divide." Varieties of this word were used in a number of European currencies. The penny (plural: pence) is from the Old English and symbolized as d, from denarius, an ancient Roman coin. There were various ways to write money amounts, but a common one was £.s.d—£10.4.8 meant ten pounds, four shillings, eight pence.

In addition to British money, there were a number of other coins in unofficial circulation. The most common was the Spanish dollar, worth eight reals (the standard Spanish monetary unit from the mid 14th century to 1868) which was sometimes cut up into eight pie-shaped pieces, each one valued as a bit. This is the derivation of the team cheer "Two-bits, four-bits, six-bits, a dollar!"

These Spanish coins were made in Mexico and Peru and were very uniform and of full weight in the amount of silver they contained. They were highly trusted, circulated widely and were common in the British colonies. Other coins such as the Dutch guilder, Portuguese crusado, French Louis d'or, German mark and many others also circulated. It took a high level of intelligence, knowledge, and calculation to do business with this mixture of coins.

In America there was always a shortage of this hard money. The theory of monetarism was prevalent in western Europe at that time. It held that the wealth of a country, and thus its prosperity and military might, lay in the amount of hard currency held within its borders. Britain was eager to take in hard money but reluctant to let any of it go, so Parliament established tariffs on goods imported into the colonies and laws prohibiting shipping hard money out of England.

Several times the royal colony of North Carolina petitioned the king to allow the importation of copper half-cents to encourage commerce, but this was denied each time. No method had been developed to move coins in quantity from one place to another, and even though these were only copper coins, this would have been a violation of the theory of monetarism.

Because of this shortage of hard money, monetary transactions were often recorded by book entry or personal note. Account books of the era show that merchants, doctors, lawyers, planters and many others had blank books in which they kept their customers' accounts and accumulated their transactions. Often the accounts were settled in December and, January when it was also customary to negotiate and sign contracts. In this way the small amount of hard money in circulation could go from hand to hand to hand, settling a whole series of debts.[2]

It is common, and attractive, to think that in these early times there was wide use of a barter system within which, say, a pound of bacon is exchanged for two pounds of wheat or some such. On the face of it this would be an awkward system as it would have required finding someone who has what you need at that time and who needs what you have to offer. We have found no contemporary evidence of such a system in general use. Rather, book entries of debit and credit were made and eventually offset against each other. Seldom was there a complete balance. One exception to this was when a miller ground corn for another farmer. He kept his toll of 5 to 10 percent of the flour as his payment.

Some debts were settled with personal notes. These could carry an interest charge but often did not. Moreover, it appears that a great many debts were never settled in hard money or notes. A few were offset by the exchange of labor or other goods, and many were settled only on the death of one of the parties. Estate papers often listed a great number of debts, credits and notes, all of which had to be settled by the executor before the estate could be closed. It sometimes took years to collect the debts and dispose of various kinds of property to settle an estate. When the movable assets of an estate were auctioned off, the payments in some cases could be by notes due in six or twelve months' time.

In 1704 Queen Anne issued a proclamation to all of the colonies establishing what came to be known as "proclamation money." This law set the value of the Spanish dollar a full 33⅓ percent above its value in silver in the hope of attracting more hard money to the colonies, which colonists would use in turn to pay their taxes and quit rents, which had to be paid in specie. Four years later Parliament extended this overvaluation to all foreign coins. Eventually the term "proclamation money," or "proc," came to be applied widely, and prices were stated in either sterling or proc.

The Value of Dollars in the several States

No. of Doll.	N. Hampsh. Massachusetts R. Island Connecticut Virginia	New-York and N. Caroline	N. Jersey Pensylvania Delaware and Maryland	S. Carolina and Georgia
1	£0..6..0	£0..8..0	£0..7..6	£0..4..8
5	1..10..0	2..0..0	1..17..6	1..3..4
10	3..0..0	4..0..0	3..15..0	2..2..6
15	4..10..0	6..0..0	5..12..0	3..10..0
20	6..0..0	8..0..0	7..10..0	4..13..4
30	9..0..0	12..0..0	11..5..0	7..0..0
40	12..0..0	16..0..0	15..0..0	9..6..8
50	15..0..0	20..0..0	18..0..0	11..13..4
60	18..0..0	24..0..0	22..10..0	14..0..0
70	21..0..0	28..0..0	26..5..0	16..6..8
80	24..0..0	32..0..0	30..0..0	18..13..4
90	27..0..0	36..0..0	33..15..0	21..0..0
100	30..0..0	40..0..0	37..10..0	23..6..8
200	60..0..0	80..0..0	75..0..0	46..13..4
300	90..0..0	120..0..0	112..10..0	70..0..0
400	120..0..0	160..0..0	150..0..0	93..6..8
500	150..0..0	200..0..0	187..10..0	116..13..4
1000	300..0..0	400..0..0	375..0..0	233..6..8

MARY BALDWIN'S ARITHMETIC BOOK, 1791. This table is in a schoolgirl's arithmetic copy book dated 12 May 1791. It shows the value of the currency of each state in Spanish dollars. These values vary from South Carolina at 4s 8d to the dollar to North Carolina at 8s to the dollar. In other words, South Carolina's currency was nearly twice as valuable as that of North Carolina. Original in the authors' possession.

In general it was not legal for the colonies to print and issue their own paper money. However, at times of war or other emergencies they were sometimes granted the ability to issue notes denominated in proc. These were a temporary expedient and were to be retired and destroyed over a few years as they came into the colonial treasury in tax payments. However, many of them were extended and continued to circulate for years, often at a highly inflated exchange rate. The currency issued in one colony was generally not accepted at face value in any other colony, which further complicated commerce. This type of paper money is known as "fiat money." It was established by government decree and was not convertible to gold or silver.

During the American Revolution fiat money issued by the Continental Congress inflated to the point where it was worth virtually nothing or, as the saying went, "not worth a Continental." The same applied to state money issued during the Revolution.

After the Revolution each state determined its own fiscal and monetary policy. State notes were issued by the state government, by individual banks and by state banks. The value of these notes varied widely from time to time compared to the Spanish dollar, which remained the reference currency as seen in a copy book of the time.

During this period most ordinary transactions continued to be by book entry or personal notes written in the currency of that state. To further confuse matters, in the antebellum period the money in circulation and in daily use was in dollars and cents, but public fines, fees and taxes continued to be denominated in pounds, shillings and pence for many years.

In looking at the old records and trying to figure out whether a person was well off or not, it is helpful to remember that during this entire time, a man's work was worth about a dollar a day for plowing, hauling and harvesting. This varied during times of war or financial panics but always returned to about the same value. Slave labor was worth somewhat less and that of a skilled craftsman, black or white, was worth more.

Remarkably the wage of a dollar a day was very much the same from the colonial period through the First World War. Eventually the United States went off the gold standard and declared that our money was no longer convertible to specie, and the currency began to inflate. We have since come to accept constant inflation, thinking that 2 or 3 percent per year is perfectly acceptable. The Federal Reserve attempts to keep inflation under control by manipulating interest rates, but from time to time inflation has been out of control, rising as high as 13 percent in 1980.

Inflation makes it very difficult to compare prices from decade to decade, much less from century to century.

L. A Confusion of Counties

TRACING COURT RECORDS, deeds and wills is made even more difficult by the fact that new counties were constantly being formed in North Carolina during these early years. As the population of a county increased due to migration from other counties or from other colonies or states, it reached a point where one county could be divided into two. Forming more counties was of benefit to people living there because the new courthouse would be closer to where they lived and because each county would have two representatives in the colonial or state assembly. In each case the assembly passed a law establishing the new county and appointed a commission to build a courthouse, prison and stocks.[1]

Anson County was formed in 1750 from Bladen County. It was named to honor George Lord Anson, admiral of the British fleet, who had sailed into the Pacific, captured a Spanish treasure ship and returned home to Britain in 1744. This new county comprised the entire territory west of the Pee Dee and Yadkin rivers. The line ran east of the Pee Dee and then continued north to the Virginia line. During the westward expansion these new county lines ran through unsettled and unexplored territory, so the boundaries were necessarily vague until they could be surveyed, which often happened many years later. The western boundary was "the Great South Sea," or the Pacific Ocean. In the backcountry the earliest settlers all lived in Anson County.[2]

By 1753 enough settlers had established themselves in Anson County that Rowan County was formed. This new county comprised all of Anson County north of the Granville County line. The eastern boundary was a line extending due north to Virginia from where the Anson County line now ended at the Granville line. The northern boundary was the Virginia line and the western boundary was the Great South Sea.[3]

The Carolina Colony was all of the land from the southern border of Virginia south to about the present-day Florida-Georgia line and extending from the "Great Ocean" (the Atlantic) westward to the Great South Sea. After King Charles II was restored to the throne in 1660 he granted all this land, in 1663, to a group of eight of his friends and supporters called the Lords Proprietors. In 1729, after trying to settle the land for 66 years, seven of the proprietors or their heirs sold their interest in the land back to King George II. One of the proprietors, Lord Carteret, wanted to keep his portion and was granted the northern one-eighth of the land. He was from a distinguished family; one of its modern descendants was Diana, Princess of Wales. Two years later Lord Carteret inherited the Granville title from his deceased mother and became the second Earl Granville.

Thus this land became known as the Granville Grant; it extended 60 miles south from the Virginia line. Although Lord Granville never set foot in America, he has the distinction of having two of North Carolina's 100 counties named for him: Carteret County on Pamlico Sound in the east and Granville County along the Virginia line in the north-central part of the state.

By 1762 there were enough settlers in the western part of Anson County that they petitioned the assembly to form a new county. A law was passed, effective 1 February 1763, forming the new county. It was all of the land south of Rowan County, north of the South Carolina line and extending to the Great South Sea. It was to be named Mecklenburg in honor of the ancestral home of the new queen of England, Princess Sophia Charlotte of Mecklenburg-Strelitz. As it happened, Admiral Anson commanded the fleet that brought Princess Charlotte from Mecklenburg to England to marry King George III in September 1761.

In 1768 Mecklenburg County was divided at the Catawba River, and the western part became Tryon County, named to honor the royal governor at the time, William Tryon. The governor had passed through this area in the fall of 1765, accompanied by the militia of Mecklenburg and Rowan counties, to negotiate a treaty with the Cherokee. He was an excellent governor for North Carolina during his tenure from 1765 to 1771. The support he received from the western counties on this expedition and during the two Wars of Regulation[4] may account for his approval of the establishment of Queens College in Charlotte in 1771.

Many place names honor him today, including Tryon County, Tryon Street in Charlotte and a number of other Tryon streets, roads and drives in North and South Carolina. Tryon Mountain marks one end of the Cherokee line that he negotiated. It is located in Polk County, where the town of Tryon, North Carolina, is today. In 1771 William Tryon was rewarded by the king for his excellent work in North Carolina and appointed royal governor of New York. He was replaced as North Carolina governor by Josiah Martin, who was not an excellent governor.

A number of counties were created during the Revolutionary War. In 1779 Tryon County was divided into two counties: Lincoln, next to Mecklenburg, and Rutherford, which is farther west. By that time Governor Tryon was an active British general in New York, and this may have contributed to the renaming of Tryon County. However, it is more likely that the name was changed to Lincoln County to honor the American general Benjamin Lincoln of Massachusetts, then commanding the Southern Army. The next year General Lincoln surrendered his army at the Siege of Charleston.

In 1788 Iredell County was formed from the western part of Rowan County, and in 1792 Cabarrus County was formed from the northeastern part of Mecklenburg. In 1842 Union County was formed out of the eastern part of Mecklenburg and the western part of Anson. In 1846 Gaston County was formed out of the southern part of Lincoln County. Some of the properties mentioned in this book as being in Lincoln County are now in Gaston County.

When the early counties were first carved from the wilderness, the land was sparsely occupied. To lay out and mark the state and county lines, a company of pioneers had to clear brush and cut trees. With no local farms or settlements the men had to bring with them all of the food required for man and beast. This added to the difficulty and expense of marking these lines, and the surveying was frequently postponed until the land was more settled and the survey party could subsist on the land.

Before these dividing lines had been marked out, it was impossible for new settlers to be sure which county or state they lived in. This caused a good deal of trouble to some of the early settlers who purchased land grants and improved their property, only to find out later they did not own clear title to their land. The most egregious example of this is the North Carolina–South Carolina line west of the Catawba River. This line was not finally agreed upon and laid out until 1771, nine years after Mecklenburg County was formed. The line was 23 miles north of where everyone knew it should have been. South Carolina termed this land "the New Acquisition," and people living in this area who had purchased their land grants from North Carolina had to buy them again from South Carolina.

These county divisions, name changes and surveys cause confusion as researchers must look in a number of places to locate the land records they need.

M. Land Acquisition by Grants and Deeds

THIS APPENDIX PROVIDES a general description of how land was acquired in the royal colony of North Carolina as well as in the State of North Carolina in the federal and antebellum periods. The details of these procedures varied from time to time during the colonial period as the king and his officers developed methods of settling this new land.

When the British colonies in North America were first established, all of the land belonged to the king, who owned it by right of conquest. The reigning monarchs at that time granted parts of the land to their supporters under the condition that they settle the land with Protestants, who would then pay an annual quitrent to the monarch.

The Carolina Colony was all of the land from the southern border of

Virginia south to about the present-day Florida-Georgia line and extending westward to the Great South Sea, or Pacific Ocean. After King Charles II was restored to the throne, he granted all this land, in 1663, to a group of eight of his friends and supporters called the Lords Proprietors. In 1729, after trying to settle the land for 66 years, seven of the proprietors or their heirs sold their interest in the land back to King George II. One of the proprietors, Lord Carteret, wanted to keep his portion and was granted the northern one-eighth of the land. When Carteret inherited the title of Lord Granville from his mother, this land was known as the Granville Grant. Land acquisition in that area was similar to that in the royal area.[1]

There were earlier methods of granting land, but by the 1750s, when people began to settle the backcountry, all land was granted as a purchase patent. A small purchase price and fees were to be paid at each step of the process. All land was subject to an annual quitrent paid to the king. A grant was the permission to purchase a certain amount of land for so many shillings per 100 acres. Most of the land Major John acquired by grant was priced at 30 shillings (one and a half pounds) per 100 acres.

To begin the process a man found a piece of land that was apparently unoccupied. He wrote out a rough description and filed an entry with the secretary of state, who presented it to the King's Council. The council approved the entry, and the royal governor issued a warrant to the surveyor general ordering him to survey the tract of land. The actual survey was performed by a deputy surveyor in the local area.

The deputy surveyor met with the potential landowner, or "grantee," to determine where the land was and who, if anyone, owned the adjacent land. Working with his survey crew, the surveyor measured out the land using a compass and a measuring chain, marked or blazed the corner trees and wrote out his description. He made a drawing of the land, which, together with the description and the estimated area, is called a plat. This listing of the land boundaries is referred to as the "metes and bounds."[2]

After North Carolina became a state in 1777, the entry was filed with the county entry taker, who ordered the county surveyor to lay out the land. The surveyor filed the plat with the secretary of state, who ensured that all fees had been paid, recorded the grant in the patent book and issued the land patent, along with a copy of the plat, to the grantee.

It was not required that the grant be registered at the county level until after 1777, though it often was done. After that time the grantee was required to register the grant with the county registrar and prove it in the county court. There was no penalty for failing to register the grant, and it was sometimes not done.

Each of these actions required payment of a separate fee. Having surveyed and registered the plot of land, the grantee now owned it in fee simple and had the right to hold, develop, sell or devise the land to his heirs.

Appendix M. Land Acquisition by Grants and Deeds 187

Land granted by the king was subject to a quitrent. This was an annual payment made by the property owner to the ling. Generally at this time it was two shillings per 100 acres per year. Quitrent was a holdover from medieval times, when favored nobles received land from the monarch and in turn owed their loyalty, including military support, whenever the monarch needed it.

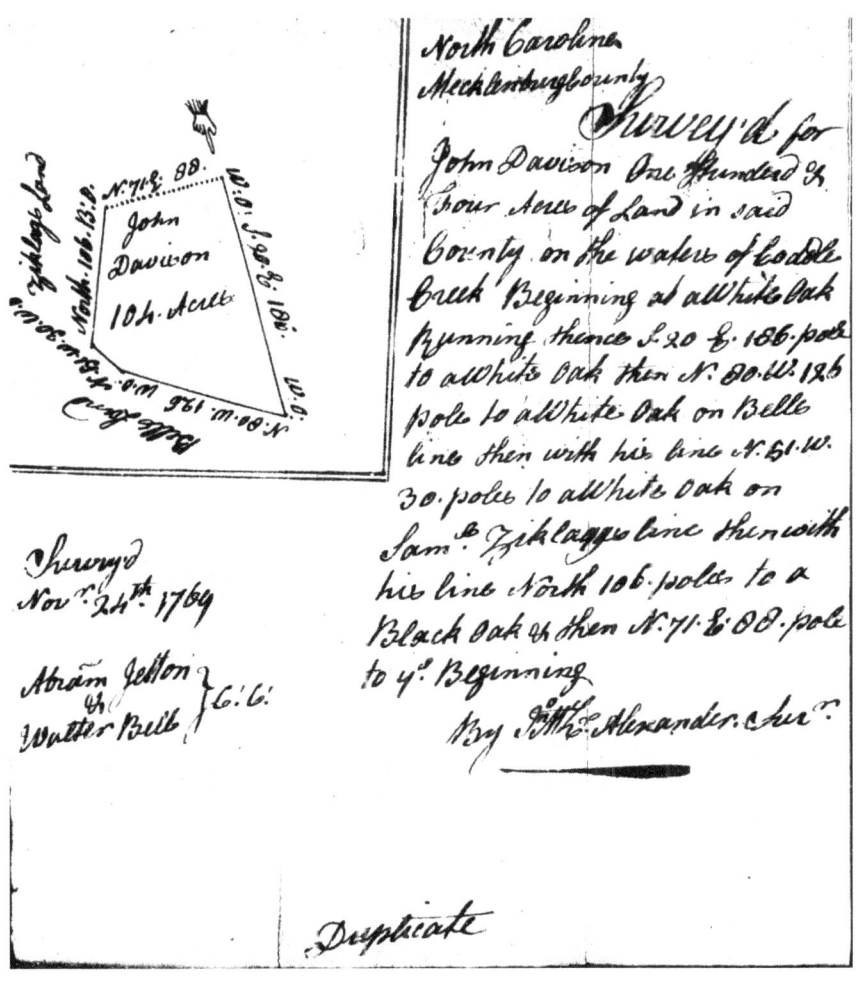

ROYAL GRANT, 24 NOVEMBER 1769, 104 ACRES. This grant on Coddle Creek to Major John Davidson may have been simply for speculation. It was acquired after he had established himself on McDowell Creek and disposed of his land on Coddle Creek. No records have been found of the disposition of this land. Image courtesy of the State Archives of North Carolina, Raleigh, NC, microfilm call # S.108.838 frame 22.

188   Appendix M. Land Acquisition by Grants and Deeds

As time went on, Britain established a standing army and the feudal system began to fade away. Military support was neither possible nor needed and was replaced by annual monetary contributions—a rent to quit the nobles of their military obligation. Quitrents were universal in the royal colonies and provided the revenue to support the colonial governments as well as the royal establishment back home. The receiver general of quitrents was a colonial official appointed by the king and had a deputy collector in

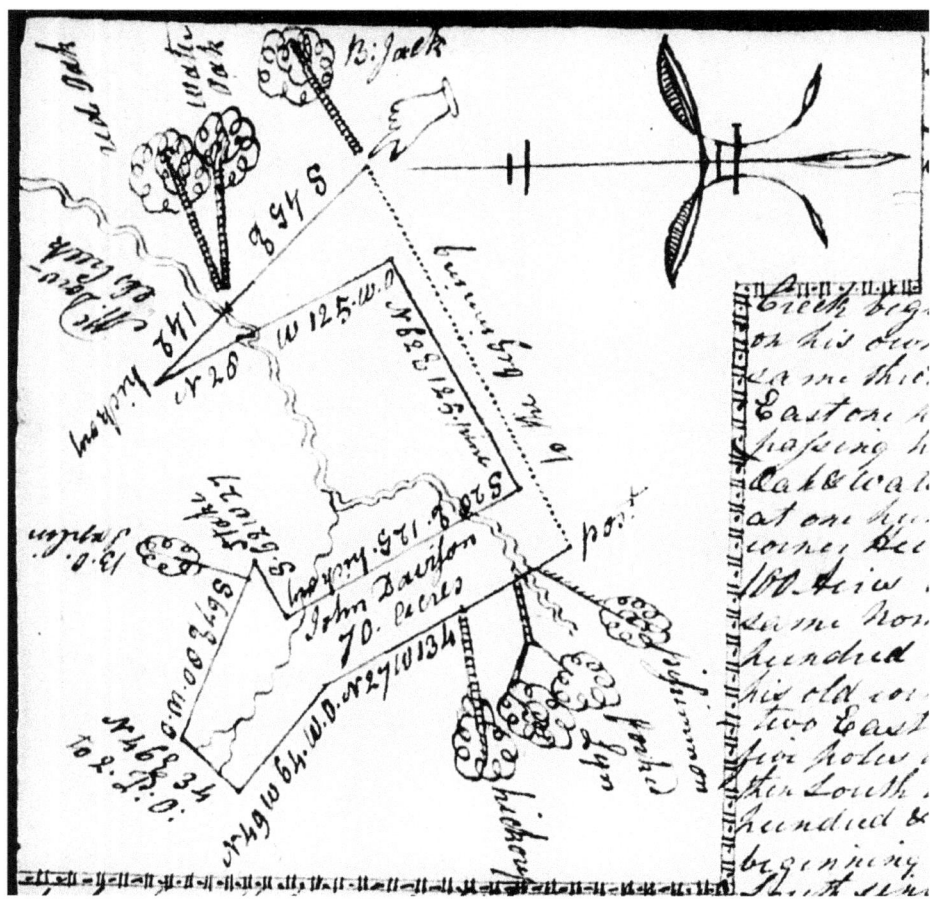

LAND GRANT TO JOHN DAVIDSON FOR 70 ACRES, 1794. In this grant on McDowell Creek, Major John claimed the vacant land surrounding his own 100 acres. The instructions to the surveyor specified that the land was "70 acres ... lying on both sides of McDowell Creek joining Richard Barry and his own 100 acres." This was sometimes known as a "fill-in" grant. Image courtesy of the State Archives of North Carolina, Raleigh, NC, microfilm call # S.108.846 frame 305.

Appendix M. Land Acquisition by Grants and Deeds

each county. The quitrents he collected were the major source of revenue for the colony. During and after the Revolution the quitrent ceased, replaced by county real estate taxes.[3]

Laws allowing the granting of vacant land continued even into the 20th century. These grants, whether issued by the King or by state governments, were signed by the governor and registered at the colony or state level.

Original grantees selected their land based on desirability: along a stream or river and suitable for farming or lumbering. As a result many of those original grants did not fully touch other grants nearby, leaving vacant land between the grants. After the land was well occupied, some enterprising individuals filed grants for the vacant land between their property and that of their neighbors. These "fill-in" grants often provide information about where the land was located. Many of the original plats still exist at the state Office of Archives and History in Raleigh, and some of these are available on the internet.

After the initial settlement of the area, land was acquired by purchase from the original grantee or from a previous owner. These purchase deeds seldom tell us anything about buildings and other improvements on the land, and when they do, they give very little information. The deed was for the land, not the house that was on the land. Some deeds mention "the Manor House," outbuildings or a mill pond, but they usually make no mention of specific improvements. As with grants, these deeds were not always recorded in the county deed books.

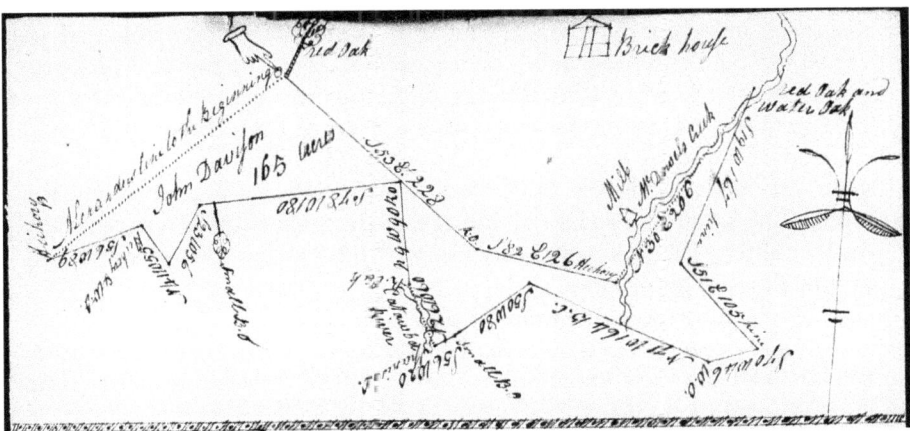

LAND GRANT TO JOHN DAVIDSON FOR 165 ACRES, 1795. This grant lay between two parcels of Major John Davidson's land and that of his neighbors David Alexander and Sam Wilson, making it another fill-in grant. Note the details of a brick house and a mill on McDowell Creek. The brick house is Rural Hill, built ca. 1788. Image courtesy of the State Archives of North Carolina, Raleigh, NC, microfilm call # S.108.846 frame 305.

The previous images show the original plats for three pieces of land granted to John Davidson; the plats were drawn and written by the prominent local surveyor John McKnitt Alexander. Note the elaborate arrows for North.

Another way to acquire land was to buy it from the University of North Carolina. When the university was founded in 1789, its charter stated that it was to receive all property that reverts to the state. This is property that comes to the state through abandonment, failure to pay taxes or from a person dying without a will and with no known heirs. The university sold this property to support its operation.[4]

As noted previously, the term "metes and bounds" refers to the surveying method used to measure the land when it is claimed or sold. The corners are marked by blazes on existing trees or by posts or rock piles. The land is described using angles and distances between these corners. This is in contrast to the later, or military, method of surveying in which the entire land is presurveyed and measured out in square-mile sections. This latter method prevailed in the new territories and states from the early part of the 19th century. Metes and bounds remained the method in the original thirteen states and is still used today.

In the very early days some of the land surveys were quite approximate. In heavily forested and undeveloped lands there was a great temptation to do an armchair or fireside survey instead of going out to mark and measure the land. A proper and complete survey required clearing all boundary lines of brush and trees in order to sight the lines and measure the angles and distances between the corners. In later years the county court often appointed a jury to procession, or remeasure, a specific piece of property to determine the correct boundaries. Often this procession found that the land contained a good deal more or less acreage than the original deed claimed. In some cases this could be as much as plus or minus 20 or 30 percent. All deeds stated the calculated or estimated acreage, and then the words "the same more or less," indicating the approximate nature of the measurement. That same phrase is used in deeds today when measurements are much more accurate.

The next image is of a modern plat from 1977.

While a grant was a document that transferred a piece of property from the king or from the state to an individual, a deed transfers property from

Opposite: A CHARLOTTE CITY DEED, 1977. **On this modern deed note that the metes and bounds are referenced to the Charlotte city streets of Wendover and Providence, the subdivision Pharr Acres and the neighboring lots. The distances are in feet, tenths and hundredths. Usually the corners are marked with steel bars driven into the ground. The surveyor H. E. McCauley has signed, sealed and dated the plat and has shown the walls of the buildings on the property. Original in the authors' possession.**

THIS IS TO CERTIFY THAT ON THE 21st DAY OF November 1977 I SURVEYED THE PROPERTY SHOWN ON THIS PLAT. AND THAT THE TITLE LINES AND THE WALLS OF THE BUILDINGS IF ANY. ARE AS SHOWN HEREON.

GENERAL SURVEYORS, INC.

SIGNED H. E. McCauley
REGISTERED SURVEYOR

NORTH CAROLINA REGISTERED L-656 LAND SURVEYOR HOWARD E. McCAULEY

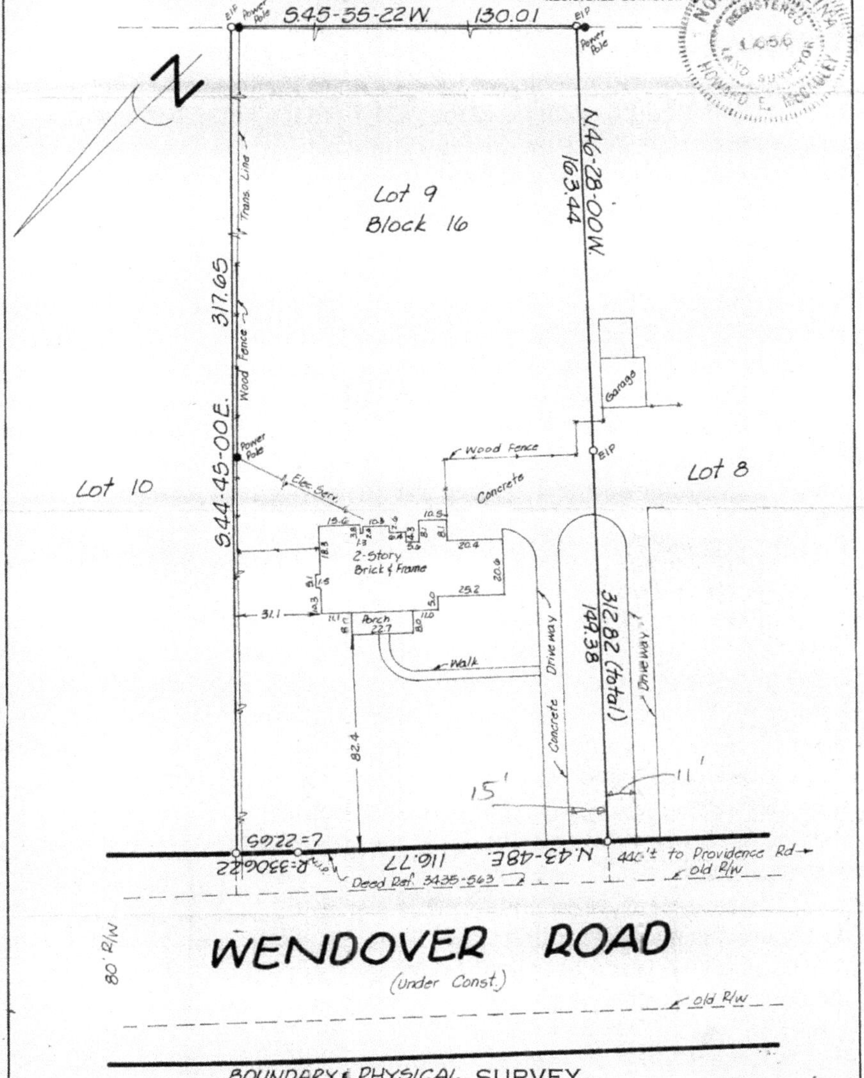

S.45-55-22W. 130.01
EIP
Power Pole
N
Trans. Line
Lot 9
Block 16
N.46-28-00W.
163.44
317.65
Wood Fence
S.44-45-00E.
Power Pole
Garage
Wood Fence
EIP
Lot 8
Lot 10
Elec. Serv.
Concrete
2-Story
Brick & Frame
Porch
22.7
31.1
Walk
Driveway
Concrete
312.82 (Total)
149.38
82.4
15'
11'
L=22.65
R=3306.22
116.77
N.43-48E.
440'± to Providence Rd
old R/W
Deed Ref. 3435-563
80' R/W
WENDOVER ROAD
(Under Const.)
old R/W

BOUNDARY & PHYSICAL SURVEY
OF

A Portion of Lot 9 Block 16 Pharr Acres

SCALE 1"=40'

CHARLOTTE, N. C.

THE PROPERTY OF James H. Williams and wife Patricia Ann Jones Williams

MAP RECORDED IN BOOK 4 AT PAGE 275 DEED RECORDED IN BOOK ______ PAGE ______

one person to another. The original deed, signed by the seller and witnesses, was kept by the buyer as proof of ownership.

In those early days the structure or organization of a deed was universal and legally required, although variations and omissions occur in some deeds. Most of that structure is still required today. It started with the date of the transaction, written out in longhand and stating both the year of the reign of the king or of the Republic and the year. Then it identified the two parties to the transaction, giving their names and stating which county and colony or state they resided in. Next it stated the amount paid for the land, that the buyer had paid the money and that the seller had received it and was fully satisfied.

Next the land was identified by listing the metes and bounds. The description started at a corner, which was, if possible, a corner of someone else's land. The description then proceeded around the land, listing the direction and distance from each corner to the next and naming property owners. Usually the description closed with the phrase "and so on to the beginning," without giving a direction or distance for this last line. Usually but not always, the description gave the estimated area of the land.

The deed closed with a long legal statement saying that the seller guaranteed to the buyer the legal right to sell the land and promised to defend the title in court if need be. The deed was signed by the seller and witnessed by two or more people.

Usually but not always, the deed was proved in court and ordered to be registered. To prove a deed in court the seller or someone who knew the seller testified that the signature on the deed was that of the seller. Often but not always, the buyer registered the deed with the county registrar, who copied it into the county deed book and returned the original to the buyer.

Occasionally a deed was registered in a different county or state than where the property was located or registered in two or more counties. Sometimes a deed was proved in court but not registered in the deed book or registered in the deed book but not proved in court.

Other types of documents were registered. Deeds of trust are legal agreements concerning things other than real estate. These could also be proved in court. Upon occasion the registrar copied miscellaneous documents into the deed books, such as proclamations by the king or by the royal governor.[5]

When a deed was proved at a county court session, only a summary of it was entered; the summary listed the names of the parties and witnesses and sometimes the acreage and price. When a deed was registered in the county deed book by the register, he copied the entire deed into the book. He sometimes made copying errors in spelling and punctuation, and phrases could be duplicated, added or dropped.

In recent years a great numbers of these deeds, court records and wills have been transcribed or abstracted for genealogical purposes. This is of great benefit to history researchers, but the abstracts sometimes leave out information vital to a complete understanding of the transactions. For very important deeds it is necessary to go to the original source and make a complete transcription. Except for a very few cases where the original deed has been preserved by the family and still exists, the county deed books are the only contemporary sources available.

Except in very few cases, the buyer of a tract was a man and only his name appears on the deed. However, the name of the seller is often accompanied by the name and signature of his wife. In some cases the wife's name appears nowhere else in the legal record, since at this time marriage licenses did not exist and no official record was kept of marriages. On some occasions a jury was appointed to interrogate the wife separately from her husband to make sure that she had signed the deed of her own free will. This was reported to the court and entered into the court minutes.

N. Major John's Earliest Land Transactions

THE EARLY HISTORIES describing John Davidson's life in the Carolina backcountry were written more than a hundred years after the fact. Original records have always existed in grants, deeds, wills and court minutes, but they have been difficult or nearly impossible to access in any meaningful manner. In recent years genealogists have abstracted or transcribed many of these original records in search of genealogical information. The books by Herman W. Ferguson, Jo White Linn, Brent H. Holcomb and others are generally reliable, but the original documents should be examined and transcribed to gain a full understanding and identify errors of fact or interpretation. Fortunately many of these records are now imaged and available online. This appendix describes some errors made by various authors regarding the earliest Davidson family land transactions.

There are a number of real estate transactions in the records of Anson, Rowan and Mecklenburg counties that document the first few years of Major John's adult life, when he was getting started as a farmer and laying the foundation for his later success. These bear looking into in some depth as they illustrate how a young man whose father had died many years before could begin life with no assets and make his way in the world.

This appendix contains summaries of eight of these deeds, followed by complete transcriptions of the originals. These deeds contain long traditional legal passages that vary slightly from deed to deed; we have replaced these passaged with ellipses, except in one case, that of the first deed on McDowell Creek.

The transcriptions of these deeds lead to a fuller understanding and in general present a very different picture of the beginnings of this family than that told in family stories and early commentaries. These old stories begin with Major John's marrying Violet Wilson in 1761 and receiving a gift of land on McDowell creek from her father. They completely ignore Major John's beginnings on Coddle Creek and get the origin of Rural Hill wrong.

John Davidson bought his first plot of land in 1759 on Coddle Creek in the Yadkin River Valley. This was in that part of Anson County that would become Mecklenburg four years later and on the border of Rowan County. He started farming this land and, after he and Violet married in 1761, continued to live there for three and one-half years. Two of their 10 children were born on that property. In 1765 John bought 250 acres of land on McDowell Creek from his father-in-law for £45. There he built the cabin later called Rural Retreat and moved his family from Coddle Creek.[1]

17 April 1759

John was 23. He was trained as a blacksmith and worked at that trade until he accumulated sufficient funds to purchase land and become established. Only then could he marry and begin his family.

This deed was for 300 acres on Coddle Creek in Anson County. He bought it from John Dunn, Esquire, and paid £50 for it. The land was on both sides of Coddle Creek, below Joseph Tanner's bridge and mill. This land is today in Cabarrus County and lies just south of the Iredell County line.

As shown in the deed, this land was originally a royal grant purchased in 1751 by Henry Hendry, who by 1759 was John's stepfather. The land grant was registered in the deed books of Anson County in 1751 but does not appear in the North Carolina Land Patent Books.

Hendry lost this land in a lawsuit brought by, among others, Samuel Wilson, John's future father-in-law. The land was auctioned by the Anson County sheriff and purchased by John Dunn, register of deeds for Anson County. The deed for John's purchase was witnessed by Henry Hendry.

The early court records of Anson County are missing so we know nothing more about the suit, but it is interesting to note that John Davidson's first purchase of property was for land that had been taken from his stepfather in a court case by his future father-in-law.

This deed is the earliest known document that refers to John Davidson as "blacksmith." This may have been to distinguish him from other John Davidsons in that county at that time.

Presumably John started farming this land while he continued his blacksmith business. He may have continued to live with his mother, sister and stepfather on an adjacent property and may have begun to build a cabin for his future wife and children.

2 June 1761

On this date, two and one-half years later, John and Violet were married and went to housekeeping on his land on Coddle Creek. Their first two children, daughters Rebecca and Isabella, were born there. Violet's family lived on McDowell Creek, about 15 miles away: these people were all close neighbors.

20 July 1762

One year after he married Violet, John purchased a small parcel of 19 acres and 20 pearches in Rowan County for £2.8 from Thomas McQuoun. This plot was part of the 640 acres owned by McQuoun adjacent to Henry Hendry. A pearch or perch is a standard measure of length equal to 16.5 feet and is also known as a rod. In this deed it refers to an area of twenty square pearchs.

16 January and 23 February 1765

Three and one-half years after his marriage to Violet, John Davidson bought land on McDowell Creek and sold his land on Coddle Creek in a total of three transactions. He spent £45 for the one and received £50.5.0 for the other two. These three transactions occurred within a period of four and a half weeks, and the conditions attached to them illustrate the sophistication of John Davidson's land transactions at a young age.

16 January 1765

On this date John Davidson purchased a plot of land from his father-in-law, Samuel Wilson, for £45. This was for 250 acres in Mecklenburg County on McDowell Creek, very near the Wilsons.

This deed is the only mention in the public record of the given name of Samuel Wilson's second wife, which is given as "Sarah his wife" throughout. Early histories say that her family name was Howard but that her given name was not known. In this deed John Davidson's name is spelled "Davison" and Samuel Wilson's name is spelled both "Willson" and "Wilson."

John Davidson built the home, later called Rural Retreat, about the same time. This piece of land and the houses built on it would be the center of the Major John Davidson's Rural Hill plantation for generations to come.

23 February 1765

Just a month after buying the land on McDowell Creek, John, along with his mother and stepfather, sold a piece of land. In this transaction Henry Hendry; his wife, Isabel; and John Davidson sold 180 acres to John Neichler for £50.5.0. The land was part of Hendry's original land grant on the west side of Coddle Creek and part of the 300 acres that Davidson bought in 1759. This deed is the only place that Isabella is identified as being married to Henry Hendry and gives no indication of how long they had been married.

In this deed John Davidson's name is spelled "Davidson" five times and "Davison" four times and his mother, Isabel Hendry, is referred to as " Isabel twice," "Esabel" three times and "Esbel," once, in her signature.

Apparently Hendry had retained some claim to this land, which started at the north end of Hendey Hendrys Lane (spelled Leann) at Thomas McQuown's Plantation, ran down to the lower survey and mentions buildings and an orchard.

A provision in this deed allowed John Davidson to build a dam on the branch, a little above the old dam, in order to water his meadow on the lower survey. This branch may have been Coddle Creek or one of its tributaries. The deed also provided that John Davidson could use a hog yard as long as an old barn "continued."

23 February 1765

On the same day as the previous transaction John Davison sold "19 acres and 20 perches" to the same John Neichler for the nominal amount of five shillings. This plot was adjacent to the land described in the previous deed but was located in Rowan County and so required a separate deed and registration in the Rowan County Deed Books.

20 October 1765

Nine months after John bought the land on McDowell Creek from his father-in-law, he and his wife, Violet, sold some of his land on Coddle Creek to James Ker and John Murphy. The land amounted to 228 acres and was sold for £140. John had owned the land for six and a half years and had originally paid £50 for 300 acres. This sale yielded him a profit of 270 percent, which is not a bad return in that short period.

LAND GRANT TO JOHN DAVIDSON FOR 104 ACRES, 1769. This is a fragment of the full plat shown in Appendix M, "Land Acquisition by Grants and Deeds." Although Major John may have farmed, or planned to farm, this land, it is probable that this was simply speculation. No records have been found of the disposition of this land. It was surveyed by the prominent local surveyor and planter John McKnitt Alexander. Image courtesy of the State Archives of North Carolina, Raleigh, NC, microfilm call # S.108.838 frame 22.

Appendix N. Major John's Earliest Land Transactions

The deed ensured that Joseph Tanner would have full use of the waters of Coddle Creek to support a mill dam and mentions a deed dated 1 May 1762. This earlier deed was not recorded in the Anson County Deed Book at the time and is not known to have survived. Although it was required that all deeds be recorded, many were not. The deed also mentions Joseph Tanner's Bridge on Coddle Creek as the upper boundary of the land.

In this deed Violet Davison signed her name rather than making her mark, indicating that she was literate.

16 December 1769

Three years later John had one more land transaction on Coddle Creek. He filed an entry for 104 acres, had the land surveyed and purchased that grant.

Abstracts and Transcriptions of the Deeds

17 April 1759
See next two pages for images of 1759 deed.

20 July 1762

This Rowan County deed was abstracted by Jo White Linn and contains a significant errors of fact. The abstract says that the land being sold is "...where sd McGuown now lives, known as Henry Hendry's plantation...." The complete transcription says that the land is that "...which the sd Tomas McQuown Now lives on, lying on the south thereof Joining to that place Commonly Known by Henry Hendry's Plantation...." The lesson is that genealogical transcriptions can be useful, but one must always make a complete and accurate transcription of the original deed to gain a full understanding.[2]

From the deed:

> This Indenture made this 20th Day of July in the year of our Lord God One Thousand Seven Hundred & Sixty Two Between Thomas McQuown of Rowan County and province af^{sd} of the one part, and John Davison Blacksmith of Anson County of S^d province of the other part Witnesseth, that the s^d. Thomas McQuoun for & in Consideration of the sum of Two pounds Eight shillings pro^c. Money ... Hath Granted Sold ... a piece or parcel of Land being part of the Plantation which the s^d Tomas McQuown Now lives on, lying on the south thereof Joining to that place Commonly Known by Henry Hendry's Plantation, and Granted to the s^d. Thomas McQuown by the right Hon^{bl} John Earl Granville, Viz Count Carteret's Deed of Sale, bearing Date the 25th Day of March in the year of our Lord 1752 Begining at a Spanish Oak on the s^d. Thomas McQuowns South Line, Running thence West 102 perches to a pine, thence North 30 pearches to a White Oak, thence running East 102 Pearches to White Oak Containing Nineteen Acres & Twenty pearches; To Have & To Hold.... Signed.... Thos McQuown ... [witnessed] James Price, Henry Hendry.... July Court ... proved ... James Price, and recorded.... John Frohock CC

31   JOHN DUNN to JOHN DAVIDSON

NORTH CAROLINA

THIS INDENTURE made this 17th day of April in the year of our Lord 1759 Between John Dunn Esqr. of Rowan County and province aforesd of the one part and John Davidson of Anson County and province aforesd black smith of the other part. WITNESSTH that the sd John Dunn for and in consideration of the sum of Fifty pounds proclamation money to him in hand paid by the sd John Davidson before the Ensealing and delivery of these presents the receipt where of he the sd John Dunn doth hereby acknowledge and himself therewith fully paid and satisfied and contented hath granted bargained sold aliened and confirmed and by these presents doth grant bargain sell alien and confirm unto the sd John Davidson his heirs and assigns all and singular the piece or parcel of land granted to Henry Hendry by his Majesty patent bearing date the 27 day of September in the 25th year of our reign A. D. 1751 and sold at publick vendue by the sheriff of Anson County by virture and strength of execution obtained and recovered in the Court of Anson at the suit of Samuel Wilson Samuel McCleary &C against the goods and chattels lands and tenements of the sd Henry Hendry and bought by the sd John Dunn at the vendue being the highest bidder the sd tract or parcel of land containing Three Hundred acres lying and being in the County of Anson Beginning at Thomas McQuawns giving line lying on both sides of Coddle Creek running down for the complement at a red oak runs Wt. 240 poles to a white oak thence So. 16 Et. 200 poles to a hickory then Et. 240 poles to a pine then to the beginning be the same more or less. TO HAVE AND TO HOLD the sd hereby bargained lands improvements buildings orchards meadows waters & watercourses and premises and every part and parcel thereof unto the sd John Davison his heirs and assigns and to his and their proper use and behoof forever and the sd John Dunn for himself and his heirs Exers. and Admrs. doth hereby covenant and grant to and with the sd John Davison his heirs and assigns that he the sd John Davison his heirs and assigns shall and may at all times hereafter have hold and enjoy the sd hereby bargained premises with the appurtenances free and clear of all former grants bargains sales dowers judgements executions incumbrences whatsoever the quitrents becoming due to his Majestybis heirs and successors only excepted and further that he the sd John. Dunn and his heirs and all and every other person & persons his and their heirs any thing having or claiming in the sd premises above mentioned or any part thereof by from or under him them or any of them their or any of their heirs except as before excepted shall and will from time to time and at all hereafter upon the reasonable request and at the cost and charges of the sd John Davison his heirs and assigns make do and execute all and every such further and other lawfull and reasonable act and acts thing and things conveyance and conveyances in law for the further better and more perfect granting conveying and assuring of all and singular the sd premises above mentioned with the appurtenances unto the sd John Davison his heirs and assigns and to his and their only proper use and behoof forever according to the true intent and meaning of the a presentses by the sd John Davison his heirs or assigns or his or thier Council Learned in the law shall be reasonably advised or required. In witness whereof the sd John Dunn..to these presents have here-

58

unto set his hand and seal the day and year first above written.
Signed sealed and delivered in the presence of us
James Gount
Henry Hendry   John Dunn   (Seal)

Opposite and above: ANSON COUNTY DEED, 17 APRIL 1759. This deed is registered in the deed books of Anson County, Volume 6, page 57 and 58, and is for the land on Coddle Creek, the first parcel of land that Major John ever purchased. He was 23 at the time and not yet married. At some point the Anson County registrar had the original recorded deeds transcribed. This is highly unusual in North Carolina and it is unknown whether the original records still exist. This transcription has some problems with typographical errors and worn or broken typewriter characters. Image courtesy of the State Archives of North Carolina, Raleigh NC, microfilm, Deeds, Anson County.

16 January 1765

This deed for the land where Major John would build Rural Retreat and Rural Hill was abstracted by Brent H. Holcomb and Elmer O. Parker. That abstract reads:

> Mecklenburg Deeds, 16 January 1765, 2:291–92. "Samuel Wilson & wf Sarah of Meck., to John Davison of same, for £45.. 250 A on McDowells Creek, about ¼ mile below his own line, adj. George Cathey, Senr. granted 1 Sept 1753 ... Samuel Wilson (seal), Sarah Wilson (seal), Wit: James Aston, Hance Mac Whorter, Hen. Hendry.[3]

Because of the importance of this deed to the Davidson family, a complete transcription by the authors follows. This transcription includes all of the legal boilerplate that is in most deeds. Most other transcriptions in this book replace this boilerplate with ellipses.

From the deed in Mecklenburg County Deed Book, 2:291–92:

> This Indenture made this sixteenth Day of January in the year of our Lord one Thousand Seven Hundred and Sixty five Between Wilson and Sarah his Wife of Mecklenburg County and province of North Carolina of the one part and John Davison of the Same County and province And afors^d. of the other part Witnesseth that they S^d. Samuel Willson & Sarah his Wife for and in Consideration of the sum of forty five pounds Current Money of the province Afors^d. to them in hand paid by the said John Davison the Receipt Where of the they s^d. Samuel Wilson and Sarah his Wife Doth hereby acknowledge and themselves there with fully Satisfied hath Granted Bargained Sold Aliened & Confirmed and by these presents Doth Grant Convey Sell Alien and

Confirm Unto the S^e. Jno Davison to him his heirs and Assigns for Ever Claim tract or parcel of Land Situate Lying and Being in y^e. County and province Afs^d. Beginning at M^r McDowels Creek about a Quarter of a mile Below his own Line at a Red oak and Runs North 40 W 8 poles to a hikory thence N 87 Wst 44 poles to a Red oak then N°. 76 W 100 poles to a Red oak thence N. 56 W. 36 poles to a hickory on the River then Down the River S. 63 W 22. poles to a Spanish oak George Cathys [illeg] Corner then along his Line So 5 W 79 poles to a Red oak then South 74 W 185 poles to a Red oak then So 20 E 100 poles to a hickory on McDowls Creek then up its Several Courses to the first Station Containing 250 acres of Land be the Same more or Less the sd. Land being Granted by his majesty Patton Bearing Date the first Day Sepr. in the year of our Lord one thousand Seven hundred and fifty Three as by the Said patent may more fully and at Large Appear together With all the profits Commodities advantages hereditaments Ways Waters Water Coursed and Appurtenances Whatsoever to the Said to the Said Tract of Land and premises above mentioned Belonging or in any Way Appurtaing and also the Reversion and Reversions Remainder and Remainders Rents and Services of the said Land and of Every part and parcel thereof and all the Estate Right Title Interest property Claim and Demand Whatsoever of them the S^d. Samuel Wilson and Sarah his Wife of in or to the S^d. tract of Land and premises and Every part thereof to have and to hold y^e. s^d. tract of Land and all and Singular the s^d. premises Above mentioned and Every parcel thereof the Quitrents Becoming Due and payable to our sovereign Lord the King his heirs and Successors only Excepted and [illeg] With the Appurtenances unto the Sd. John Davison [next page] Davison his heirs and Assigns to the only higher Use and Behoof of him the Said John Davison his heirs and Assign for Ever and the said Samuel Wilson and Sarah his Wife for them and their heirs ye s^d. land and premises and Every part and parcel thereof Ag^{n}st them and their heirs & Assigns & against all & Every person and persons Whatsoever to the S^d. John Davidson to him his heirs Exr^s. Adm^{rs}. or assigns Shall and Will Warrant and for Ever Defend and upon the Reasonable Request Cost and Charges in the Law of the S^d. John Davison his heirs or Assigns Shall and Will Sign Seal and Deliver any [illeg] further and other Reasonable Instruments or of Writing Whatsoever for the further and better Assurences and Conssideration of the hereby Granted Premises With the Appurtenances Unto the said John Davidson his heirs or assigns as by him or Them or by his or their Counsel Learned in the Law Shall or may Be Reasonably advised or Required In Witness Whereof the Sd. Samuel Wilson and Sarah his Wife hath hereunto set their hands and Seals the Day and year first Above Written

Signed Seald and Delivered }	Samuel Wilson (Seal)
	Sarah Wilson (Seal)
In presence of	
James Aston	Mecklenburg County
Hance MacWhorter	The Clerks record of the probate
Hen. Hendry	of this Deed is lost
	Test Wm B Alexander Clk

23 February 1765

This deed was abstracted by Holcomb and Parker, but the abstract is wrong in an important way. It makes it appear that Henry and Isabel Hendry sold the land to John Davidson and John Niechler.[4] A close reading of the

Appendix N. Major John's Earliest Land Transactions

deed makes it clear that the Hendrys and John Davidson sold the land to John Niechler. For this reason a complete transcription follows.

Note that John had purchased 300 acres on Coddle Creek for £50 six years before this date. In this transaction he sold 180 of those acres for £50, which replenished the £45 he had used to buy the land on McDowell Creek just one month earlier.

Also note that Isabel Hendry signed with a mark, perhaps indicating that she was not literate. This is the usual interpretation applied by many historians to such a mark.

From the deed in Mecklenburg County Deed Books, 2:268.

This Indenture Made this 23^d Day Feby in the Year of our Lord one thousand Seven hundred and Sixty Five Between Henry Hendry and Isabel his Wife and John Davison all of the Province of North Carolina in Mecklenburg County of the one Part and John Neichler of the Same Province and County of the Other Part Witnesseth that the said Henry Hendry and Isabel his Wife and John Davison for and in Consideration of the Sum of Fifty Pounds Current Money of the said Province Paid to them in hand by the said John Neichler.... Hath Granted Bargained sold Aliened and Confirmed.... Unto to the said John Neichler to him his heirs Ex^{rs} and assigns forever a Certain Tract or Parcel of Land Scituate Lying and being in the Province and county Af^{sd} on the West Side of Coddle Creek being Part of the Two Surveys Granted to the said Henry Hendy by his Majesties Patent the Lower Survey being Taken by Virtue of an Execution Directed to the Sherriff of Anson County and sold by the said Sheriff unto M^r. John Dunn attorney the Said John Dunn sold the said Survey unto the Within Mentioned John Davidson by Deed of Conveyance as by the said Deed may More fully and at Large appear Containing in the Whole one hundred and Eighty acres of Land be the same more or Less Beginning at a Sasafras at the North End of the Leann known by the Name of Henry Hendrys Learn and Joining To Thomas McQuowns Plantation Runing thence S° 20 W. 48 Poles to a stake thence S° 12 W 34 Poles to a hickory thence S° 20 W 96 Poles to a White Oak Corner of the Lower Survey then N. 75 W 128 Poles to a Then N 45 W 30 Poles to a White Oak then N 5 E 100 Poles to a Black Oak thence to the Beginning Together With all the Buildings Orchards ... of them the said Henry Hendry & Esable his Wife and John Davison of in or to the said Tract of Land and Premises and every Part and Parcel thereof of the Quit Rents Becoming Due and Payable to our Sovereign Lord the King his heirs and Successors only Excepted and [illeg] its Further Excepted unto the said John Davison to him his heirs & assigns forever full Power Priviledge and Liberty to Erect Build and support a Damm on the Branch a Little above the Old Dam in Order to Water Meadow Ground on the Lower survey as also the Benefit of Hog yard During the Continuance of the Old Barn With all the Rest of the Appurtenances unto the John Neichler his heirs and assigns forever.... In Witness Whereof the said Henry Hendry Esable his Wife and John Davidson Hath hereunto Set their hands and seals the Day & year above Writen

Signed Sealed & Delivered	Henry Hendry (seal)
	her
In Presence of	Esbel X Hendry (seal)
Thomas M'Quown	mark
Hugh M'Quown	John Davison (seal)

Mecklenburg County
The Clerks record of the
Probate of this Deed
Is lost
Test W^m. B. Alexander Clk

23 February 1765

On the same day that John Davidson with his mother and stepfather sold the land to John Neichler, John Davidson sold "19 acres and 20 perches" to the same John Neichler for the nominal amount of five shillings. This plot was adjacent to the previous deed but was located in Rowan County and was recorded in the Rowan County Deed Books.

Rowan County Deed Book, 6:310. From the deed:

> This Indenture made this 23^d Day of Feb^r in the year of our Lord 1765 between John Davison of the province of North Carolina in the County of Mecklenburg of the one part and John Neichler of the same province & County of the other part Witnesseth that the s^d John Davidson for & in Consideration of the Sum of five Shillings Proc^l paid ... by the s^d John Neichler ... hath granted sold ... land in Rowan County & province af^{sd} being part of the Tract of Land Thomas McQuown now lives on and Joining to a Tract of Land now Granted & Sold by Henry Hendry & the S^d John Davison by Deed of Conveyance bearing Even Date with these presents Beginning at a Spanish Oak on the Sd Thomas McQuown's South line.... Containing Nineteen Acres & twenty perches.

20 October 1765

From the deed in Mecklenburg County Deed Books 1:202–204:

> This Indenture made this Twentieth Day of October one thousand Seven hundred and Sixty five Between John Davison and Violet his wife of the Province of north Carolina & Mecklenburg County of the one Part and James Kerr and John Murphey of the said Province and County a^f.s^d. of the other Part Withesseth that for and in Consideration of the Sum of one hundred and forty Pounds Current money of the Said Province Paid to them in hand by the Said James Kerr and John Murphey.... Hath Granted Bargained sold alienated and Conformed ... a Certain Tract or Parcel of Land.... Beginning at Thomas McQuowns Giving Line on both sides of Coddle Creek Runing ... Down Said Creek ... [metes and bounds] ... to a lain known by Henry Hendrys Lain at a Sasafras ... [metes and bounds] ... East Side of Coddle Creek below Joseph Tanners Bridge from thence to the Beginning Containing by Estimation Two hundred and Twenty Eight acres ... being Part of a Tract of Land Granted by his majesties Patent to Henry Hendry Bearing Date the 27th Day of Sept. in the year of our Lord one thousand Seven hundred and fifty one and then the Said Land and Premises Sold at Public Vendue by the Sherriff of Anson County by Virtue and Strength of an Execution obtained and Recovered in the Court of Anson a^f.s^d. at the Suit of Samuel Wilson & Samuel McCrory &c ... and bought by John Dunn Esqr. At s^d. Vendue being the Highest Bidder and then Sold by the Said John Dunn Unto the Said John Davison by Deed of Conveyance Bearing Date the 17th Day of April in the Year of our Lord one thousand seven hundred and fifty Nine.... Together With all the Hereby Bargained Land Buildings houses Orchard Meadows Water and Water Courts ... the Quit Rents becoming Due and Payable to our Sovereign Lord the King only Excepted and [illeg]

its also Excepted Unto Joseph Tanner full [illeg] Privilege and advantage of the aters of Coddle Creek in order for the Supporting of the Mill Dam as the same is bounded Granted and Conveyed by John Davison unto the Said Joseph Tanner by Deed of Conveyance Bearing Date the first Day of may 1762 ... In Witness Whereof the said John Davidson and Violet his Wife have hereunto Set their hands and Seals the Day and year above Written

<table>
<tr><td>Signed Sealed & Delivered
In the Presence of
Thomas McQuown
Henry Hendry</td><td>John Davison—Seal
Violet Davison—Seal</td></tr>
</table>

O. Land Acquisition by Robert Davidson

DURING HIS LIFE Robin Davidson acquired a great deal of land, including a number of fisheries on the Catawba River. His land acquisition and ownership, as documented primarily in grants and deeds, gives an interesting view of his life.

Robin began, at the age of 23, by filing for a state grant for 93 acres of vacant land adjacent to his father's plantation. He filed for the grant in 1792 and it was issued two years later. Seven months after he received the grant, he sold one-third of that land to his father for the nominal sum of five shillings. On that same day he received a very large gift of land from his father.[1]

This was the only land Major John ever gave away until he retired and dissolved his holdings in 1823. He gave Robin "for & in consideration of the love & affection which he hath & beareth towards the sd Son & for other considerations" 430 acres of improved land "on the Cataba river including his own improvements" in three tracts. The metes and bounds of this land show a good deal of river frontage, and this may have been for a fishery as well as a plantation.

Eleven months later Robin joined with a man named Samuel Wilson to buy a fishery on the Catawba River. This was probably Robin's uncle, who was 46 at the time. The land was below Tool's Ford, where Robin's land lay, and was 23 acres, mostly underwater. They bought it at a sheriff's auction for 25 shillings. This was the only time that Robin ever went into a partnership with anyone, and he may have done it to learn the business of harvesting and selling the annual shad run. There is no recorded deed showing when or how this partnership was dissolved.[2]

Robin continued to buy property and by the age of 32, shortly after he was married, owned 1,221 acres, more land than his father owned at the time. In 1819, at the age of 50, Robin gave 40 acres to his brother Jacky, "for love and affection." This was the same year that Major John made provisions for his two other sons, and this may have been part of that complicated land swap and sale. At the age of 56 Robin bought one large island and several small ones in the Catawba below Cowan's Ford. He may have been continuing to expand his fishery, as the same year he bought a tract of 300 acres on the Catawba, including a fishery. He continued to build his plantation up to the age of 77 when it reached a total of 2,615 acres, or four square miles of land.

The details of Robin's land acquisition illustrate the arc of his life and the building of his fisheries.

- 1794, age 25, 93 acres by state grant as mentioned previously.
- 1795, age 26, the sale to and gift from his father. The sale was for the nominal sum of 5 shillings. The gift was free.
- 1796, age 27, in partnership with Samuel Wilson. 25 Shillings.
- 1798, age 29, 375 acres on McDowell Creek from the University of North Carolina for £200.

The law establishing the university gave it title to all abandoned land. When someone died with no living heirs or left the area without disposing of their land, their property reverted to the university, which then could sell the land to support itself.

- 1801, age 32, 303 acres from Adlai Osborne for $140.
- 1801, 51 acres on McDowell Creek near Hugh Torrence from William Waddle for $50.
- 1807, 155 acres on the Catawba River from Isaac Alexander for $1,000.
- 1807, 175 acres on McDowell Creek from Francis and Jane Bailey for $2,700. Considering the prices paid for these two plots in 1807, they may have made up another "fishing."
- 1819, a state grant of 70 acres on the Catawba River for 35 shillings.
- 1819, Robin gave 40 acres on the river to his brother Jacky "for love and affection." Jacky was 40, and the deed was dated within a week of Robin's 50th birthday.
- 1821, 10 acres on McDowell Creek from the estate of John McKnitt Alexander for $10.
- 1824, 130 acres on the headwaters of McDowell Creek from John Kenmer of York, South Carolina, for $400.
- 1825, 177 acres on the Catawba River from Abner Franklin of Iredell County for $1,200. Perhaps another fishery.[3]

- 1825, 29 acres containing the big island and several small islands in the Catawba River at Cowan's Ford from Abner Franklin of Iredell for $50. Despite the small price this may have been a fishery. He may have farmed the big island which was part of the ford and therefore accessible although that was probably subject to flooding in times of high water.
- 1825, 300 acres including fisheries on the Catawba River in four surveys from the estate of Wm. Henderson for $7,740 in three equal annual installments. This amount seems extraordinarily high but the amount is very clearly written in the deed. The fisheries must have produced a very good income to justify this high a price.
- 1836, 169 acres from Solomon Sifford for $597.
- 1843, A parcel of land on the Catawba for $4,000. The recorded deed does not state the acreage but it was purchased from William Johnson of Lincoln County and in his will Robin states that the "Johnson tract" was 200 acres.
- 1846, 115 acres on McDowell Creek from David A. Caldwell for $200.[4]
- 1852: Robin wrote his will at the age of 83 and made almost all of the bequests effective as of that date. In this way it was more a retirement distribution than a will. In 26 bequests he distributed 2,131 acres of land in nine tracts plus one tract of 500 to 600 acres and one tract for which he did not state the acreage.

P. Courts and Legal Structure

IN THE ROYAL COLONY of North Carolina the laws and legal structure were modeled on that of England and on "The Fundamental Constitutions of Carolina," written by John Locke in 1669. The Lords Proprietors attempted to follow Locke's constitution but finally gave up the effort in 1702. By the time the Carolina backcountry was settled, the laws of North Carolina were based on English common law with appropriate variations for local conditions.[1]

Less than one year after William Tryon became governor in 1765, he had Patrick Duff Gordon, a prominent lawyer in Newbern, write a report describing the laws and court structure of the colony, which the governor sent on to the Board of Trade in England.[2]

Gordon was an interesting person. Of a wealthy and prominent family in Scotland, he was trained in the law and became a prominent lawyer in Edinburgh. He married well and had one child, but both his wife and child died early. Gordon began gambling and soon lost his entire fortune and the fortunes of his friends. Marrying a household servant, he fled to America where he changed his name from Patrick Gordon Duff to Patrick Duff Gordon. He came to Newbern, where he prospered, serving a short time in the assembly and practicing law.[3]

The common laws of North Carolina changed from time to time, usually based on the ideas of the governor, council and assembly as to what was fitting and proper. Some of the laws were in effect only until the next meeting of the assembly, when they were renewed, often with minor changes. As the colony grew and population increased, with new counties being formed, the laws needed to be changed to accommodate and match the new structure. Gordon's description applies to the operation of the laws in 1750 and as they remained until 1777.

In 1748, under Governor Gabriel Johnston, the assembly passed a law establishing the fees for all public offices and services. Tables of these fees were to be posted in public places, and all officers were to charge these fees and none other. From the wording of the law it appears that excessive fee taking had been going on, causing upset in the province. This excessive fee taking was one of the main factors that led to the Regulator movement in Orange County 20 years later.[4]

There were a total of 242 fees listed for 24 types of offices, giving an interesting view of how the courts operated. Some of these offices, such as the clerk of chancery and the chief justices had little occasion to earn fees. Others, like the county offices of clerk, sheriff and register had numerous fees. These officers were generally busy and could gather a great amount of fees. Since these positions were of necessity political, a man with the right connections could get very rich very quickly. It is often seen in the court minutes and deeds that a man who owned little land could serve a year or two as sheriff, clerk or registrar and then be able to buy a great deal of land. It was not the only way to get rich in the early days, but it was a good, quick one.

The county clerks collected 28 different fees while the sheriffs collected 18 separate ones. Among sheriffs' fees are those for whipping any person (two shillings, eight pence [2.8]), pilloring (5.0), putting in the stocks and letting out again (seven pence), and for arresting a person (5.4). The sheriff also received one shilling per day for each person in jail to provide one pound of bread, one pound of roasted or boiled flesh and two quarts of water.

The primary officers of the legal system were the justices of the peace. They were appointed in the king's name on the recommendation of the royal governor after being recommended by the local representative in the assembly. These recommendations were seldom refused by the governor or by the king. They were chosen from among the better sort of men, who were educated to some degree and owned property. Appointment as a justice of the peace was for life, on good behavior—that is, a justice could be removed from office by the governor or the assembly but seldom was.

A justice of the peace was given the honorary title of esquire and was empowered to settle minor cases in his court. These cases included small fines but not corporal punishment such as branding or whipping. There were a variable number of justices in each county. When Gordon wrote the report documenting the court structure in 1765, there were 516 justices of the peace in the 29 counties, averaging 18 per county. They were to meet annually during court week to elect the sheriff, set tax rates and other such business. At this time they also selected three or four of their number to preside over the quarterly court sessions. They had great power, both individually and as a court, and served without salary or fees of any type, taking an oath to that effect.

In each county the justice of the peace presided over the court of common pleas and quarter sessions, which were held for one week every three months. The time for holding court was assigned by the assembly so that the various counties in a district held court on different weeks. This allowed the lawyers to ride the circuit from court to court and appear and represent clients in each court in their district. At this time there were about 45 licensed lawyers in the province to cover the 29 counties. The district, or superior, court met twice a year and decided the most important cases, including those in which a convicted defendant was subject to hanging. The district court for the backcountry was held in Salisbury, which was by far the largest and most important town in the area.

The county courts decided all civil cases involving amounts up to £20 plus criminal cases in which conviction carried fines up to £20 and corporal punishment, including the pillory and whipping but not extending to the taking of life or limb. The powers and authorities of this court were many and important. These courts had jurisdiction over wills, trusts and estates, and over orphans and guardians. Deeds for personal property (any goods of value other than real estate) and real estate were proved in this court, which issued orders for recording them. County courts annually recommended three people from among whom the governor appointed the sheriff for the following year, and they supervised and audited the sheriff's accounts. These courts also appointed and administered a number of county offices.

The county court levied taxes for building and repairing bridges and repairing courthouses, jails and other public works. The county courts authorized the operation of public grist mills and ferries and licensed taverns and the retailing of spirituous liquors. They appointed the overseers of roads and the constables of the county. They settled all questions regarding servants, slaves, apprentices and their complaints. They appointed jurors to the county and district courts. Most of the men elected to the assembly were justices of the peace and were among the leading men of the county.

The primary county official was the high sheriff. He was appointed by the governor and served for an indefinite period of time, although he could not serve past the second year unless his books had been settled. Mecklenburg County records indicate that many sheriffs served only one year but that a few served for long periods of time.

The sheriff maintained a list of polls (heads) for the county who were the primary taxpayers. A poll was a man over the age of 16 or a slave, male or female, over the age of 12. The sheriff collected the province poll tax and the county poll tax. Taxes on slaves were assessed of their masters. There was a province vestry tax but since there was no Church of England in the county, this tax was not collected in Mecklenburg.

If taxes were not paid, the sheriff could seize property and auction enough of it off to pay the taxes. On this he received a fee of 2.5 percent of the value of the property sold. He received an 8 percent commission on taxes collected and various fees for services rendered such as delivering court papers, collecting fines, executing punishment, and so on.

Other county officers such as the treasurer, coroner, overseers of the poor, inspector (auditor) and others served without pay for the good of the county. Some of them received fees for their services.

There were a number of royal offices in the province. Some of these offices carried a salary and all of them charged fees. Those who held these offices were generally rich and influential to begin with and became more so from their power, salary and fees. The governor's council was made up primarily of these officers.

The Gordon report refers frequently to an act passed in April 1748 "which is the general law for the regulating officers fees in the province." Unfortunately this is one of those laws for which a copy has not been found. All we have is the title of the act, so we have little information about the salaries and fees for many provincial officers.

The governor received a great number of fees. All that is known about them is that there were fees for "all patents or grants of the King's lands, for letters of administration, probates of wills, registers of shipping, testimonials under the colony seal, commissions for civil offices, letters patent of denization together with his fees in chancery."

There were two treasurers, northern and southern, who collected taxes from the sheriffs and settled with the assembly for the poll taxes. The fee for this was 5 percent of the monies collected.

The receiver of quitrents had a deputy or two in each county. They collected the annual quitrents and distributed them according to the wishes of the king. For this they received a percentage of the receipts.

The assembly was the colony's primary governing body. Most counties had two representatives who were elected by the voters in the county. Through long-standing tradition several of the older, smaller counties in the northeast of the colony had five representatives and one had three. The larger cities were designated as boroughs and had one representative elected by the citizens of that city. Other cities could have their own representative as soon as their population reached 60 families, but few did. Salisbury was one of these boroughs.

Voters had to be male, 21 or older, and own a certain amount of land. The franchise did not extend to women, children, Indians, slaves, free blacks or those men who did not own land.

The assembly met when called by the governor. This was every year or two, often in December or January when the elected representatives' farming activities were light. These assembly sessions generally took a month or two. Occasionally the governor would prorogue a session, that is, he would postpone the assembly before its work was done and call the members back into session at a later time. This could happen when there was extraordinary business that required the governor's attention or when the governor was not happy with the bills the assembly had passed.

The council, or upper house, was a small body of men appointed by the king on the recommendation of the governor or other powerful men. They served for life or until they resigned or were removed by the king. Although neither the assembly members nor the councilors were paid a salary or any fees, the councilors generally held other government positions that paid very well. Since the council had to pass every law and its members were appointed by the king, it served as a check on both the assembly and the governor.

During assembly sessions the members requested permission to introduce a bill and then read it out to the assembly. The bill was read out two more times and voted on. If passed, it was carried to the council, which sat at the same time. If the council passed the bill, it was sent to the governor. Often a bill was amended and passed back and forth between the assembly and the council until agreement was reached. At the end of the assembly session the governor called the two houses to wait on him. He addressed the assembly and told them which bills he had approved and which ones he had disallowed.

The approved bills were engrossed, or written out in a clear hand, and sent by the governor with his recommendations to the Board of Trade in England, which had direct authority over the colony. The board submitted the bills, with their recommendations, to the king's privy council, which presented them, with its recommendations, to the king. The king either allowed or disallowed each bill, and word was sent back through the privy council and Board of Trade to the governor and thus to the colony. It could take up to two years after a bill was passed to determine whether it was a law or not. In practice the bills were considered to be laws until "the King's pleasure be known." A very few bills included a suspending clause that said that the bill did not go into effect until the king's approval had been received.

The colonial records contain most of the minutes of the assembly and council meetings. The bills introduced and voted on are named but not included in detail or even described. Many bills were introduced that did not pass, and it is not known what these bills said except for their titles. There were also a number of laws that were approved by the king that have been lost, leaving no record of them except their titles.

From 1886 to 1890 William Saunders searched through records in America and in England to find copies of the laws, which he included in *The Colonial Records of North Carolina*.[5]

Q. The Court House Law of 1774

LAWS OF 1774, in Clark, *State Records of North Carolina*, 23:966.[1]

CHAPTER XIV.

An Act for establishing the Court House in the Town of Charlotte, in Mecklenburg County, and for regulating the said Town.

Whereas, by an Act entitled an Act for dividing the County of Mecklenburg and other Purposes, The Court of the County was directed to be held in the Courthouse then Built during the Term of Seven Years, which said Term is near expiring, and it having been represented that the removal of the Seat of the Court from the said Courthouse and the disposal of the same agreeable to the before recited Act, would be inconvenient to many of the Inhabitants of the said County and discourage the Trade and Commerce of the said Town.

I. Be it therefore Enacted by the Governor, Council and Assembly, and by the Authority of the same, That from and after the Passing of this Act the said Courthouse already built in Charlotte Town be, continue and remain the Courthouse of the said County of Mecklenburg and the Inferior Court of the said County shall hereafter be constantly held therein; any thing in the said Act contained to the Contrary notwithstanding.

II. And whereas the frequent firing of Guns, Running Horse Races and playing at Long Bullets in the said Town is found to have a dangerous Tendency to prevent which,

III. Be it Enacted by the Authority aforesaid, that from and after the passing hereof no Person whatsoever shall shoot with a Gun except it be to kill Cattle or Hogs, or immoderately ride or strain any horse or horses, or play at Long Bullet within the Limits of the said Town under the Penalty of paying the Sum of Twenty Shillings for each Offence, to be recovered by a Warrant before any Justice of the Peace of the said County, by one of the Trustees.

IV. And whereas by an Act for Establishing a Town in Mecklenburg County, every Person having a deed for any Lot in the said Town of Charlotte is required to Build a house of the dimensions in the said Act specified within three years after the date of the Conveyance for the same, which is found to be injurious to the Inhabitants of the said Town.

V. Be it Enacted by the Authority aforesaid, That no Person or Persons shall forfeit his or their Lot or Lots for not building on the same, except such Lots shall front on one of the Main Streets in said Town, any Law Usage or Custom to the contrary notwithstanding.

VI. And be it further Enacted by the Authority aforesaid, That every Taxable Person in the said Town shall be obliged to work on the Streets thereof six days in every year if required by the Overseer, or find some Person to work for him, under the Penalty of Five Shillings for every day he shall refuse or Neglect, to be recovered as is herein before directed.

VII. Whereas some of the Trustees of the said Town are Dead and others removed out of the Province, Be it Enacted by the Authority aforesaid, That Jeremiah McCafferty, Robert Elliot, William Paterson and Isaac Alexander be added to the Trustees formerly appointed and they are hereby invested with the same Powers and Authorities as the other Trustees, anything to the Contrary notwithstanding.

VIII. And be it further Enacted by the Authority aforesaid, That all fines arising in virtue of this Act shall be applied towards clearing and repairing the Streets in the said Town of Charlotte.

Notes

Chapter 1

1. Chalmers Gaston Davidson, *Major John Davidson of "Rural Hill," Mecklenburg County, N.C., Pioneer, Industrialist, Planter* (Charlotte: Lassiter Press, 1943), 1–5.
2. Brent H. Holcomb, *Anson County, North Carolina Deed Abstracts, 1749–1766, Abstracts of Will & Estates, 1749–1795* (Baltimore: Genealogical Publishing Co., 1980), s.v. "Hendry, Henry"; Herman W. Ferguson, *Mecklenburg County, North Carolina Minutes of the Court of Common Pleas and Quarter Sessions 1774–1780* (Rocky Mount, NC: 2007) (hereafter *Mecklenburg Minutes*), s.v. "Hendry, Henry."
3. William L. Saunders, ed., *The Colonial Records of North Carolina* (Raleigh, N.C.: 1886–90), 5:575.
4. Robert J. Cain, ed., *Colonial Records of North Carolina (Second Series)* (New York: AMS Press, 1968–72), s.v. "Hendry, Henry."
5. Mecklenburg County Deed Books in the Office of the Registrar of Deeds, Mecklenburg County, NC, image accessed at http://meckrodindex.com 5:165.
6. For a discussion of the spelling of names, see "Naming Conventions and Other John Davidsons" in appendix G.
7. Davidson, *Major John Davidson*, 1–5. See also J. B. Alexander, *The History of Mecklenburg County from 1740 to 1900* (Charlotte, NC: Observer Printing House, 1902), 24, and Charles William Sommerville, *The History of Hopewell Presbyterian Church* (Charlotte, NC: Hopewell Presbyterian Church, 1939).
8. As to the date of 1740, the town of Salisbury was not laid out until 1755 (Saunders, *Colonial Records of North Carolina*, 5:355).

Chapter 2

1. Samuel Wilson was born about 1711 and died 13 March 1778.
2. Sommerville, *History of Hopewell Presbyterian Church*, 195; C. L. Hunter, *Sketches of Western North Carolina, Historical and Biographical* (Raleigh, NC: Raleigh News Steam Job Print, 1877), 84; Alexander, *History of Mecklenburg County*, 10; Davidson, *Major John Davidson*, 6.
3. There is a family story that Mary Winslow was the daughter of Benjamin and Mary Winsley or perhaps their granddaughter, born of Moses and Jean Osborne Winslow. There is some evidence that both Samuel Wilson and Benjamin Winsley came to Anson County from Lunenburg County, Virginia, about the same time. See Landon C. Bell, ed., *Sunlight on the Southside; Lists of Tithes, Lunenburg County, Virginia, 1748–1783* (Philadelphia: George S. Ferguson, 1931). Lunenburg County is in the Southside area of Virginia

near the North Carolina border. Samuel Wilson, Benjamin Winsley and Benjamin Winsley, Jr., appear in the Lunenburg County list of tithes for 1748. By 1749 Benjamin Winsley is gone, and by 1750 they have all left Lunenburg County. It is possible that these are the individuals who arrived in Anson County about that time.

4. Hunter, *Sketches*, 84. Baker's Graveyard, on the southern edge of Iredell County, contained graves for Samuel, Margaret, John and Benjamin. This is the best source for birth and death dates for these people, although the transcriptions contain some errors. When Charles William Sommerville wrote *The History of Hopewell Presbyterian Church* in 1939, he transcribed these stones, saying they were "hardly legible." Lake Norman was made in this area in about 1964; before the lake was filled, the graves were moved to Centre Church Graveyard, where they reside today.

From Sommerville: "Samuel Wilson died March 13, 1778 (or 1788) in his 68th year." The death date of 1778 is confirmed by his will. His birth year would have been 1711. "Margaret Wilson, born February 12, 1804, died at 58 years of age." This birth year is certainly a misreading of the tombstone. The third wife of Samuel Wilson died in 1804 at age 58. Her birth year would have been 1746, which agrees with other records. "Benjamin Wilson, born August 4, 1800, 56 years of age." This too is a misreading of the tombstone. He did die in 1800 at age 56, but this eldest son of Samuel Wilson and Mary Winslow Wilson would have been born in 1744. "John Wilson, born June 12, 1795(?), died in his 43rd year." This is the youngest son of Samuel Wilson and Mary Winslow Wilson and is also a misreading of the tombstone. He died in 1795, as confirmed by his will; if he died at age 43, his birth year would have been 1752. However, Samuel Wilson's will indicates that John was a minor in 1778, requiring a birth year of 1757 or later. John's mother, Mary, died in 1758, so John must have been born in 1757 or 1758. The existence of an infant child could explain why Samuel Wilson remarried so quickly. J. B. Alexander and Sommerville both list a seventh child from the first marriage, a girl named Sally. No corroborating evidence of this child has been found. Hunter also lists a seventh child, a girl named Rebecca. He says she married and had two children. Then, while on the way to Tennessee, she and her husband were murdered by Indians. Hunter says that the two children survived. This may be true, but since there is no corroborating evidence, she is not on the list above.

5. Mecklenburg Estate Files in North Carolina Estate Files, 1663–1979, at http://FamilySearch.org, accessed 10 February 2017.

6. Saunders, *Colonial Records of North Carolina*, s.v. "Wilson, Samuel."

7. Hunter, *Sketches*, 85.

8. Mecklenburg County Will Books, Mecklenburg County Courthouse, imaged by FamilySearch at www.familysearch.org F:211–214 ; Mecklenburg Estate Files.

9. Helen F. M. Leary, ed., *North Carolina Research, Genealogy and Local History* (Raleigh: North Carolina Genealogical Society, 1996), 36; Saunders, Acts of the North Carolina General Assembly, 1784, in *Colonial Records of North Carolina*, 24 :578.

10. These five children were, in birth order:

- Violet, born August 1742, wife of Major John Davidson;
- Benjamin, born in 1744, who bought 340 acres from his father in 1769 for £5;
- Mary, called Maria, born in 1746, wife of Ezekiel Polk;
- David, born in 1748, who bought 297 acres from his father in 1769 for £5;
- Samuel, born 1750, who bought 300 acres from his father in 1772 for £10.

11. For a recent and complete telling of the story of the Mecklenburg Declaration of Independence, see Scott Syfert, *The First American Declaration of Independence? The Disputed History of the Mecklenburg Declaration of May 20, 1775* (Jefferson, NC: McFarland, 2014).

12. Hunter, *Sketches*; David L. Swain, ed., *North Carolina State Pamphlet on the Mecklenburg Declaration of Independence* (Raleigh, NC: State of North Carolina, 1831).

13. Typescript, box 1, folder 20, Davidson Family Papers, Special Collections, Atkins Library, University of North Carolina at Charlotte (hereafter UNCC).

Chapter 3

1. Ferguson, *Mecklenburg County Minutes, 1780–1800*, 4:129, 130; J. B. Alexander, *Biographical Sketches of the Early Settlers of the Hopewell Section* (Charlotte, NC: Observer Printing and Publishing House, 1897); Thomas Hugh Spence, *The Presbyterian Congregation on Rocky River* (Concord, NC: Rocky River Presbyterian Church, 1954). See "The Lunacy of the Rev. Alexander Caldwell" in appendix D.

2. Mecklenburg County Deed Books, 15:23, 20:31–32, Office of the Registrar of Deeds, Mecklenburg County, NC. See "A Marriage Deed of Trust" in appendix F.

3. Chalmers Gaston Davidson, 'Benjamin Wilson and Elizabeth Latta Davidson of 'Oak Lawn' Mecklenburg County, N.C.," copy in the authors' collection.

4. Ibid. See "Naming Conventions and Other John Davidsons" in appendix G.

5. Saunders, *Colonial Records of North Carolina*, 9:462, 493, 588.

6. Saunders, *Colonial Records of North Carolina*, 9:763, 23:966, Acts of the North Carolina General Assembly, 1774, chapter XIV.

7. Acts of the North Carolina General Assembly, 1768. "An Act for dividing the County of Mecklenburg, and other Purposes": https://docsouth.unc.edu/csr/index.php/document/csr23-0049; Acts of the North Carolina General Assembly, 1774. "An Act for appointing Commissioners for building a Court House, Prison and Stocks for the County of Tryon, and for establishing a Boundary Line between the Counties of Tryon and Mecklenburg": https://docsouth.unc.edu/csr/index.php/document/csr23-0054.

8. David Hackett Fischer, *Albion's Seed, Four British Folkways in America* (New York: Oxford University Press, 1989), 738. Long Bullets was an ancient and popular British sport that involved two contestants throwing cannon balls on a set course of several miles. After throwing the ball, the player walked forward, picked up the ball and threw it again. The winner was the man who required the fewest throws of the cannon ball to cover the distance. This sport is still played today in some English villages. It probably seemed much more enjoyable if it followed a few noggins of flip or some other spirituous drink. Flip was a popular 18th-century drink made of beer and rum with sugar and egg and served hot.

9. Saunders, *Colonial Records of North Carolina*, 9:783.

10. Ibid., 23:964. "An Act for … building a Court House … the County of Tryon, and for establishing a Boundary Line between the Counties of Tryon and Mecklenburg. … II. And whereas sundry disputes have arisen relative to the Boundary line between the said County of Tryon and the County of Mecklenburg, to prevent which for the future … the River Catawba be and is hereby declared the Boundary line between the said Counties."

11. Saunders, *Colonial Records*, 10:206, 531.

12. Pension application of Samuel Wilson, Southern Campaign American Revolution Pension Statements and Records, S7915 fn36NC, http://revwarapps.org/s7915.pdf, accessed 30 May 2012.

13. Lawrence E. Babits and Joshua B. Howard, *"Fortitude and Forbearance": The North Carolina Continental Line in the Revolutionary War, 1775–1783*. (Raleigh: North Carolina Division of Archives and History, 2004), 257.

14. Saunders, *Colonial Records of North Carolina*, 23:994.

15. Ibid., 10:186.

16. Swain, *North Carolina State Pamphlet on the Mecklenburg Declaration*; Syfert, *First American Declaration of Independence?*; V. V. McNitt, *Chain of Error and the Mecklenburg Declarations of Independence* (New York: Hampden Hills Press, 1960).

17. See "Naming Conventions and Other John Davidsons" in appendix G.

18. See "Samuel and Mary Wilson, Parents of Violet Wilson Davidson," chap. 3 in Mecklenburg County Will Books, F:211–14.

19. Mecklenburg County Deed Books, 14:449.

20. Ibid., 18:21.
21. Mecklenburg County Will Books, G:34. See "The Story of Plum, Enslaved Man, Freedman, Property Owner" in appendix E.
22. For the details of these early transactions and some of the deeds themselves, see "Major John's Earliest Land Transactions" in appendix N.
23. Charlotte-Mecklenburg Historic Landmarks Commission, s.v. "Oak Lawn," http://landmarkscommission.org, accessed 12 January 2018.

Chapter 4

1. The Brevards lived in that part of Rowan County that was formed into Iredell County in 1788.
2. William S. Powell, *Dictionary of North Carolina Biography* (Chapel Hill: University of North Carolina Press, 1979), 1:218.
3. See a discussion of iron making in Lincoln County in notes 11 and 12 of this chapter and "Iron Making in North Carolina" in appendix J.
4. Keziah Goodwyn Brevard, *A Plantation Mistress on the Eve of the Civil War*, ed. John Hammond Moore (Columbia: University of South Carolina Press, 1993).
5. The family genealogy gives a birth date that makes Peggy 41 years old when they were married, but this is probably in error. It would have her bearing four children between the ages of 42 and 47.
6. Diary of Juliana Margaret Conner from June 10 to Oct. 17, 1827, original and transcript in Conner Papers #174, Southern Historical Collection, Wilson Library, University of North Carolina Library, Chapel Hill.
7. William A. Graham, *General Joseph Graham and His Papers on North Carolina Revolutionary History* (Raleigh, NC: Author, 1904).
8. See appendix J.
9. William Hill, *Col. William Hill's Memoirs of the Revolution*, ed. A. S. Salley (Columbia: Historical Commission of South Carolina, 1958).
10. Lincoln County Deed Books, 19:78, in the Office of the Registrar of Deeds, Lincoln County, North Carolina.

11. Land Grants, North Carolina Office of Archives and History, grant 835, book 84, 27, images from http://nclandgrants.com/home.htm, accessed 21 April 2017; Lawrence E. Babits and Joshua B. Howard, *Long, Obstinate, and Bloody: The Battle of Guilford Courthouse* (Chapel Hill: University of North Carolina Press, 2009); Powell, *Dictionary of North Carolina Biography*, s.v. "Forney, Peter," 2:222; Walter Clark, ed., "An Act to Encourage the Building of Iron Works in this State," in *The State Records of North Carolina* (Raleigh, NC: Trustees of the Public Libraries, 1895), 24: 978–79, Other laws encouraging ironworks had been passed during the Revolution with varying degrees of success. This bill was introduced by the representative from Burke County, located north of Lincoln County and west of the Catawba River.
12. In addition to John Davidson, Joseph Graham, Alexander Brevard, and Peter Forney, a number of other iron makers are mentioned in Lincoln County deeds. These include Abram Forney, Abram Earhardt, John Fulenwider, Turner Abernethy, John Smith, Adam Costner, John Sloan, John Atkinson and Daniel Bourdeaux. Ironworks mentioned include Mount Carmel Forge on Mountain Creek, Mount Welcome furnace, Rehoboth furnace, High Shoals Iron Works, Aetna Forge, Lincoln Forge, and Washington Furnace. Other forges and furnaces were mentioned but not named.
13. Lincoln County Deed Books in the Office of the Registrar of Deeds, Lincoln County, NC.
14. For a detailed description of this process, see appendix J. Also see Kay Moss, *Journey to the Piedmont Past, Source Book* (Gastonia, NC: Schiele Museum of Natural History, 2001), 119.
15. Machpelah Cemetery, North Carolina Historical Marker, https://www.ncmarkers.com/Markers.aspx?MarkerId=O-58, accessed November 2016.
16. Davidson, *Major John Davidson*, 41:2.
17. Fischer, *Albion's Seed*, 655.
18. Davidson, *Major John Davidson*, 45.
19. A. Brevard Davidson, Rural Hill Journal, 1834–54, 113–24, box 1, unfoldered, Davidson Family Papers, UNCC;

photocopy of John Matthew Davidson's letterbook in box 1, folder 1, also in Davidson Family Papers, UNCC. The original is in the John Matthew Davidson Papers, Southern Historical Collection, Louis Round Wilson Special Collections Library, University of North Carolina at Chapel Hill.

20. Mecklenburg County Deed Books, 21:55–56, image at http://meckrodindex.com, accessed 20 February 2017.

21. Mecklenburg County Will Books, G:74, imaged by FamilySearch at www.familysearch.org.

22. Mecklenburg Estate Files in North Carolina Estate Files, 1663–1979, www.familysearch.org, accessed 20 February 2017.

Chapter 5

1. John Hill Wheeler, *Reminiscences and Memoirs of North Carolina and Eminent North Carolinians* (Columbus, OH: Columbus Printing Works, 1884), 292.

2. Michael Hill, "Crowfield Academy," NCpedia, 2006, http://www.ncpedia.org/crowfield-academy, accessed 15 May 2017. Crowfield Academy was located within the bounds of Centre Presbyterian Church near the home of Alexander Osborne from 1760 to 1788 in what is today southern Iredell County.

3. Herman W. Ferguson, *Mecklenburg County, North Carolina Minutes of the Court of Common Pleas and Quarter Sessions, Volume II: 1801–1820* (Rocky Mount, NC: Herman W. Ferguson, 1997), 5:308, 7:211.

4. Ferguson, *Mecklenburg Minutes, 1780–1800*, 4:19; Ferguson, *Mecklenburg Minutes, 1801–1820*, 4:295.

5. Saunders, *Colonial Records of North Carolina*, 24 :902–3.

6. Banks R. Cates, Jr., "Mecklenburg Fisheries," *Olde Mecklenburg Genealogical Society Quarterly* 20, no. 2 (2002): 18

7. "A Natural and Cultural History of Shad," http://www.brandywineconservancy.org/shad-history.html, accessed 7 May 2012.

8. Ferguson, *Mecklenburg Minutes, 1774–1780*, 4:57.

9. Ibid., 4:148.

10. Saunders, *Colonial Records of North Carolina*, 5:141–144b.

11. Ibid., 5:579–84.

12. Copies of these maps can be viewed in the Robinson Spangler Carolina Room collection at the Charlotte Mecklenburg Library.

13. Graham, *General Joseph Graham and His Papers*, 216fn.

14. Hugh F. Rankin, *Greene and Cornwallis: The Campaign in the Carolinas* (Raleigh: North Carolina Department of Cultural Resources, Division of Archives and History, 1976).

15. Cowan's Ford Wildlife Refuge, https://www.meckrc.gov/ParkandRec/StewardshipServices/Pages/NPTextDetail.aspx, accessed 6 October 2018.

16. For more detail see "The Lunacy of the Rev. Alexander Caldwell," appendix D.

17. For information on land grants, see "Land Acquisition by Grants and Deeds," appendix M.

18. Herman W. Ferguson, *Mecklenburg County, North Carolina Will Abstracts, 1791–1868, Books A–J, and Tax Lists* (Rocky Mount, NC: Herman Ferguson, 1998).

19. For details of Robin's land acquisitions see "Land Acquisition by Robert Davidson," appendix O.

20. Beth Eakes, daughter of L. Garner Eakes, personal communication.

Chapter 6

1. Mecklenburg wills I:214–224, transcribed by the authors from images on microfilm in the Robinson-Spangler Room, Charlotte Mecklenburg Public Library.

2. Mecklenburg estate files in North Carolina Estate Files, 1663–1979, at http://FamilySearch.org, accessed 17 September 2017.

3. See "The Lunacy of the Rev. Alexander Caldwell," appendix D.

4. Herman W. Ferguson, *Mecklenburg County, North Carolina Minutes of the Court of Common Pleas and Quarter Sessions, Volume III: 1821–1830* (Rocky Mount, NC: Herman W. Ferguson, 1998).

5. Mecklenburg Estate Files on Family Search.

6. A steelyard was a three-foot-long

balance for weighing commodities such as cotton, corn and wheat. A carryall is a type of wagon.

7. Brevard Davidson was still alive in 1859. He was "the late" in 1924 when Osborne wrote his autobiography. Alexander Caldwell was David Alexander Caldwell, also still alive in 1859.

8. Autobiography of Edwin Augustus Young Osborne, folder 170, Edwin Augustus Osborne Papers, 1832–1928, Southern Historical Collection, Louis Round Wilson Special Collections Library, University of North Carolina at Chapel Hill, transcribed by Josephine A. Osborne, Charlotte, 1947, copy in the authors' personal collection. Jacky was 79 in 1859.

9. Powell, *Dictionary of North Carolina Biography*, 4:401, s.v. "Osborne, Edwin Augustus."

10. This is not the present-day Historic Rosedale Plantation but another located farther north, near the Croft settlement, which burned in 1967.

11. Osborne, autobiography.

12. Today this land makes up the Little Sugar Creek Greenway and Central Piedmont Community College.

13. Mecklenburg Wills on Family Search, J:180–3.

14. Wheeler, *Reminiscences and Memoirs*, 293; Graham, *General Joseph Graham and His Papers*.

15. Mecklenburg estate files North Carolina Estate Files, 1663–1979, http://FamilySearch.org, accessed 28 May 2017; Ferguson, *Mecklenburg Minutes, Vol. VII, 1861–1868*, 11:718.

Chapter 7

1. Davidson, *Major John Davidson*, 72–80.

2. Chalmers Gaston Davidson, (1928) plantation files, 1907–94, Archives and Special Collections, Davidson College, Davidson, North Carolina.

3. Chalmers Gaston Davidson, "Benjamin Wilson and Elizabeth Latta Davidson of 'Oak Lawn' Mecklenburg County, N.C.," unpublished paper, copy in the authors' collection.

4. Ann Williams, *The Rural Hill Farm Journals of Adam Brevard Davidson, 1834–1856* (Charlotte, NC: Antebellum Books, 2017).

5. This information on slave ownership is based on an analysis of the U.S. decennial censuses for Mecklenburg and surrounding counties for the years 1790 to 1860.

6. The ten children of Jacky and Sallie were:

- John Matthew (or Matthews) Winslow Davidson—9 November 1801–16 November 1879;
- Mary Winslow Davidson—19 September 1803–31 December 1832;
- Violet Wilson Davidson—24 January 1806–23 January 1877;
- Adam Brevard Davidson—13 March 1808–4 July 1896;
- Robert Hamilton McWhorter Davidson—2 October 1810–25 October 1841;
- Isabella Sophia Graham Davidson—11 June 1813–3 August 1888;
- Augustus W. Davidson—2 June 1815–25 October 25 1837;
- William Speight MacLean Davidson—2 November 1817–15 December 1873;
- Edward Constantine Davidson—17 February 1820–13 May 1892;
- Sarah Rebecca Davidson—6 May 1822–14 February 1841.

7. These education records are located in the Torrance-Banks Family Papers and the Davidson Family Papers, both of which are in Special Collections, Atkins Library, UNCC.

8. The Reverend John M. M. Caldwell was called to Sugar Creek in 1837 when Robert Hall Morrison resigned to become the founding president of Davidson College. Caldwell served at Sugar Creek until 1845.

9. The spelling of this church name had been Sugar Creek since its founding in about 1755. It was changed to Sugaw Creek in 1924, leading to confusion ever since. Apparently this spelling was taken from the Rev. William Foote, *Sketches of North Carolina Historical and Biographical*, 1843. There are many different spellings of this church's name in the historical record, but Foote is the only one who uses this spelling.

10. Harry Gardner Cutler, ed., *History of Florida, Past and Present* (New York: Lewis, 1923); Neill Roderick McGeachy, *A History of Sugaw Creek Presbyterian Church, Mecklenburg Presbytery, Charlotte, North Carolina* (Rock Hill, SC: Record Print, 1954) (Second printing Charlotte 2005), 164–67.

11. Cutler, *History of Florida, Past and Present*, 114.

12. Davidson Family Papers, 1813–1937, Southern Historical Collection, Louis Round Wilson Special Collections Library, University of North Carolina at Chapel Hill, #204. The letters mentioned in this section are photocopies in the collection of family papers at Rural Hill Historic Site. Their source is unknown.

13. Davidson Family Papers, 1813–1937, UNC Chapel Hill.

14. Torrance-Banks Family Papers, UNCC. Ingleside has been designated a historic landmark by Mecklenburg County. See http://landmarkscommission.org/wp-content/uploads/2018/05/Ingleside-SR.pdf.

Chapter 8

1. Katherine Wooten Springs, *The Squires of Springfield* (Charlotte, NC: William Loftin, 1965).

2. Davidson Family Papers, 1813–1937, UNC Chapel Hill.

3. Ibid., series 1, Loose Papers, 1827–1935, #204, transcribed by the authors.

4. Adam Brevard Davidson, Rural Hill Journal, 1834–54, and 1856, Davidson Family Papers, UNCC; ; Williams, *Rural Hill Farm Journals of Adam Brevard Davidson*

5. Karen McConnell, Janet Dyer, and Ann Williams, eds., *A Life in Antebellum Charlotte: The Private Journal of Sarah F Davidson, 1837* (Charleston, SC: History Press, 2005), 141.

6. Chalmers Gaston Davidson, *The Plantation World Around Davidson* (Davidson, NC: Mecklenburg Historical Association, 1973).

7. Torrance-Banks Family Papers, UNCC.

8. *Charlotte (NC) Journal*, 24 May 1844 and 31 May 1844.

9. W. R. Myers, age 26 at that time, had settled in Charlotte the year before and was developing a successful law practice. Two years later he married Sophia Springs, daughter of John Springs III, making him Brevard's brother-in-law as they had married sisters. Myers rose to prominence in the law, in farming and in banking. He served in the Civil War and afterward donated the land on which Biddle Institute, now Johnson C. Smith University, is located. His son John Springs Myers was a successful cotton farmer and developer of Myers Park.

10. E. Jennifer Monaghan, *Learning to Read and Write in Colonial America* (Worcester, MA: American Antiquarian Society, 2005); Davidson Family Papers, series 1, Loose Papers, 1827–1935, UNCC.

11. Chalmers Gaston Davidson, *The Plantation World Around Davidson* (Davidson, NC: Mecklenburg Historical Association, 1973).

12. *Charlotte Journal*, 8 April 1847.

13. Powell, *Dictionary of North Carolina Biography*, s.v. "Davidson, Chalmers."

14. Historic Rosedale Plantation in Charlotte was reroofed with cedar shingles in 2017. Considering the area of Rosedale and the number of shingles used, the roof at Dickson Plantation may have had an area of about 3,000 square feet.

Chapter 9

1. The source of the information about Harry Worke asked to remain anonymous.

2. Katherine Wooten Springs, *The Squires of Springfield* (Charlotte, William Loftin, 1965).

3. Mary Laura Davidson was born 3 February 1837 and died 8 May 1902.

4. John Springs Davidson was born 6 August 1838 and died 7 August 1899.

5. For the history of Rosedale Plantation see Caldwell-Davidson Papers, Historic Rosedale Plantation, Charlotte, NC.

6. Robert Augusta Davidson was born 13 March 1842 and died 31 March 1865. These papers are in the authors' collection, received from the estate of Alice Davidson Abel.

7. Sarah Harper Davidson Journal, 1868–77, private collection.

8. The travel journal is in private hands.

Sallie Davidson was born 16 August 1845 and died 26 March 1935.

9. Leroy Springs Davidson was born 19 August 1855 and died 15 September 1915.

10. Edward Lee Baxter Davidson was born 7 November 1858 and died 10 October 1944.

Chapter 10

1. *Encyclopædia Britannica; or, a Dictionary of Arts and Sciences*, by a Society of Gentlemen in Scotland (Edinburgh: Macfarquhar 1771), 1:40–70.

2. Williams, *Rural Hill Farm Journals of Adam Brevard Davidson*; A. Brevard Davidson, Rural Hill Journal, 1834–1854, Davidson Family Papers, UNCC.

3. A. Brevard Davidson, Rural Hill Journal, 1856, Davidson Family Papers, UNCC; *Plantation and Farm: Instruction, Regulation, Record, Inventory, and Account Book*, by A Southern Planter (Richmond, VA: J. W. Randolph, 1852).

4. Constance McL. Green, *Eli Whitney and the Birth of American Technology* (Boston: Little Brown, 1956).

5. Stephen Yafa, *Big Cotton* (New York: Viking, 2005).

Stuart Bruchey, *Cotton and the Growth of the American Economy: 1790–1860* (New York: Harcourt, Brace & World, 1967).

6. Ibid.

Chapter 11

1. Davidson Family Papers, UNCC. Edgeworth Academy was located in Greensboro, NC. Salem Academy, where so many of the Davidson girls were educated over the years, is still in operation in Salem, NC.

2. *Charlotte Observer*, 5 November 1886.

3. Davidson, *Major John Davidson*.

4. Mary Louise and Alice sold the land and property to Historic Preservation of North Carolina in 1985. The North Carolina chapter of the National Society of the Colonial Dames of America raised money to purchase the property and restore the house, and the society established the Historic Rosedale Foundation. The Junior League of Charlotte did research and raised money to open the house, staffed with a director and members of the Mecklenburg Historical Association Docent Committee. The house was opened to the public in 1993.

5. Based on papers in the collection of the authors, a gift from the estate of May Davidson, Jo's sister.

6. Ibid.

7. Personal correspondence.

8. From a printed copy of this elegy in the possession of a family member.

Appendix B

1. Jan Blodgett and Ralph B. Levering, *One Town, Many Voices: A History of Davidson, North Carolina* (Davidson, NC: Davidson Historical Society, 2012), 3.

2. Mary D. Beaty, *A History of Davidson College* (Davidson, NC: Briarpatch Press, 1988) 328.

Appendix C

1. Sommerville, *History of Hopewell Presbyterian Church*.

Appendix D

1. Spence, *Presbyterian Congregation on Rocky River*; Ferguson, *Mecklenburg Minutes, 1780–1800*, 4:129–30.

2. Ferguson, *Mecklenburg Minutes, 1821–1830*, 6:396.

Appendix E

1. Mecklenburg County Will Books, F:211–14.

2. Ibid., G:34–37.

3. Ferguson, *Mecklenburg Minutes, 1780–1800*, 3:245, 266.

4. Ibid., 4:74.

5. Ibid., 4:247.

Appendix G

1. Saunders, *Colonial Records of North Carolina*, 15:162 .

Appendix H

1. Sarah Frew Davidson, Journal (1837), box 1, folder 9, Caldwell and Davidson

Family Papers, Special Collections, UNCC. This journal has been transcribed and published, with extensive notes, as *A Life in Antebellum Charlotte*, ed. Karen M. McConnell, Janet S. Dyer, and Ann Williams (Charleston, SC: History Press, 2005).

2. A. Brevard Davidson, Rural Hill Journal, 1856, Davidson Family Papers, UNCC.

Appendix I

1. Saunders, *Colonial Records of North Carolina*, 7:489. This informaton is from a report written by Patrick Duff Gordon and sent by Governor Tryon to William Petty, Marquis of Lansdown, in 1767. It describes how all parts of the government functioned at that time: the courts, laws and office holders, including an accounting of salaries and some of the fees.

2. David A. Norris and Robert E. Ireland, "Roads," *NCPedia*, 2006, http://www.ncpedia.org/roads, accessed 10 March 2017.

3. See chaps. 5 and 6 for more complete discussions of the Catawba River fisheries.

Appendix J

1. This appendix is based on the following sources: Lester J. Cappon, "Iron-Making—A Forgotten Industry of North Carolina," *The North Carolina Historical Review* 9, no. 4 (1932): 331; *Encyclopaedia Britannica* (1771), 2:82–83; W. Hill. *Col. William Hill's Memoirs*; Paul Archambault, "The Iron Industry of Lincoln and Gaston County, North Carolina," unpublished paper, pages not numbered.

Appendix K

1. Alan D. Watson, *Money and Monetary Problems in Early North Carolina* (Raleigh, NC: Department of Archives and History, 1980).

2. Davidson Family Papers, UNCC.

Appendix L

1. David Leroy Corbitt, *The Formation of the North Carolina Counties 1663–1943* (Raleigh: North Carolina Division of Archives and History, 2000).

2. Ibid., 8.

3. Ibid., 185.

4. From 1768 to 1771(and long before and after) there was unrest in the backcountry, primarily in Orange County. This had many causes but a lack of hard currency and the custom of seizing property and auctioning it off for non-payment of taxes were two of the major ones. Royal Governor William Tryon supported by militia, went there twice. In 1768 he calmed things down and caused the superior court to be held. Several court officers were convicted and fined. In 1771 he returned with more militia because the regulators had threatened to march on New Bern and burn the town. He met the regulators at Alamance Creek and defeated them soundly. As soon as the battle was over Tryon departed for a new assignment in New York. Several good books have been written on the wars of the Regulators in North Carolina. Some refer to these wars as the immediate precursor to the Revolution. One of the best is Marjoleine Kars, *Breaking Loose Together, The Regulator Rebellion in Pre-Revolutionary North Carolina* (Chapel Hill: UNC Press, 2002).

Appendix M

1. William S. Powell, *The Proprietors of Carolina* (Raleigh, NC: Carolina Charter Tercentenary Commission, 1963).

2. Margaret M. Hoffmann, "Land Grants," in *North Carolina Research, Genealogy and Local History*, ed. Helen F. M. Leary, chap. 31 (Raleigh: North Carolina Genealogical Society, 1996).

3. Saunders, *Colonial Records of North Carolina*, 5:19–21.

4. Clark, "Acts of 1789," chap. 21, in *State Records of North Carolina*, 25 :24.

5. For an example of these, see a royal proclamation and a proclamation by Governor Tryon, both regarding the boundary line between North Carolina and the Cherokee Indians, in Mecklenburg County Deed Books, 3:318–21.

Appendix N

1. Davidson, *Major John Davidson*, 9.

2. Jo White Linn, *Rowan County, North Carolina Deed Abstracts* (Salisbury, NC:

Mrs. Stahle Linn, Jr., 1972), s. v. Davison, John.

3. Brent H. Holcomb and Elmer O. Parker, *Mecklenburg County, North Carolina Deed Abstracts 1763–1779* (Greenville, SC: Southern Historical Press, 1979), 49.

4. Ibid., 48.

Appendix O

1. North Carolina Land Grants, file 1915, 14–195, State Archives of North Carolina, http://nclandgrants.com/home.htm, accessed 5 September 2018; Mecklenburg County Deed Books, 15:78.

2. Mecklenburg Deed Books, 15:160.

3. For the 10 transactions on this page, see Mecklenburg County Deed Books 16:5, 16:586, 21:299, 18:346, 18:355, 17:311, 21:298, 21:300, 22:96, and 22:165.

4. For the five transactions on this page, see Mecklenburg Deed Books, 22:165; 22:195; 27:32; 1, 2d ser.:510; 2, 2d ser.:105.

Appendix P

1. Saunders, *Colonial Records of North Carolina,* 1:187–206.

2. Ibid., 7:472–91. This is a report written by Patrick Duff Gordon and sent by Governor Tryon to William Petty, Marquis of Lansdown, in 1767. It describes how all parts of the government functioned at that time: the courts, laws and office holders, including an accounting of salaries and some of the fees.

3. Powell, *Dictionary of North Carolina Biography,* s.v. "Gordon, Patrick Duff," 2:319–20.

4. Clark, *State Records of North Carolina,* 23 :275.

5. Saunders, *Colonial Records of North Carolina,* vols. 23, 24, and 25 .

Appendix Q

1. Clark, *State Records of North Carolina,* 23 :966.

Bibliography

Notes on Early Sources

This account of Major John Davidson, his extended family and Rural Hill is principally based on the primary sources of land grants, wills, deeds, estate files, court records, newspapers and census records plus other early records contained in *The Colonial and State Records of North Carolina*. It is fleshed out with family journals, letters and other papers preserved in collections at the University of North Carolina at Charlotte, Davidson College and UNC Chapel Hill.

There are a number of early histories of the Carolina backcountry that touch in one way or another on the Davidson family of Rural Hill. Although these can provide information that is not available elsewhere, they should be considered carefully and verified against other sources wherever possible.

The earliest useful history is the Rev. William H. Foote's *Sketches of North Carolina Historical and Biographical*. This is a history of the Presbyterian faith in North Carolina and as such contains a good deal of information about the backcountry, where so many Scots-Irish Presbyterians settled. It was compiled to some extent from Presbyterian church and ecclesiastical records and other printed sources.

For a period of seven years from 1838, Foote was the secretary of foreign missions for North Carolina for the old-school Presbyterian Church and so visited most of the Presbyterian congregations in the state. As he met and stayed with these pastors, he asked about the old days, later writing down these stories as he remembered them. These were, of course, memories of the stories that had been told to them by their fathers and grandfathers. A number of these were published in *The Watchman of the South*, a Presbyterian newspaper published weekly in Richmond from 1837 to 1845. This elicited other stories from the readers of that paper.

In 1844 the North Carolina Presbytery asked Foote to publish his stories as a book to "show the influence of Presbyterian doctrines, habits, and population, upon the past and present generations of citizens of the North State, and in some degree also upon the population of those States which owe much to the emigration from Carolina."

Another who wrote about these early days was John Hill Wheeler, lawyer, politician, diplomat and author, who was raised in Murfreesboro and later settled in Lincoln County. In addition to his many accomplishments, he was appointed superintendent of the Charlotte branch of the U.S. Mint for four years by President Andrew Jackson.

Later, while serving as treasurer of North Carolina, Wheeler took steps to acquire copies of vital historical documents from the British archives. Finally, he devoted himself to recording a history of the state, which he published as *Historical Sketches of North Carolina from 1584 to 1851.* This broad overview of North Carolina history is notorious for its inaccuracy and errors and of little value in researching the history of Mecklenburg County. His *Reminiscences and Memoirs of North Carolina and Eminent North Carolinians* was published after his death. This contains a few articles of interest regarding the backcountry but must always be verified by comparison with original records.

The papers of General Joseph Graham, Major John's son-in-law, were published in 1904 by his grandson. The portion of this book written by General Graham between 1820 and 1829 for Judge Murphey is concerned with correcting errors in others' accounts of the Revolution in the South and is accurate and important. The first part of the book, written by Wheeler's grandson, contains some family information that is generally accurate but must be verified by reference to other sources.

C. L. Hunter was a noted physician and scientist of Lincoln County. He was born near present-day Mount Holly and married a daughter of Peter Forney's. Forney had partnered with Major John and his sons-in-law in the iron-making business. Hunter lived near Iron Station and is buried in the Machpelah Church cemetery. He was an accomplished scientist with the best library in that part of the state, and his collection of more than 200 species of North Carolina trees was exhibited in Venice, Italy. He was the developer of the Catawba variety of wine grape that is widely used today in wine making in the northeastern United States. His extensive mineral collection was exhibited at the Centennial Exposition in Philadelphia in 1876. After the Civil War Hunter became interested in history and his *Sketches of Western North Carolina, Historical and Biographical,* was published in 1877. Several of these are original, but many others are taken from Wheeler's *Sketches.*

Samuel A'Court Ashe was a prominent lawyer and politician after the Civil War and owner and publisher of the *Raleigh News and Observer.* His seven-volume *Biographical History of North Carolina* (1906) is a valuable reference for the lives of early settlers, especially those whom history has otherwise forgotten.

J. B. Alexander was a doctor in the Hopewell area of Mecklenburg County. In 1890 he moved his family to Charlotte, where he continued to practice and operate a drugstore until retiring in ill health in 1898. In his retirement he wrote three histories, of Mecklenburg County, of the Hopewell section and of his experiences in the Civil War and during Reconstruction. The first two of these are stories he gathered during his medical practice and are widely quoted. Many errors in the earlier histories are repeated here.

Daniel Augustus Tompkins was an engineer, industrialist and newspaper publisher in Charlotte at the beginning of the 20th century. His two-volume *History of Mecklenburg County and the City of Charlotte from 1740 to 1903*, published in 1903, is widely referenced but often unreliable.

After extensive training and experience as a mechanical engineer, designer and machinist, Tompkins came to Charlotte as a commissioned salesman of steam engines. He succeeded so well that he soon opened his own company for founding, building and operating textile mills of various kinds. Within 20 years his company had built 250 cotton oil mills, 150 electric plants and 100 cotton mills.

Beginning in 1892, Tompkins became publisher of the *Charlotte Daily Observer* and the *Charlotte Evening News*. His Observer Printing House published a number of books and countless pamphlets and speeches under his name. In addition to his *History of Mecklenburg County*, these included five technical books on the textile industry. According to his biographer, "Tompkins apparently did not write the books and articles on which his name appeared as author but employed ghostwriters. The *History* was written by Charles Lee Coon, Alexander J. McKelway, and Bruce Craven. E. W. Thompson, an engineer in Tompkins's employ, wrote the technical books."

If information in Tompkins's *History* cannot be positively confirmed in other publications, it should be ignored. If it can be confirmed, the original source should be referenced instead of Tompkins.

The Reverend Charles W. Sommerville, D.D., author of *The History of Hopewell Presbyterian Church*, was the pastor of Hopewell from 1926 until his death in 1938. His *History* was published in Charlotte by the church in 1939. It is quite reliable, with the exception of the family stories he gathered and included or that may have come from earlier Mecklenburg histories.

Sommerville was highly educated, with a doctoral degree from Johns Hopkins, where he lectured in colonial history. He received a doctoral degree in divinity from Hampden-Sidney College, where he had received his bachelor's degrees many years before. He taught Latin, Greek and Hebrew in addition to history, founded a number of schools and academies, and was teaching the Bible at Queens-Chicora College in Charlotte when he was called to Hopewell.

At the urging of Mrs. Jo Davidson, and the support of Colonel E. L. Baxter Davidson, of the Rural Hill Davidsons, Sommerville gathered traditions, memories and firsthand knowledge from the Hopewell congregation for this history. He consulted a number of Presbyterian church libraries and archives and the Library of Congress for additional information. He died in 1938, leaving the book not yet completed. His second wife, Betty, and Jane Carson completed the book, working from his extensive notes and documentation.

Finally, the *Dictionary of North Carolina Biography*, six volumes, edited by William S. Powell, is comprehensive and generally quite reliable. However, to the extent that the authors of the various articles have relied on genealogies and early published sources, additional verification is recommended.

The works of the late Dr. Chalmers Gaston Davidson, Davidson College history professor, have contributed greatly to this history. Davidson was a family descendant and wrote several histories of the area and biographies of some of his ancestors. Most were written from the 1940s to the 1970s; some were published, others exist only in manuscript form. Davidson was director of the Davidson College Library and, in retirement, college archivist. His work was well researched and documented, but many resources are available today that were not readily accessible when he did his work. Davidson died in 1994 and is buried in the Rural Hill Burying Ground.

An extensive and thoroughly researched Davidson genealogy has been compiled by Dr. Douglas Marion of Chester, South Carolina. Marion, also a Davidson descendant, has spent many years on this project and regularly corrects and updates his records as new information becomes available.

Manuscript and Image Sources

Southern Historical Collection, Louis Round Wilson Special Collections Library, University of North Carolina at Chapel Hill
- Davidson Family Papers, 1813–1937
- Conner Papers

Archives and Special Collections, Davidson College, Davidson, North Carolina
- Chalmers Gaston Davidson, (1928) plantation files, 1907–94

Special Collections, Atkins Library, University of North Carolina at Charlotte
- Davidson Family Papers
- Torrance-Banks Family Papers
- Caldwell and Davidson Family Papers

State Archives of North Carolina
- Mecklenburg County Will Books, https://archives.ncdcr.gov/documents/mecklenburg-county-wills
- North Carolina Estate Files, 1663–1979, http://FamilySearch.org

- North Carolina Land Grants, http://nclandgrants.com/home.htm

North Carolina Historical Markers, https://www.ncmarkers.com/Markers.aspx?MarkerId=O-58

Historic Rosedale Plantation, Charlotte, North Carolina
- Caldwell-Davidson Papers

Lincoln County Deed Books, Office of the Registrar of Deeds, Lincoln County, North Carolina, http://72.15.246.181/LincolnNC

Mecklenburg County Deed Books, Office of the Registrar of Deeds, Mecklenburg County, NC, http://meckrodindex.com

Revolutionary War Pension Applications, http://revwarapps.org

Charlotte-Mecklenburg Historic Landmarks Commission, http://landmarkscommission.org

Newspapers

The Charlotte Journal
Watchman of the South

Books and Articles

Alexander, J. B. *Biographical Sketches of the Early Settlers of the Hopewell Section* (Charlotte, NC: Observer Printing, 1897).

———. *The History of Mecklenburg County from 1740 to 1900* (Charlotte, NC: Observer Printing, 1902).

———. *Reminiscences of the Past Sixty Years* (Charlotte, NC: Ray Printing, 1908).

Ashe, Samuel A'Court. *History of North Carolina* (Greensboro, NC: Charles L. Van Noppen, 1908).

———, ed., *Biographical History of North Carolina from Colonial Times to the Present* (Greensboro, NC: C. L. Van Noppen, 1905–17).

Babits, Lawrence E., and Joshua B. Howard. *"Fortitude and Forbearance": The North Carolina Continental Line in the Revolutionary War, 1775–1783* (Raleigh: North Carolina Division of Archives and History, 2004).

Bell, Landon C., ed. *Sunlight on the Southside; Lists of Tithes, Lunenburg County, Virginia, 1748–1783* (Philadelphia: George S. Ferguson, 1931).

Blodgett, Jan, and Ralph B. Levering. *One Town, Many Voices: A History of Davidson, North Carolina* (Davidson, NC: Davidson Historical Society, 2012).

Brevard, Keziah Goodwyn. *A Plantation Mistress on the Eve of the Civil War*. Edited by John Hammond Moore (Columbia: University of South Carolina Press, 1993).

Cain, Robert J., ed. *Colonial Records of North Carolina (Second Series)* (New York: AMS Press, 1968–72).

Cappon, Lester J. "Iron-Making—A Forgotten Industry of North Carolina." *The North Carolina Historical Review* 9, no. 4 (1932): 331.

Cates, Banks R., Jr. "Mecklenburg Fisheries." *Olde Mecklenburg Genealogical Society Quarterly* 20, no. 2 (2002): 18.

Clark, Walter, ed. *The State Records of North Carolina*. 16 vols. (Raleigh, NC: Trustees of the Public Libraries, 1895).

Corbitt, David Leroy. *The Formation of the North Carolina Counties 1663–1943* (Raleigh: North Carolina Division of Archives and History, 2000).

Cutler, Harry Gardner, ed. *History of Florida, Past and Present* (New York: Lewis, 1923).

Davidson, Chalmers Gaston. *Major John Davidson of "Rural Hill," Mecklenburg County, N.C., Pioneer, Industrialist, Planter* (Charlotte, NC: Lassiter Press, 1943).

———. *The Plantation World Around Davidson* (Davidson, NC: Mecklenburg Historical Association, 1973).

Encyclopædia Britannica; or, a Dictionary of Arts and Sciences. By a Society of Gentlemen in Scotland. 3 vols. (Edinburgh: Macfarquhar 1771).
Ferguson, Herman W. *Mecklenburg County, North Carolina Minutes of the Court of Common Pleas and Quarter Sessions 1774–1780* (Rocky Mount, NC: 2007).
_____. *Mecklenburg County, North Carolina Minutes of the Court of Common Pleas and Quarter Sessions, 1780–1800* (Rocky Mount, NC: Herman W. Ferguson, 2000).
_____. *Mecklenburg County, North Carolina Minutes of the Court of Common Pleas and Quarter Sessions, Vol.2: 1801–1820* (Rocky Mount, NC: Herman W. Ferguson, 1997).
_____. *Mecklenburg County, North Carolina Minutes of the Court of Common Pleas and Quarter Sessions, Vol. 3: 1821–1830* (Rocky Mount, NC: Herman W. Ferguson, 1998).
_____. *Mecklenburg County, North Carolina Minutes of the Court of Common Pleas and Quarter Sessions, Vol. 4: 1831–1840* (Rocky Mount, NC: Herman W. Ferguson, 2002).
_____. *Mecklenburg County, North Carolina Will Abstracts, 1791–1868, Books A–J, and Tax Lists* (Rocky Mount, NC: Herman Ferguson, 1998).
Fischer, David Hackett. *Albion's Seed, Four British Folkways in America* (New York: Oxford University Press, 1989).
Foote, the Rev. William H. *Sketches of North Carolina Historical and Biographical*, 3d ed. Edited by Harold J. Dudley (1846; New Bern, NC: Owen G. Dunn, 1966).
Graham, William A. *General Joseph Graham and His Papers on North Carolina Revolutionary History* (Raleigh, NC: Author, 1904).
Green, Constance McL. *Eli Whitney and the Birth of American Technology* (Boston: Little Brown, 1956).
Hill, Michael. "Crowfield Academy." *NCpedia*, 2006. http://www.ncpedia.org/crowfield-academy.
Hill, William. *Col. William Hill's Memoirs of the Revolution.* Edited by A. S. Salley (Columbia: Historical Commission of South Carolina, 1958).
Holcomb, Brent H. *Anson County, North Carolina Deed Abstracts, 1749–1766, Abstracts of Will & Estates, 1749–1795* (Baltimore: Genealogical Publishing, 1980).
Holcomb, Brent H., and Elmer O. Parker. *Mecklenburg County, North Carolina Deed Abstracts 1763–1779* (Greenville, SC: Southern Historical Press, 1979).
Hunter, C. L. *Sketches of Western North Carolina, Historical and Biographical* (Raleigh, NC: Raleigh News Steam Job Print, 1877).
Kars, Marjoleine. *Breaking Loose Together, The Regulator Rebellion in Pre-Revolutionary North Carolina* (Chapel Hill: UNC Press, 2002).
Leary, Helen F. M., ed. *North Carolina Research, Genealogy and Local History* (Raleigh: North Carolina Genealogical Society, 1996).
Linn, Jo White. *Rowan County, North Carolina Deed Abstracts* (Salisbury, NC: Mrs. Stahle Linn, Jr., 1972).
McConnell, Karen, Janet Dyer, and Ann Williams, eds. *A Life in Antebellum Charlotte: The Private Journal of Sarah F. Davidson, 1837* (Charleston, SC: History Press, 2005).
McNitt, V. V. *Chain of Error and the Mecklenburg Declarations of Independence* (New York: Hampden Hills Press, 1960).
Monaghan, E. Jennifer. *Learning to Read and Write in Colonial America* (Worcester, MA: American Antiquarian Society, 2005).
Moss, Kay. *Journey to the Piedmont Past, Source Book* (Gastonia, NC: Schiele Museum of Natural History, 2001).
Norris, David A., and Robert E. Ireland. "Roads." *NCPedia*, 2006. http://www.ncpedia.org/roads.
Powell, William S. *The Proprietors of Carolina* (Raleigh, NC: Carolina Charter Tercentenary Commission, 1963).
_____, ed. *Dictionary of North Carolina Biography* (Chapel Hill: University of North Carolina Press, 1979).
Rankin, Hugh F. *Greene and Cornwallis: The Campaign in the Carolinas* (Raleigh: North Carolina Department of Cultural Resources, Division of Archives and History, 1976).

Saunders, William L., ed. *The Colonial Records of North Carolina*. 10 vols. (Raleigh, 1886–1890).
Sommerville, Charles William. *The History of Hopewell Presbyterian Church* (Charlotte, NC: Hopewell Presbyterian Church, 1939).
Spence, Thomas Hugh. *The Presbyterian Congregation on Rocky River* (Concord, NC: Rocky River Presbyterian Church, 1954).
Springs, Katherine Wooten. *The Squires of Springfield* (Charlotte, NC: William Loftin, 1965).
Swain, David L., ed. *North Carolina State Pamphlet on the Mecklenburg Declaration of Independence* (Raleigh: State of North Carolina, 1831).
Syfert, Scott. *The First American Declaration of Independence? The Disputed History of the Mecklenburg Declaration of May 20, 1775* (Jefferson, NC: McFarland, 2014).
Tompkins, D. A. *History of Mecklenburg County* (Charlotte, NC : 1903).
Watson, Alan D. *Money and Monetary Problems in Early North Carolina* (Raleigh: North Carolina Department of Archives and History, 1980).
Wheeler, John Hill. *Historical Sketches of North Carolina from 1584 to 1851* (Philadelphia: Lippincott, Grambo, 1851).
_____. *Reminiscences and Memoirs of North Carolina and Eminent North Carolinians* (Columbus, OH: Columbus Printing Works, 1884).
Williams, Ann. *The Rural Hill Farm Journals of Adam Brevard Davidson, 1834–1856* (Charlotte, NC: Antebellum Books, 2017).

Unpublished Papers

Archambault, Paul. "The Iron Industry of Lincoln and Gaston County, North Carolina." Original in the collection of the Schiele Museum, Gastonia, NC.
Baldwin, Mary. "The Copy Book of Mary Baldwin, May 12, 1791." In the authors' collection.
Davidson, Chalmers Gaston. "Benjamin Wilson and Elizabeth Latta Davidson of 'Oak Lawn' Mecklenburg County, N.C." In the authors' collection.
Davidson, Sarah Harper. Journal, 1868–77. Private collection.
Osborne, Edwin Augustus Young. "Autobiography." In folder 170, Edwin Augustus Osborne Papers, 1832–1928, Southern Historical Collection, Louis Round Wilson Special Collections Library, University of North Carolina at Chapel Hill, transcribed by Josephine A. Osborne, Charlotte, 1947. Copy in the authors' collection.

Index

Numbers in ***bold italics*** indicate pages with illustrations

Abel, Alice Davidson 125
Alexander, Col. Adam 31
Alexander, Dr. Annie Lowery 71
Alexander, Annie May 149, 152
Alexander, Dr. John Brevard 12, 15, 71, 225
Alexander, John McKnitt 26, 33, 57, 59, 61, 159, 165, 190, 196, 204
Alexander, Robert Davidson 71
Alexander, Violet Davidson 26, 71, 153
Alexander, William Bain 26–27, 45, 48, 71, 153, 163–165, 200, 202
Anson, Admiral 183–184
Anson County 10–16
apple trees 139
apprentices 5, 19, 23, 59, 67, 81, 93, 97, 207

Bailey, Francis 35, 60, 204
Baker's Graveyard 15*n*4
Baldwin, Mary 229
Bank of North Carolina, Bank of the State of North Carolina 58, 66, 68, 71–77, 85, 87, 161
Barry, Miss Jane 118
Barry, Richard 16, 117, 188
Beal, Amanda "Maude" Davidson *see* Davidson, Amanda "Maude" Beal
Beaver Dam Plantation 24, 46–47, 110
blacksmith 5, 6, 10, 23, 33, 45, 62, 69, 75, 131, 145, 167, 171, 174, 178, 194, 197
Bladen County 56, 183

Blythe, John viii
boll weevil 141
Boyer, Mary vii
Boyte, Jack 63
Brabham, Robin vii
Brevard, Alexander 25, 35, 37–38, 40–42, 71, 88, 153, 176
Brevard, Ephraim 51, 112
Brevard, Franklin 38
Brevard, Keziah Hopkins 38
Brevard, Mary Winslow 88
Brevard, Rebecca Davidson 37–38, 71–72, 153
Brevard, Robert 71
Brevard, Sarah 6, 28, 42
Brevard, Theodore 71
Brevard County Florida 38
Brevard Family 10
Bronson, the Rev. Benjamin 82
Brumby, Mary 72
Brumby, Richard T. 72
Byars, James Smith 35
Byars, Julia 85
Byars, Nancy Cecelia Osborne 85
Bynum 83

Cabarrus County 10, 24, 26–27, 30, 124, 162–165, 184, 194
Caldwell, the Rev. Alexander 26, 58–59, 65, 110, 153, 159–161, 168
Caldwell, Alice 148
Caldwell, Baxter 148

Index

Caldwell, David Alexander 26, 58–59, 68–69, 71–72, 74–75, 77, 131, 159–161
Caldwell, Dr. David Thomas 93, 113, 124, 147
Caldwell, Edward 79
Caldwell, John Hancock 26, 58–59, 159–161
Caldwell, John Madison McKnitt 93
Caldwell, M.A. 86
Caldwell, Sally 79, 86
Caldwell, the Rev. Samuel Craighead 26, 58–59, 158–161
Caldwell, Sarah Davidson 47, 65, 110
Caldwell-Davidson Family Papers 227
Cambridge College (Harvard) 93–94, 97
Cashen Quarry 119
Catawba River 2, 5–6, 10, 12, 22–23, 29–31, 35, 41, 44, 49, 51, 53–60, 62, 78, 85, 98, 107–108, 114–115, 118, 120, 128, 157, 167, 175, 184–185, 204–205, 224
Catawba Springs 22
Chapel of St. Mary 83
Charlotte Agricultural Society Fair 116, 131
Charlotte and South Carolina Rail Road 71, 76, 114–115, 122; *see also* Rail Road
Civil War 2, 3, 26, 38, 42, 63, 76–78, 80–81, 98, 122, 147, 225
Coddle Creek 6, 10–12, 23–25, 34, 187, 194–197, 199, 201–203
College of New Jersey (Princeton) 51
communion 109
Conner, Henry 39
Conner, Juliana 99
Connor, Margaret "Peggy" 38
corn 18, 45–46, 75, 91–92, 95, 103–104, 107, 117–118, 120–121, 131–133, 138–141, 180
cotton 3, 24, 45, 60, 62, 75, 90–92, 94, 107–109, 114, 117, 121, 131–141, *134, 135*, 145, 174, 225
cotton gin 60, 62, 69, 75, 90, 107, 116, 133–138, *136, 137*
cotton harvest 90–91, 95, 105–106, 108, 114, 134, 137–138, 174
Craighead, Alexander 159
Crowfield Academy 51*n*2
Cunningham, the Rev. H.B. 109, 111, 113

Davidson, Adam Brevard 2, 79–80, 89–90, 99–118, *100*, 119–129, 130–146, 154, 156, *157*, 168–174
Davidson, Adam Brevard, Jr. 155

Davidson, Amanda "Maude" Beall 109, 114, 126, 154–155
Davidson, Augustus W. 96, 106, 154
Davidson, Austin Richard 109, 155
Davidson, Baxter Craighead 124, 148–149, 155
Davidson, Benjamin Howard 68–69
Davidson, Benjamin Wilson 28, 36, 68–69, 116, 154
Davidson, Betsy 6
Davidson, Blandina 155
Davidson, Brevard *see* Davidson, Adam Brevard
Davidson, Chalmers 12, 28, 44, 62, 109, 114–115, 226
Davidson, Cornelia Elmore 123
Davidson, Edward Constantine 72, 80, 93, 97, 154
Davidson, Edward Lee Baxter 114, 124, 127, *128*, 129, 155, 157, 226
Davidson, Elizabeth 116, 150, 155
Davidson, Elizabeth (Betsy) 28
Davidson, Fanny Baxter 110, 155
Davidson, George 9–10, 23
Davidson, Isabella *see* Graham, Isabella Davidson
Davidson, Isabella Ramsay 9–13, 24
Davidson, Isabella Sophia 96
Davidson, Jane Elizabeth Torrance 97, 111, 154
Davidson, Jo Graham 123, 149
Davidson, Jo Graham, Jr. 149, *150*, 155, 226
Davidson, Maj. John 2, 5–7, 9–13, 16, 23–36, 117, 153, 158–159, 162–165, 187, 190; in Assembly 28–31; iron making 175–178; land ownership 33–36, 193–203; *see also* Davidson, Violet Wilson
Davidson, John (Jacky) 80, 88–98, 154; Florida connection 94–95
Davidson, John ("Long Headed Jacky") 68, 160
Davidson, John Matthew 94, 154
Davidson, John, other 9–10, 58, 160–162, 165–168
Davidson, John Ramsay 69, 77
Davidson, John Springs (son of Brevard and Mary Davidson) 44, 123–125, 147, 154–155
Davidson, John Springs (son of Jo Graham Davidson) 79, 106, 149, 151–152, 155
Davidson, Leroy 124, 127

Davidson, Margaret "Minnie" Caldwell 124, 147, 154–155
Davidson, Margaret (Peggy) Osborne (wife of Robert [Robin] Davidson) 27, 39, 50–65, 66–87, **79**, 90, 111, 153–154, 159, 162–165, 203–205
Davidson, Martha "Patsy" Caldwell 26, 58–59, 159–161, 168
Davidson, Mary Laura Springs (wife of Adam Brevard Davidson) 2, 79–80, 89–90, 99–118, 119–129, 130–146, 154, 156–157, 168–174
Davidson, Mary Louise 125, 143–149
Davidson, Mary (Polly) 25, 71, 153
Davidson, Mary Winslow 66
Davidson, May 7, 150, **151**, 156
Davidson, Minnie 46, 124–125, 147–149, 154–155
Davidson, Richard Austin 155
Davidson, Robert Augustus 125, 154–155
Davidson, Robert F. 69, 74
Davidson, Robert H.M. 95, 154
Davidson, Robert, other 9, 23
Davidson, Robert (Robin) 27, 39, 50–51, **52**, 53- 65, 66–87, 90, 111, 153–154, 159, 162–165; fisheries 53–56; property 59–63, 203–205; will and estate 66, 73
Davidson, Sarah (daughter of Jacky and Sally Davidson) 98, 154
Davidson, Sarah (daughter of Maj. John and Violet Davidson) see Caldwell, Sarah
Davidson, Sarah (Sallie) Harper Brevard 88, 98, 126–127, 154–155
Davidson, Sarah Williams Vosburgh 129
Davidson, Violet (daughter of Maj. John and Violet Wilson Davidson) see Alexander, Violet
Davidson, Violet Wilson (wife of Maj. John Davidson) 2, 5–7, 9–13, 16, 23–36, 117, 153, 158–159, 162–165, 175–178, 187, 190, 193–203
Davidson, Gen. William Lee 16, 23, 28, 156
Davidson, William Lee (son of Brevard and Mary Davidson) 107, 155–157
Davidson, William Lee, Jr. 6, 24, 28, 45–46, 110
Davidson, William Speight MacLean 97, 111, 154
Davidson and Moss Store 75
Davidson and Springs Store 107

Davidson College 22, 39, 72, 89, 93, 97, 106, 114, 119, 156–157
Davidson Family 1–2, 5–7, 153–156
deeds see grants and deeds
Dickson, Joseph 101
Dixon (Dickson) Plantation 101–104, 107, 116–117, 135, 142–144, 168–173
Doby 96, 154
dowry 18, 26, 101–104, 143, 168–169, 172–173
dowry of Mary Laura Springs (bride of Adam Brevard Davidson) 101–104
Duffy, Mr. 102–103

Eakes, L. Garner 63
Ebenezerville, Ebenezer Academy 114–115
Edgefield 38
Edgeworth Female Seminary 113–114, 147
Elmira, NY, prison camp 122, 125–126, 147
Elmwood cemetery 122

farm journals see Rural Hill Farm Journals
farming 1–2, 36, 45, 50, 67, 69, 81, 88, 91–92, 99, 104, 106–108, 116, 122, 130–146, 189, 209
fisheries 53–55, 175
Fissel, Jeff vii
Fite, Mr. 78
Flanigain, Osborn 107
Florida 38, 44, 94–96, 183, 186
Forney, Peter 35, 40, 41n12, 55, 176, 178, 224

Gaston County 25, 80, 178, 184–185
Germans, Palatine 2, 176
Gilead Church 158
Gordon, Patrick Duff 175n1, 205n2, 206–208
Graham, Isabella Davidson 25, 39, 47
Graham, Joseph 25, 35, 37–40, 42, 85, 153, 176, 224
Graham, Malvina Sophia 85
Graham, Robert Davidson 71
Graham, Gov. William 39
grants and deeds 1–2, 10–12, 14–15, 21, 24, 27, 33–36, 40–41, 45, 47, 49, 56–61, 71, 162–165, 133, 185–186, **187, 188, 189, 191**, 192–205, 208, 211, 223

Hagler, King 56
Hale, Adeline 86

Harris, Maj. James 26–27, 153, 162–165
Harry, J.F. 77
Harvard *see* Cambridge College
Henderson, Jane Violet 98, 154
Hendry or Henry, Henry 9–13, 24, 194–197, 201–202
Hill, Gen. D.H. 39
Hill, William 41, 175–176
Hiss, John 119
Holly Bend Plantation 6, 25, 35, 39, 50–87, **64**, 110–111, 131, 160–161
Hopewell Church 71–72, 76–77, 79, 97, 109–111, 113, 151, 158–159, 225–226; Academy 50, 88, 92–93, 99
horses, mules 18, 49, 109, 126, 136–138, 144–145, 210–211
Houston Panthea Lemira 85
Huck, Christian 175
Hutcheson, Cyrus 107–116
Hutcheson, S. Nye 87

infare, infair 101, 111
Ingleside Plantation 97
Iredell County 23, 25, 28, 35, 50, 55, 85, 120, 184, 194
iron making 1–2, 24–25, 35, 37–42, 75, 175–178, 224, 227, 229
Irwin, James Patton 80
Irwin, John 70, 80
Irwin, Mary Ann 70, 80, 101, 111

Jack, James 16–21, 32–33
Jack, Margaret *see* Wilson, Margaret Jack
Jack, Patrick 15, 17–21
Jack family 20–21
Jackson, Andrew 94, 224
Jackson, Anna Morrison 39
Jackson, Gen. Stonewall 39
Jasper and Larkin Store 74
Johnson, James 116
Johnson, Jane vii
Johnson, William 205
Johnston, Gabriel 206
justice of the peace 2, 31–32, 51–52, 206–207

Kenmer, John 204
Kerns, Robert 78
King, A.E. 87
Kings Mountain 101, 178

Leeper's Creek 42
Lincoln County 2, 24–25, 35, 37–41, 55–56, 71–72, 85, 96, 99, 101, 103, 113, 116, 168, 176–178, 184–185, 205, 224
Little Sugar Creek 82–84
Locke, John 205
Logan, G.W. 77
long bullets 30n8, 210
Long Creek 71, 73, 75–76
Lundergain, Edwin 121
Lunenburg County, Virginia 14n3

Machpelah Cemetery and Church 42, 224
Mackay, Miss Elizabeth 82
Marion, Dr. Douglas viii, **52**, **68**, **79**, 127, 226
Mathews, W.M. 87
McAdam, John 53, 175
McDowell Creek 6, 11, 14, 16, 23, 25, 33–34, 36, 42, 57, 60, 118, 187–189, 194–196, 201, 204–205
McLean, Ed vii
McLean, Jennie 80
McLean (Maclean), Dr. William B. 71, 73, 80
McLean, Mary (Polly) Davidson (wife of Dr. William McLean) 47, 71, 73, 80
McLean, Robert 71
McLean, Warren 80
McQuoun (McQuown) 195, 197, 201–203
Mecklenburg Agricultural Society 116, 131
Mecklenburg County 2, 5, 7, 12, 14–15, 20, 23, 28–32, 39, 48, 55–56, 59–62, 70–73, 184–185, 193–194, 224–225
Mecklenburg Declaration of Independence, Resolves 19–21, 24, 32, 39, 51, 111
Mecklenburg Historical Association 83
Mecklenburg Monumental Association 111–112
Medical College of Charleston 93, 97
Mexican War 72, 97
Miller, Jane (Jenny) Davidson 109, 113–114, 155
mills 33, 54, 71, 73, 75, 85, 108, 116–117, 119–121, 137, 139, 146, 173, 177, 189, 194, 197, 203
Mint, U.S. Branch 68, 70, 224
money, value of 17, 19, 21, 72, 82, 87, 127, 133, 179–180, **181**, 182
Moore, Fanny Swan 81
Moore, Harriet C. 86
Moore, Isabella 86, 96

Moore, James W. 74, 77, 113, 154
Moore, Sally 79
Moore, Thomas J. 78
Moore, Warren 72, 79, 86, 96
Moore's Ferry 58, 98
Morrison, Isabella 39
Morrison, Mary Graham (wife of Robert Hall Morrison) 28
Morrison, Robert Hall 39, 42, 156–157
Mount Tirza Forge 42
Myers, W.R. 112n9, 123

naming conventions 165–167
negroes *see* slaves
Neichler, John 195–196, 201–202
New Acquisition 185

Oak Lawn Plantation 28, 36
Oates, John E. 124
Oates, R.M. 123
orphans, orphanages 5, 67, 69, 81, 82, 160, 207
Osborne, Adlai 50, 56, 64, 70
Osborne, Edwin A. 63, 77–86, 229
Osborne, Edwin J. 67, 70, 80, 86
Osborne, Ephraim B. 85
Osborne, James W. 67, **68**, 69–70, 72, 74, 76–80, 85–87, 111–112
Osborne, Margaret (Peggy) *see* Davidson, Margaret (Peggy)
Osborne, Marry Ann Irwin Moore 70, 80, 86, 111
Osborne, Robert Davidson 71

Pain, Isaac 120
patroller 12, 51
Pee Dee River 11, 114, 183
pig iron 38, 42, 176–178
plum 22, 33, 161–162
Polk, Mary (Maria) Wilson 15
pork, hogs, pigs 75, 138, 141–142
Prim, John D. 117

Queens College 25, 29, 39, 184, 226
Quincy, Florida 94–96

Rail Road, Charlotte and South Carolina 70, 76–77, 95, 114–115, 122, 145
Reed, Rufus 69, 70
Revolutionary War 18–21, 25, 31, 37, 39–40, 51, 94, 112, 156, 176–177, 184
Riley, Jacob 116
river work 52, 54, 174–175
road work 12, 41, 52–56, 174–175

Rock Island Manufacturing Company 85
Rosedale Plantation 93, 113, 117n14, 124–125, 147–148, 149n4, 152
Rowan County 10, 12, 16, 20, 23, 30–31, 37, 51, 78, 166, 183–185, 193–194, 197
Rural Hill Burying Ground 7, 96, 98, 123, 126–127, 129, 149–152, 226
Rural Hill Farm Journals 95, 104–111
Rural Hill, Rural Retreat 1–2, 5–7, 11, 13, 25–26, 28, 34–37, 42–45, **46**, 47, 57–58, 62–63, 65, 68, 72, 88–89, 92, 95–99, 101, 104–111, 115–118, 125–126, 130–149, 152, 157, 159–161, 168–174, 189, 194–195, 199, 223

Sadler, Robert A. 92–93
St. Mary's Chapel 83
Salem Female Academy 93, 100, 103, 113–114, 124, 147
Sarazin School 100
scientific farming 1–2, 104, 116, 122, 130–146
shad *see* fisheries
Sharpe, T. A. 86
Sigman, Martin 120
Sinclair, the Rev. Alexander McLean 124–126, 154
Sinclair, Mary Laura Davidson (wife of the Rev. Alexander McLean Sinclair) 106, 124, 162–165
slaves by name: Aaron 116; Adam 169–170, 174; Adeline 170; Alek 102, 104; Alexander 169–170; Alfred, Alphred 169–171; Alice 170; Amy 86, 170–171, 173; Andy 172; Ann 102–104, 142, 168, 170, 172–173; Austin 103, 172; Ben 80; Bet 163; Bill 102, 170; Bob 170, 172; Burrow 104, 168, 172; Caroline 163; Celia 103, 170, 172–174; Charles 69, 110, 173; Cuff 68; Dave, David 169, 171–172, 174; Davie 170; Dick 76, 170–172; Dilsi, Dilsie 170–172; Dina 163; Eliza 86; Evaline 170–171; Fanny 102–103, 163, 172; George 104, 121, 169, 172; Ginci 170; Green 170, 173; Hampton 169, 170–171, 174; Hannah 64, 103, 170, 172–174; Harrison 124, 169–172; Henry 102, 104, 173; Humphrey 69, 103, 172–173; Iby 170; Jack 170, 172; Jef 170; Jerry, Jerrie 136, 169–172, 174; Jim 170–171; Jincy 170–171; Joe 169–172; John 170; Julia 102–104, 142, 145, 168, 170, 172, 174; Lemuel 104, 172; Lidia 173; Liza 170–171; Logan 136,

169, 171; Martha 75; Melanda 163;
Molly 170; Monrow 170; Moses, Mose
169–174; Nancy 103, 170, 172–173;
Patt 68; Peggy 102–104, 168; Peter 17,
110, 173; Phil 169–171, 174; Plum 22,
33, 161–163; Polly, Poly 142, 170–171,
173–174; Rachael 75; Rhody 103, 172–
173; Rufus 170–171; Sarah 170–171;
Sinai, Sina 104, 168, 170, 172; Stephen
172; Susan 124, 170–171; Thomas,
Tom 103–104, 121, 168–172; Umphrey
169–170; Vergil 163; Wheeler 102;
Wilbert 102–103, 172
slaves, family groups: at Rural Hill in
1856 169–170; at Rural Hill in 1864
170
Sloan, John 41, 176
Smith, James Madison 176
spelling 12, 93, 146, 163, 171, 192
Springfield Plantation 99, 102, 121–122
Springs, Elizabeth Hill 122
Springs, John III 99, 101–102, 104, 107,
110, 113, 116, 122, 171
Springs, Katherine Wooten 100
Springs, Leroy 90, 96
Springs, Mary Laura *see* Davidson,
Mary Laura Springs
Springs family 100
Sugar Creek Academy 89, 93, 97, 113
Sugar (Sugaw) Creek Church 93*n*9, 113,
157–159
Sylvester, Joseph Howard 95, 154
Sylvester, Mary Jerusha 94, 154

Tanner, Ibzan 117
Tanner, Joseph 194, 197, 202–203
Thompson, Lewis 82
Thompson's Orphanage 82–83, 78
Tiffany Jewelers 127
Tools Ford, Matthew Tool 56–57
Torrance, James 97, 134
Torrance, Jane Elizabeth *see* Davidson,
Jane Elizabeth Torrance
Torrance, William 97
Torrence, Hugh 162, 204
trepanning 92
Tryon, Gov. William 184, 205
Tryon County 29–31, 184
Tryon Street 30, 93, 184
Tuckaseegee Ford 101

Union County 30, 184
Unity Academy 113
Unity Church 96, 113
University of North Carolina 2, 34, 39,
70, 101, 190, 204

Vesuvius Furnace 37, 40, 42, 178
Vinson, Jeff vii

Wadle Place 73
West Point 89, 93, 96, 106
Whatley, Robert D. 72
wheat 18, 75, 91–92, 120, 131, 133, 139–
140
White, Sallie Caldwell 79–80
Whitney, Eli 133, 138
Williamson, James 74
Williamson, the Rev. John 93, 110, 158
wills and estates 1, 15, 17, 19, 34, 45, 64,
66–87, 119–129, 166, 207–208, 223
Wilson, Benjamin 11, 15, 22, 36, 49, 154
Wilson, Benjamin, painter 14, 22
Wilson, David 15
Wilson, John 15, 33
Wilson, Margaret Jack 14–16, 21
Wilson, Mary (Maria) Polk *see* Polk,
Mary (Maria) Wilson
Wilson, Mary Winslow or Winsley *see*
Winslow
Wilson, Robert 14, 18
Wilson, Rocinda 118
Wilson, Samuel 6, 11, 13–22, 24, 33,
161–162, 194–195
Wilson, Samuel, Jr. 15–16, 31, 53, 60,
203–204
Wilson, Sarah Howard 15
Wilson, Violet *see* Davidson, Violet
Wilson
Wilson, William Jack 15
Winslow 14–15
Worke, Harry 119–120

Yadkin River 10–11, 34, 183–184
Young, John Augustus 85–87
Young, Mary E. 86
Young, Mary Lloyd Osborne Sharp 85–
86
Young, Malvina Sophia Graham 85

www.ingramcontent.com/pod-product-compliance
Ingram Content Group UK Ltd.
Pitfield, Milton Keynes, MK11 3LW, UK
UKHW041941140426
5217IPUK00014B/602